Night's Black Angels

Night's Black Angels

The Forms and Faces of Victorian Cruelty

by

RONALD PEARSALL

David McKay Company, Inc.

New York

Night's Black Angels

LIBRARY OF CONGRESS CATALOG CARD NUMBER: 74-28934

ISBN: 0-679-50496-6

MANUFACTURED IN THE UNITED STATES OF AMERICA

There is nothing that revolts our moral sense so much as cruelty. Every offence we can pardon, but not cruelty. The reason is found in the fact that cruelty is the direct opposite of compassion—viz., the direct participation, independent of all ulterior considerations, in the sufferings of another, leading to sympathetic assistance in the effort to prevent or remove them; whereon, in the last resort, all satisfaction and all well-being and happiness depend. It is this compassion alone which is the real basis of all voluntary justice and all genuine loving-kindness.

ARTHUR SCHOPENHAUER
(1788-1860)

Contents

8 *Contents*

I DOMESTIC AND SOCIAL CRUELTY

Introduction

THE CAPACITY FOR cruelty is only found in mankind, and no other creature is capable of deriving conscious satisfaction from the infliction of intellectually conceived suffering. It might be that the improvement of *homo sapiens* as a species can be measured by the growth and enlargement of compassion, and the confinement of cruelty within narrow limits. This is not so simple as it might appear, for cruelty is not all of a piece. Some kinds of cruelty can be explained as a manifestation of morbid aberrations of the sexual impulse, but others derive from the primal urge to achieve mastery over the environment or other creatures. The aggressive drives of the individual organism are towards survival.

The threat of violence engenders fear, and the vigour of the response will be proportionate to the amount of fear experienced, and the capacity to retaliate. If the fight-back is successful there is relief from tension, and a consciousness of mastery over the threat. In the case of animals it ends there, but man savours the experience, and once enjoyed the feeling may be sought again, even when there is no provocation. The human tendency is towards excess in situations from which pleasure is obtained.

The weaker the victim the less chance there is of premeditated cruelty failing, and it follows that the most frequent targets of cruelty are children, animals, women, the poor, and men whose capacity for retaliation is curbed by being equipped with inferior defence mechanisms (prisoners in a gaol) or by being conditioned to suffer violence without protecting themselves (soldiers in an army).

If an individual can be cruel, so can a society or a section of society.

Corporate cruelty is frequently provoked when a rival society is credited with a destructive potential that has no relation to the facts. The result of this is over-reaction, though this is only apparent with hindsight. The Victorian period is far enough away for us to look at it objectively, and observe acts of cruelty by man and society for what they were, not necessary actions to uphold law and order, retain social stability, or enforce exploded dogma. Cruelty amongst primitive peoples can be explained by saying that they did not know any better; but the Victorians did, though in one respect—religious controversy—their record is a good deal cleaner than their predecessors'. Only rarely did they over-react, as the Catholic Church did at the time of the Inquisition, as the Romans did to Christianity, and the Jews to Jesus Christ. Fear was, and is, the common denominator of religious cruelty, the fear of a take-over by an alien creed.

Threats against law and order also resulted in over-reaction. The criminal law of the Middle Ages was rich in atrocity. The wheel, the cauldron of boiling oil, burning alive, burying alive, flaying alive, tearing apart with wild horses, all these were sparked off by fear, barbaric rituals enacted as examples to others. An Anglo-Saxon law punished a female slave convicted of theft by forcing eighty other slaves to each bring three pieces of wood and burn the thief to death. In the Customs of Arques (1231) an accomplice concubine of a thief was buried alive (if pregnant, sentence would wait until the child was born). King Frederick II of Germany (1194–1250) encased rebel captives in lead so as to roast them more slowly on the fire. Old German law prescribed breaking on the wheel for arson and murder; old French law recommended burning women alive for felony, boiling to death for coining, while Jews were hung upside-down between two savage dogs and torn to pieces.

The criminal code of Charles V, issued in 1530, is a pornographic treatise of blinding, mutilation, burning alive, tearing with red-hot pincers, and breaking on the wheel. English prisoners were boiled to death as late as 1542, hanging, drawing and quartering were commonplace, and burning alive continued until 1789. The only concession to women was that after being burned alive for high treason they were not drawn and quartered. As Sir William Blackstone (1723–80) said in support of this anomaly, 'For as decency due to the sex forbids the exposing and publicly mangling their bodies their sentence is, to be drawn to the gallows and there to be burnt alive.'

There were no limits to absurdity in setting examples to others. In 1457 a sow was hanged for the murder of a five-year-old child, in 1474 a cock was burned at the stake for the unnatural crime of laying eggs, in 1565 a mule was burned alive after its feet had been mutilated for the crime of bestiality. This crime, never particularly uncommon in country districts (in the late 1870s there were more than a hundred men in English prisons convicted of this offence), received its martyr in June 1662 when a man named Potter was executed, along with his companions in crime—a cow, two heifers, three sheep, and two sows.

Corporate cruelty was self-perpetuating. It was too easily accepted that the mob viewing punitive acts would go away vowing never to commit crimes, and that ritual slaughter was accomplishing its purpose. It is doubtful whether the horrible acts perpetrated in the name of justice did very much to counter crime. There were no newspapers until the *Publick Intelligencer* of 1659 to publicise these events, and although the seventeenth century saw broadsheets in the form of 'execution notices' these reached only a tiny minority of the population. In a land without an organised police force people stole food when they were hungry, clothes when they were cold, and raped and pillaged when the opportunity arose.

Corporate cruelty by state and church was accepted as an essential part of life. The executioners and torturers were not regarded as masters of infamy; they were merely considered as men carrying out their job, though in some cases the agent did something to ameliorate agony—women burned alive frequently had their necks broken beforehand. This was not always accepted by the mob, for many people found that they enjoyed watching the agonies of fellow human beings being boiled alive, being pelted to death in the pillory, being drowned on the ducking stool, or undergoing hanging, drawing and quartering. They had the pleasures of cruelty without the risk or the inconvenience of carrying out the cruelty themselves.

Cruelty by proxy resulted in a relief from tension, a feeling of well-being, and a sense of satisfaction. So ecstatic were these experiences that the connoisseurs did everything possible to recapture them as often as possible, and these amateurs of suffering were to be found at every occasion where someone was being ritually murdered, mutilated, or tortured. There were not enough men and women to go round to satisfy the gory appetite of the cognoscenti, and until the 1820s there were all kinds of spectator sports, such as bear-baiting, bull-baiting, and cock-throwing where Richard Dean declared in 1768, 'cruelty is exercised in all its hideous forms and varieties'.

Cruelty by proxy was exhibited by the low raffish mob that gathered around Newgate for a public execution, that arrived by special excursion trains in Liverpool for executions there, and swarmed from the East End rookeries, regarded the public hangman as hero, and were not in the least awed by the occasions. There was no pretence that it was a solemn event, a time for spectators to take stock of their souls. The basis of cruelty was lost far in the past; there was no threat, no fear, but cruelty for pleasure sanctioned by a government.

There is no ambiguity about direct physical cruelty by one person on a weaker to demonstrate power and domination, or corporate cruelty by a body, and few would argue about the reality of cruelty by proxy. Non-physical cruelty is less sharply defined. It can take many forms, from callous bullying to the social snub. It can be an instrument of class, putting people in their rightful places, or a subtle torture. It reached its peak in the nineteenth century, when social mobility brought in by the aftermath of the industrial revolution created problems of caste. People could score marks by their ability to judge to a nicety where they were on the social ladder, whom they could snub and whom they could not, and the degree of vulnerability of equals and inferiors.

During the Victorian period attitudes were changing towards cruelty. The Reform Bill of 1832 gave a new rising social class self-respect. It did not want pillories, stocks, gallows in every city, bull-baiting and bear-tormenting, young children hanged for trivial offences, nor did it want every homosexual strung up outside Newgate Prison. The middle classes wanted peace and prosperity, an end to abuses, and a fair deal for all those who deserved it. They demanded an end to legislative absurdity, and often got it. Those who were appointed to juries discharged prisoners committed on minor charges rather than find them guilty and thus subject to extravagant punishment. In the years 1817–20 there were 312 executions; in the years 1837–40 there were 62.

A fair deal to all who deserved it. But there were some people whom the dominant classes of the nineteenth century thought were not worthy of too much mercy and compassion—criminals and the poor. Although a man was not hanged for stealing a sheep, he was still a wrongdoer who must be punished, and if possible reformed and rehabilitated, and to do this new instruments of cruelty were fashioned, such as the crank and the treadmill. The casual brutality and neglect of the old prisons were replaced by systematic discipline. And similarly the poor were kept in line, for the good of themselves, and society. They were no longer left to starve in their hovels, their plight eased by hand-outs from the parish, but were placed in workhouses, wives separated from husbands and mothers from children, kept alive on subsistence rations.

Public opinion decided that cruelty was a bad thing, but what was public opinion and what was cruelty? Public opinion was a combination of statesmen, the middle classes, and journalists working together. Much of the credit for nineteenth-century reforms lies at the hands of the politicians who governed immediately prior to Queen Victoria's administrations. Many offences carrying the death penalty were abolished, bills were passed forbidding cruelty to animals, and judicial torture was abolished. Slavery was ended in the colonies. But it was not at home. Reformers could not go too far too quickly.

In the factories and the mines brutality triumphed, with cruelty for profit as the theme. The middle classes, kind to their families and their pets, upholders of the Queen and the *status quo*, were also factory-owners, industrialists, and employers of child labour. Although they knew what cruelty was, there was a dichotomy between their beliefs and their actions. Hypocrisy accounted for a good deal of Victorian cruelty; money and social order were more important than a thoroughly thought-through attitude towards life.

In a sense, there is a further category—cruelty by default, distress caused by apathy and ignorance. Much of industrial cruelty was initiated not by factory and colliery owners but by their agents—the foreman, the managers, and the charge-hands. There was no communication between the top and the bottom. Similarly, cruelty in workhouses, lunatic asylums, prisons, reformatories, prison ships, the army and the navy, was largely due not to the administrators in Whitehall but to the middle men—the workhouse masters, the asylum superintendents, and the prison governors. And if they were put to the question—and in an age so self-questioning as the Victorian they often were—they blamed those beneath them, the workhouse paupers who lorded it over their companions for an extra pint of ale, the poorly paid male nurses of the asylums, the vengeful attitude of prison warders, and over-zealousness by junior N.C.O.s in the army.

When ghastly instances of Victorian cruelty were brought to light, no one knew anything about it or whom was responsible—and those who suffered had few defenders anyway. It sometimes seems that the only people who were concerned were newspaper reporters and crusading novelists.

Despite the feeling that things were getting better cruelty during the Victorian period was not abolished; in some fields it increased. But because of the growth in newspaper readership and the social stigma of being a tyrant it went undercover—like sex. Cruelty was not an open wound any more, but a boil that needed lancing. Reformers compared the situation as it was with what it could be like, believing that people could be transformed by exhortation and precept, underestimating the complexities of the situation and the numbing effect of an inefficient bureaucratic machine on people at the bottom of the social scale. Sentimentality was read as compassion, and credit was given to legislators who passed anti-cruelty laws with the cynical knowledge that they could not be implemented and were merely sops for the faint-hearted.

Legislation was passed to protect children from the more tyrannical employers, and eventually the more outrageous tasks—such as the work done by the boy chimneysweeps—passed into history. But if no great outcry was heard, the government preferred to leave matters as they were. Administrations preferred to remain in office than perform as avenging angels. They had a rule of thumb: cruelty was that which made the people who put them in power angry, and this was the voice to which they paid heed. The middle classes were not greatly concerned with the trials and tribulations of the poor, the savage conditions existing in prisons, or the cruelty existing in workhouses and asylums. They were, up to a point, concerned with cruelty to animals, and cruelty to children, but if the continued prosperity and stability of the country depended on the exploitation of child labour, then child labour would remain. If prisons were run by poorly-paid half-illiterate warders then this showed that the government was not throwing its money away in aimless charity. Workhouses should be run economically to avoid being a burden on the rates.

Politicians, most of whom were middle class themselves, could predict what would arouse middle-class anger, and the bulk of laws passed were to pacify the sensibilities of this the dominant social group. Failure to grapple with the roots of the matter still has an effect on inter-social attitudes. Not that it was a one hundred per cent failure. There were conscientious politicians, understanding employers, philanthropists not concerned with their own image, and, above all, realists such as doctors, lawyers and aristocrats who could stand apart and try to remedy abuses in the system, who participated in Parliamentary Inquiries.

The lesson was slowly learned that it was not possible to put down cruelty by legislation. It needed a change of attitude, a change of climate. Cruelty proliferated in bad living conditions. Improve the conditions and the incidence of cruelty would dwindle. Drunkenness, for instance, produced cruelty. Regulate the outlets for drink and opening hours and drunkenness would diminish. The poor were often cruel because of their hopeless situation. If their situation was more hopeful, the cruelty would level off. Cruelty was the product of boredom, viciousness, unchannelled aggression, and discontent. It still is. It is easy to forget that it is also due to apathy and ignorance, and the propensity of civilised man to push out of mind matters that are not of personal concern. There are lessons to be learned in this account of Victorian cruelty.

Domestic Cruelty

BEFORE THE MATRIMONIAL Causes Act of 1857, a divorce could not cost much less than £700. Even after the act, the expenses involved made divorce a rarity, and the number of divorces per year did not exceed eight hundred until the twentieth century. Unwilling partners had to put up with their marriages as best as they could, and even if she had the money a wife could not be granted a divorce without proving a train of misfortunes. Since a man had the right to chastise his wife, a wife going to law was uncertain whether or not the grounds she put forward would be interpreted as just chastisement.

In the case Smallwood versus Smallwood of 1861, Mr. Smallwood had taken his wife viciously by the throat and thrown her to the floor, but she did not get her hoped-for divorce for one violent act under excitement did not constitute cruelty. Cases such as this, widely reported in the Sunday press, confirmed the opinion of the poor that there was one law for them and one for the rich, and that the marriage lines were unalterable—till death us do part really meant that.

The only hope for a wife married to a tyrant was to get through life with as little aggravation as possible, relying on the police court for some alleviation when matters became too desperate. Sometimes the police arrived too late. Wives were too terrified to appeal to the police in many cases, for a magistrate would often admonish a defendant or impose a trivial fine, leaving the man free to wreak his revenge on the woman who had humiliated him. There was one case in 1850 where a husband admitted 'that boxing his wife's ears and kicking her were among his habits' and that he was accustomed to 'bolting her down' at night. She was found one morning in a 'pitiable state from ill-usage and want of rest' with her left ear bruised and her hair full of matted blood. When reproved by neighbours the husband took no notice. Eventually the woman died, and the husband was charged with manslaughter.

There were certain towns and areas of the country where it was accepted that domestic cruelty was so widespread that nothing could be done. Cruelty was sparked off by bad housing conditions, drink, and high unemployment. In Glasgow there were some streets where every other house was a drink-shop. In the same city in 1885, of 114,759 families 40,820 were living in one room. Parts of London were no better. In System Place, Neckinger Street, Southwark, a room nine feet square was occupied by a man, wife, four children aged sixteen, thirteen, nine, and six, plus a married woman and her baby.

What went on in these surroundings was nobody's business but the people who lived there, and those who penetrated into these urban hell-holes often wished that they had not. There were those who thought that given a square deal the poor would pull themselves together, and who took over entire slices of London with the object of re-furbishing tenements and courts. Many of them honestly considered that the plight of the poor and their shocking environment were due to the machinations of slum landlords, who took the rents and did not do anything to the houses, allowing the rain to come through broken roofs and windows, ignoring rat-infestation, and closing their eyes to the evils of sub-tenancy.

That many of the landlords were doing the best they could under the conditions was revealed when do-gooders such as Octavia Hill, who started her work of improving the homes of working men in the slums in 1864, took over a squalid court and found that, although the weekly rental of all the houses only amounted to £15, the total arrears were £200. This meant that no matter how altruistic private landlords were (and there are many cases of landlords being compelled to live no better than their tenants because of low rental income) they were prevented from putting their property in order by lack of money.

The *Saturday Review* came out with an attack on slum property landlords. 'The fetid nests of half-naked and wholly savage people, living in "Rents", represent so many pounds a year in the pocket of somebody and yield some callous capitalist fifty or sixty per cent.' The humorous journal *Moonshine* took up the cry ('sung by a Callous Capitalist'):

The conditions of the poor were often too desperate for anyone to cope with. (*Graphic*)

Bah! what do I care for the way tenants dwell,
  The dirt and the crowding and such?
They may live in a pig's-stye, 'midst noise, filth, and smell,
  That don't trouble *me* over-much.
The stairs may be rotten, the walls damp with slime,
  For the poor, ease and comfort ain't meant;
I 'go in' for bargains—a slum pays me prime,
  And soon I grow fat on its rent.

It was a vicious circle. Unemployment meant no money to pay the rent, leading to hopelessness on the part of the tenant. The landlords were being deprived of their income and could not plough any back to improve the amenities. The absence of a water-closet or the presence of rats exacerbated the existing disinterest of the occupants, an apathy only disturbed by the intake of drink. Drink took what little money was available, and the question of paying rent was further shelved.

Amongst the people who lived in the slums marriage between couples was not expected, and in irregular unions the cruelty quotient was higher, especially when there were children of mixed or uncertain parentage. Such children were convenient scapegoats, expected to starve, to bring in a little money, to fetch and carry. Of all the inhabitants of the dark side of London the children were the most vulnerable to the cruel onslaughts of their parents or quasi-parents.

In 1868 Mary Thomas, aged eleven, was put by her mother on bread and water, had her hands caned and then had salt put on them. Her hands were then tied behind the bed and she was severely whipped. The case came to the magistrate's court with the medical report that Mary Thomas was heavily marked about the abdomen and thighs with deep, old scars, and that in addition she was emaciated. The mother was fined £3. She told the court that during the caning of her daughter her two other children had encouraged her, saying, 'That's it, beat her more; that isn't half enough.'

These things did not necessarily always happen in the slums. Adelaide Lomax lived in respectable Margate, and in 1868 she was sentenced to twelve months' imprisonment for ill-treatment of her daughter Agnes, aged seven. Agnes was held under the water-pump, and beaten with a fist and a hairbrush, and often had her hands tied behind her for hours on end, or all night.

Domestic cruelty also encompasses cruelty to servants. The most exploited servants were those 'on loan' from the workhouses; they had no defenders, the workhouse masters being glad to get rid of them. They were a charge on the rates under the Poor Law Amendment Bill of 1834, and a bulging workhouse was not welcomed. The workhouse masters could not throw the poor out, for under the terms of the act 'it is obligatory on the guardians of the poor to afford sufficient relief to all persons unable to maintain themselves; refusal an indictable offence'.

When the chance arose, therefore, to place workhouse children as domestic servants inquiries into the status or disposition of the new employer were not pursued too arduously. Unquestionably many of the children obtained easy berths with considerate families, but others were thrust into hell-holes. One of these unfortunates was Sarah Ann Baker, aged twelve, who was sent to work for farmer Joseph Hankins from Weobley Workhouse, Hertfordshire. At haymaking the girl was beaten with a horse whip, at apple-picking she was again assaulted with a horse whip as well as being cut across the shoulders with a holly stick and smashed on the head with a shoe-brush. When she tried to

Workhouse servants were frequently cruelly dealt with, and savage beatings were not uncommon. (*Old and New London*)

run away, Mrs. Hankins kicked her and knocked her over the pump trough. On the instructions of his mother, the son Charles stripped the girl to the waist and beat her with a birch in what was described as an indecent manner. The girl had tried to run away six times.

The vulnerable position of the workhouse servant, or, as he or she was officially called, the parish apprentice, received attention in the notorious panegyric in praise of flagellation, *The Rodiad* (anonymous, possibly by George Colman the younger):

> Whatever maid her mistress calls a fool
> Pinches and spanks him till her rage is cool:
> Odd men and charwomen about the place
> Punish his buttocks for their own disgrace:
> 'What's all that row downstairs?' I often cry,
> 'We're whipping Work'us [i.e. servant from
>   workhouse] sir, 's the safe reply;
> All right—the more the merrier, say I.
> The butler whips him when he's full of ale,
> The footman whips him when the beer is stale,
> The housemaids whip him their hot lust to slake,
> The porter whips to keep himself awake;
> There's not a groom nor horse-boy in the stable
> But has a cut at Work'us when he's able;
> The gardener, from this window, I can see
> Whipping him now beneath the old birch tree.
> He's licked for breakfast in the pantry small,
> He's thrashed for dinner in the servants' hall,
> The supper time's more beating time than all.

The lines from *The Rodiad* point out the utility of the parish apprentice as a general scapegoat to everyone in a household. Acts of cruelty towards paid servants were carried out, but on a more restricted scale. What Florence Nightingale stigmatised as the 'petty grinding tyranny of a good English family' usually took the form not of beating servants but of overworking them, treating them as slaves, or discharging them without notice. With a superfluity of domestic servants on the market, many housemaids would have preferred to take a beating rather than be thrown on the streets.

For fear of losing their places, many servants kept quiet about the conditions under which they lived and worked. Many were unhappy because they did not have the inner resources to cope with the loneliness. One girl ran away from service and entered a factory, and when asked why she replied: 'Well, missus always sat in the parlour, and I always sat in the kitchen, and I felt lonesome. Then missus used to go out at night, and leave me all alone in the house, and I got scared and runned away. I won't go back, no, not for nobody.'

This desire for companionship was widespread, and many young girls preferred to work as 'day-maids', going home to sleep, though wages were generally much lower. Many girls in the East End were employed by well-to-do Jewesses, and passed from house to house, receiving a penny or two for washing up, scrubbing and odd jobs. Because there was more happening, servant girls preferred working in lodging houses to the better paid but more lonely life in a private house.

The wages of general servants in London varied from £12 to £18 a year, but the slaveys were lucky if they received more than £7, out of which they had to buy their clothes, boots, and a variety of small items. The top rate for a slavey in a lodging house was probably £5 a year, but she would expect to pick up a shilling or two a week from tips. As a servant girl usually had only one full day a month off, and occasional afternoons, there was difficulty in finding a regular boy-friend, and soldiers let themselves out by the hour on Sundays to friendless slaveys, charging between 1s and 5s per hour for their company.

The mistress always had control over the servant because the law of master and servant was on her side (a law rescinded in 1875) and she could discharge a girl without a character.

Punch was not *Punch* without a weekly cartoon illustrating the 'servant problem'. But is was a problem in the minds of neurotic women rather than in reality, women who treated their servants like machines instead of creatures of flesh and blood. In the 1880s the journal *British Weekly* encouraged servant girls to write to it stating their grievances. One girl came to London in 1874, and was told by her new employers that she would be treated as one of the family. She soon found that this was not so, was worked from six in the morning until ten at night for £6 a year, and forbidden to leave the house.

Another girl, who called herself 'Cleopatra', complained that her mistress forced her to go to Church of England services when she herself was a Dissenter. One letter, by a servant who entitled herself 'Crystal Palace', is worth presenting in full, as it demonstrates the idle psychological cruelty of the middle-class mistress:

My opinion is ladies have not enough work themselves, and that is why they like to call us servants lazy. My mistress does fancy needlework, and yet she can't let me have time to mend my own stockings. If I sit down a minute she rings the bell or calls out above the kitchen steps, and last week I caught her at a mean trick, for I was watching her over the banisters, and I saw her upset the visiting-cards on the hall-table *on purpose*. Then she rang the bell, and told me to go and put the cards straight. And again, she was angry with me because I opened the door to a visitor before she had time to settle herself on the drawing-room soffer, and she said the lady would think she didn't sit there, only in the parlour. I've no patience to write more.

Servants were forced to live in cellars or cold attics, often three in a bed. In one house there were twenty-five occupants, including sixteen men, catered for by four servants. In such households, servant girls were fair game, and in aristocratic houses it was understood that adolescents should try their sexual mettle on the prettier servants.

In this situation, servant girls were at their most vulnerable, and whether they were seduced or raped made little difference. Servant girls who complained that they were raped were treated with contempt in the court of law; it was considered that they were getting their own back on the dominant class, and the distinctions between seduction and rape were too narrow to be worth looking into.

In the domestic environment there was also a fine distinction between incest (not necessarily cruel) and rape. When the House of Lords appointed a select committee in 1882 to look into the law relating to the protection of young girls, there were some shocking revelations, especially from the Reverend J. W. Horsley, chaplain of Clerkenwell Prison:

There was a case of a man who was charged with an offence [incest] upon his daughter; she and he and two other children slept in the same bed. Another man was charged with an assault upon his daughter, aged 13; he and his wife, and two children, aged two and six, slept in one bed. There was another bed in the same room with a boy of 16, a girl of 13, and a boy of 11. It is almost invariably the case that it is due to overcrowding.

When asked if he thought incest was very common, Horsley said that he considered it common though not 'very common' and when asked if he knew of children of very tender years having or attempting to have sexual intercourse, he surprised their lordships by answering 'At seven or eight years childish fornication is by no means uncommon, especially in the country.'

The association of pleasure and pain in sex makes it difficult to assert how much cruelty there was involved in the cases cited by the Reverend Horsley. There was a moral cruelty, certainly, but in some of the instances there was probably an element of seduction on the part of the daughter. Horsley does not mention incest of a mother with a son, though there is every evidence that this, too was commonplace.

Cruelty can only be assigned to those incest cases where actual physical damage was done. In 1895 a man named Crowley raped his daughter Catherine, aged four. In 1893 Samuel Chambers raped a girl in the household aged four and a half. Chambers was sentenced to twenty months' imprisonment with hard labour.

The ambiguities of sexual cruelty in the domestic context are not restricted to the violation of virgin daughters. Except from a moral standpoint, the violation of a virgin wife on her wedding night is not so much different. Defloration was one of the perquisites of the bridegroom. One Berlin doctor declared in 1889 that his case-book contained 150 instances of women who had been to see him on account of injuries they had sustained on their wedding-night. If infliction of pain is the criterion of cruelty, then such injuries were the result of cruel behaviour. The right of a man to commit rape upon his wife is enshrined in the marriage laws; small wonder that divorce cases involving cruelty were treated by lawyers with a good deal of circumspection.

Lawyers, being men, regarded the wife's refusal to consummate a marriage as more reprehensible than a man demanding his rights with a vehemence bordering on savagery. Divorces were granted on the grounds of 'latent incapacity arising from hysteria', and wives went through the humiliation of a searching medical examination and wide publicity in the press.

Domestic cruelty is a topic about which it is impossible to be dogmatic. Until the coming of the psychoanalysts and their evaluation of the pleasure/pain principle there were few who could make sense of the inconsistencies and contradictions of human sexuality. A conundrum might be posed:

When is domestic cruelty not domestic cruelty?
and answered:
When it is enjoyed.

2

The Disciplinarians

'ALL CORPORAL PUNISHMENTS whatsoever, and upon whomsoever inflicted, are hateful and an indignity to our common nature, which (with or without our consent) is enshrined in the person of the sufferer. Degrading him, they degrade us.' So declared Thomas de Quincey, but he was much ahead of his time, and corporal punishment was a valuable weapon to the disciplinarians, whether they were parents, prison governors, magistrates, or headmasters.

Flogging was punitive, degrading and ultimately useless; there were few punishments that aroused greater hatred in the victim and few that had such a deleterious effect on those carrying out the punishment. Herman Melville, author of *Moby Dick*, wrote that 'the law that authorises flogging does but put a scourge into the hands of a fool'.

1817 saw the abolition of the flogging of women in public and in a report of a committee looking into criminal law in 1843 a thoroughly modern attitude is beginning to peep through:

We think that, so far from extending this species of punishment, it would be better to reject it, except in the instance to which we have alluded [offences against the person of the Queen], and a few, if any, others which it may be proper to mark with signal reprobation. It is a punishment which is uncertain in point of severity, which inflicts an ignominious and indelible disgrace on the offender, and tends, we believe, to render him callous, and greatly to obstruct his return to any honest course of life.

In 1862 the corporal punishment of adults disappeared from the criminal law of Scotland. But not so in England and the rod was wielded with almost as much energy as ever before. Where there were official plans to abolish flogging altogether there arose a chorus of protest. Atavistic instincts were never brought out more easily than when the flagellation topic was raised, and the newspapers were bombarded with letters demanding flogging for hooligans, wife-beaters, train-wreckers, and burglars. Even Queen Victoria declared that those women demanding the vote should be whipped. On one occasion the advocates of flogging won; in 1863 the Security from Violence Act was passed authorising flogging for robbery with violence, following an outbreak of mugging in the London streets.

The advocacy of flogging was often associated with anger, passion, and the inability to listen rationally to the dictates of reason. It was also associated with repression and a delight in cruelty for its own sake. And when asked to defend their attitudes, the friends of flogging reverted to one catchword, discipline. The maxim 'Spare the rod and spoil the child' was fondly believed to be enshrined in the Bible, though actually it was a quotation from Samuel Butler's *Hudibras*.

One of those who actually used this phrase to the victim was the father of Edmund Gosse. Young Gosse, aged six, was naughty 'for which my Father, after a solemn sermon, chastised me, sacrificially, by giving me several cuts with a cane. This action was justified, as everything he did was justified, by reference to Scripture. I suppose that there are some children, of a sullen and lymphatic temperament, who are smartened up and made more wide-awake by a whipping,' though he did not regard 'physical punishment as a wise element in the education of proud and sensitive children'.

The mother of Lady Emily Lytton justified her cruel conduct to her children in these words: 'Children who are bullied always love their parents more than the children who have been petted.' It was typical of a kind of mentality that no middle path could be seen between the two extremes.

If one compares flogging with other disciplines, there is an ambiguity about it that one is at a loss to find elsewhere. Flogging was looked upon as positively medicinal by doctors; it was supposed to improve the circulation of the blood. The flagellant sects in the church were part of history, and during the Victorian period the mania received a boost when fustigation became one of the penances of the nunneries of the ritualist wing of the Church of England. In 1878 Dr. E. Pusey gave respectability in his *Manual for Confessors* to 'the Discipline' for mortifications. The Discipline was believed by many to be an instrument of spiked steel, though in *Nunnery Life in the Church of England*, written about 1880, it was revealed as cat-o'-seven-tails.

Many and various as were the opportunities to flog, the number of adults disciplined (for pleasure or with pain) was infinitesimal compared with the children who were whipped at home or at school. The widespread use of the rod cannot always be assigned to cruelty. Often it was lack of imagination. Children were often regarded as an alien species or as miniature adults; they were slotted into convenient pigeon-holes. Parents were not to be inconvenienced by them. Disobedience, cheek, arrogance, these were the ominous signs that life was treating the children too well, and these defects had to be eradicated.

In well-off families the boys were usually sent away to public or other boarding schools and the business of discipline was mercifully taken out of the hands of parents. Daughters were another matter. Authorities on the subject claimed that girls were more artful than boys, and therefore had to be treated more rigorously, for otherwise habits of lying and deceit become deep-rooted. Some parents discovered that they were not able to whip their own daughters, but fortunately for their peace of mind the advertisement columns of newspapers contained the answer—a chastisement service.

The establishments which advertised were highly respectable and often situated in the best parts of town. They were regarded as useful places, and the birching was carried out with a dignity that is difficult to reconcile with the circumstances. There was an elaborate ceremony of removing dress, corsets, and drawers and the donning of a dressing-gown back to front before the ritual laying on of six strokes (this was usually deemed enough by the mistresses of these houses). The proprietors of these spanking houses would have been indignant if it had been suggested that they were behaving in an indecent manner, and when their credentials were questioned the brethren and sisterhood of the birch closed ranks.

The new middle classes were torn between their wish to emulate their betters and native good sense. Their attitude towards their children was inconsistent. They were impressionable, and when an article in the magazine *Home Chat* stated that 'birches are coming into fashion again' and that a birch may be obtained by 'a special messenger'

Children were often regarded as miniature adults, and if they did not react to reason they were beaten. (Engraving by J. Barnard)

who brought it to the house 'carefully wrapped up to look like something else' the readers happily bought and used them.

This, the dominant class of the nineteenth century, did have the opportunity to decide whether to chastise its children physically. The men of the superior classes did not; they had been inculcated into flogging at school. To get through a public school—especially Eton—without a swishing was an achievement indeed. So much kudos was associated with the ceremony that the Eton Block Club was instigated, membership of which was confined to those who had been thrashed at least three times. Not to have been flogged was considered to be missing out on something. It was an initiation ritual, and the men who presided were destined for legend—Busby of Westminster, Keate of Eton, Goodford of Eton. Stories woven around John Keate (1773–1852) lived on well into the present century—how he once dealt with ninety transgressors in one go, how he administered the birch to a number of

candidates for confirmation and how when they protested he retorted,
'You are only adding to your offence by profanity and lying'.

Sensitive boys from kindly families who were despatched to the
public schools were horrified by not only the disciplines employed, but
by the squalid conditions in which they lived, by the lop-sided
curriculum based on parrot-like learning of the classics, and by the
brutality of other boys. James Brinsley Richards related:

> When I first came to the school [Eton], and was told how culprits
> were dealt with, I fancied I was being hoaxed. I never quite
> believed the stories I heard until I actually saw a boy flogged; and I
> can never quite forget the impression which the sight produced upon
> me. . . . I felt as I have never felt but once since, and that was when
> seeing a man hanged.

The rod, imagined as a handful of twigs, was neaɪɪy five feet long,
three feet of handle and two of 'bush'. The sound of the lashes was
'like splashings of so many buckets of water'.

An Eton boy did not have to do anything actually wrong to receive
a swishing. As the approaches to the local shops were out of bounds,
any boy who bought anything or who went to cash a money-order was
subject to discipline. A way was found round this by 'shirking'. When
a boy saw a master approaching he would dart into a nearby shop and
the master would pretend not to notice. This ludicrous procedure,
hallowed by tradition, was considered preferable to changing the rules.
A boy who was slow off the mark or who happened to meet a master
who disliked him was reported and beaten for 'not shirking'.

In the 1860s there was a Parliamentary Commission into the public
schools. They were no longer monastic or private corporations but
'the great seminaries of learning in this land. . . . Their welfare and
progress concerns in the highest degree the Empire itself.' The public
schools of this time were nine in number—Eton, Harrow, Winchester,
Shrewsbury, Westminster, St. Paul's, Merchant Taylors', Charterhouse
and Rugby. The schools were praised for 'cultivating the capacity
to govern others and to control themselves, their aptitude for combining
freedom with order, their public spirit, their vigour and manliness of
character, their strong but not slavish respect for public opinion,
their love of healthy sports and exercise.' The report, published in

1864, was an exercise in whitewashing, and little attention was paid to the more reprehensible features of public-school life.

The schoolmasters felt no more opprobrium than the proprietors of the spanking houses. Canon Thomas Butler considered that such a boyish attribute as a flagging memory was 'an ill-weed which would grow apace, unless it were plucked out immediately, and the only way to pluck it out was to whip him, or shut him in a cupboard or dock him of some small pleasure of childhood'. In British India, the punishments were even savager. Schoolchildren in Bengal in 1869 were hoisted by the Reverend J. Long to the ceiling in sacks filled with stinging nettles. Sabine Baring-Gould, the hymn-writer, was no disdainer of the more mundane pleasures of the birch. As one of his pupils recorded: 'I was sent to Mr. Baring-Gould. He gave me thirty-two cuts and went back to writing Onward Christian Soldiers.'

In 1877 William Gibbs, aged twelve, was sent to Christ's Hospital after being taught at a Hertford prep school. He was so ill-used that he ran away, and was flogged, whereupon he ran away again and was locked in the school infirmary, where he hanged himself from a cord suspended from a ventilator. This could not be kept within the family, and was discussed in hushed whispers in common rooms. The headmaster of Christ's Hospital, the Reverend Charles Lee, claimed that he did not know anything at all about the matter.

If that were true, Lee must have been the only headmaster in the country who did not realise what went on in his school; that masters beat boys, and that the boys themselves tried their hands against their weaker contemporaries. The masters became as degraded as the boys. The author of *Eton under Hornby* (Hornby became headmaster in 1868) wrote in 1910 that 'pity is perhaps due not so much to the boy who has to undergo this extremely stupid and nasty form of punishment, as to the master, a gentleman and a scholar, who has to inflict it, and still worse, who can bring himself to believe that it is right and decent to do so'.

Although countenancing fagging, the monitorial system, and brutality between boy and boy, the disciple of muscular Christianity and headmaster of Rugby, Thomas Arnold, ostensibly disapproved of flogging. Nevertheless, he used the birch as the ultimate deterrent, though it is fair to say that during his regime there was not the orgy of flagellation that made 1872 Winchester memorable.

Both the psychological and the physical effects on flogged boys were disregarded. In a lecture on corporal punishment in schools Dr. J. F. Sutherland pointed out that many children suffer from heart and lung disease, nervous diseases such as epilepsy, and that in schools there should be the necessity for a medical certificate of fitness, as demanded when boys were birched by police-officers by order of sheriffs and magistrates.

The boys of the public schools usually took their punishment stoically. One enterprising lad painted a portrait of his executant on his buttocks. There was often a sadomasochistic pact between flogger and floggee. At one birching the master enquired politely, between lashes, of the boy's parents. The lower master of Eton, Austen Leigh, was known affectionately as 'the Flea' (because he drew blood). Not surprisingly it was considered bad form to protest. Complaints to parents were rare, and often when the parents complained to the governors they were coldly scorned. The implications were that if they were not satisfied with the disciplinary methods they could move their maudlin child to one of the new-fangled schools where corporal punishment was not practised.

It was very rare for a boy to refuse to take a birching. In 1856 an Eton schoolboy, Morgan Thomas, was caught smoking, but summoned to the block he denied the headmaster, Dr. Goodford, his time-honoured perquisite. Goodford promptly expelled the boy, expecting compliance from the boy's father, but Mr. Thomas not only demanded the return of his son to Eton but made the matter public, and an extensive correspondence spread through the sober columns of *The Times*. Most of the writers were choleric supporters of Dr. Goodford, and, whether from expediency or not, *The Times* came out against Mr. Thomas.

Punch, under the later editorship of Mark Lemon an insipid sop, was the voice of commonsense: 'When we find a manly sentimentalist advocating the rod, we generally discover that he has been at a public school; and we see pretty clearly that his eulogy of flogging proceeds from an opinion that it has made an exceedingly fine and clever fellow of himself; an opinion sometimes very erroneous.'

Although the physical result of a school flogging was rarely as horrible as a flogging inflicted upon a soldier or a sailor, severe injuries could be inflicted, as they were on a boy named Blount who was flogged for taking lumps of sugar from the monitors' sugar basin. Blount was flogged on the back rather than the buttocks, and his back was 'one mass of lacerated flesh'. Twelve pieces of birch rod were found imbedded in the flesh, there were fifteen mild wounds and fifteen serious wounds on the back, plus fifteen elsewhere.

Psychologically a schoolboy could be crippled by being flogged, and could not forget the shame and humiliation of being thrashed in front of his companions. George Borrow, the novelist, author of *Romany Rye* and *Lavengro*, and an authority of gypsies, was once flogged at his school at Norwich in the presence of his school-fellow James Martineau. Fifty years later the recollections still smarted enough for him to avoid any social gathering to which Martineau had been invited.

The minor public schools did their best to emulate the Etons and the Harrows, and at the schools for the poor the boys were starved and bullied into subjection. Inmates were so hungry that they caught crows and cooked them on a stove, there were no soap or towels and all was filth and frugality, the boys had their own clothes taken away and were forced to wear workhouse clothing, and there were no holidays and no visitors. At one of these schools, at Bowes in the north of England, mysterious deaths were not inquired into too assiduously, and an ominous relic of the times was the Bowes burial ground, where there were twenty-nine unmarked graves.

Such schools existed in London as well as in the inaccessible north. At Mr. Drouet's establishment in Tooting (fl. 1849) the *Examiner* reported 'a great deal of severity, not to use a harsh term, had been exercised'. Charles Dickens, who looked into the matter, was more willing to be explicit: the boys were 'knocked down, beaten, and brutally used'. Even in Scotland, well-known for its fine educational record and establishments, there were deplorable schools. In Edinburgh 130 children were taught by a one-armed Irish labourer; three of these children could read one-syllabled words. A Royal Commission in 1861 discovered private schools where the teachers consisted of discharged servants, barmaids and washerwomen.

Considering the conditions prevailing in schools for rich and poor, the aims of education, enunciated in William Johnston's *England As It Is* (1851) were laughable—the gentle and kindly sympathies, the sense of self-respect, and of the respect of fellow-men, the free exercise of the intellectual faculties, the gratification of curiosity, the power of regulating the habits and business of life, the refining and tranquillising enjoyment of the beautiful—what had these to do with the squalor of the great public schools (it was said that Winchester had not been cleaned since Queen Elizabeth died), the pedantic instruction, or the cruelty endlessly dealt out by the strong against the weak, whether the strong were masters or boys?

When the masters were apparently without self-control, the examples they set were in all cases bad ones. The coarser and more brutal boys did not hesitate long in copying them, and when they were officially brought into the system as prefects and monitors there was no limit to the cruelties they could inflict.

Fagging (from 'fag' meaning weary) was defined by Dr. Arnold as 'the power given by the supreme authorities of the school to the Sixth Form to be exercised by them over the lower boys, for the sake of securing a regular government among the boys themselves, and avoiding the evils of anarchy; in other words, of the lawless tyranny of brute force'. It was a convenient way of getting the boys to do what the masters were paid to do—keep order. But it did not work out like that; the big boys had a subject race in the persons of the small boys. It was a self-propagating licence to bully; the young boys when they got into the sixth form (the fifth form at Eton) revenging themselves on the quivering newcomers.

Until the Victorian period had run its course the fag's duties included blacking boots, brushing clothes, lighting fires, cooking meals, and, if they were pretty, offering their bodies to the fag-master. It was customary for such lads to be given feminine names—the name given to Dean Stanley, writer and theologian, at Rugby was Nancy. These boys were accepted as the 'bitches' of the older boys. The one advantage of being a 'bitch' was that one had a protector, and many new boys at the public schools gave in to the homosexual advances of sixth formers merely to survive.

There was a good deal of competition for the more attractive boys, not only from other sixth formers but from the masters. 'Spooning' between master and boy was accepted as part of the scheme of things, and Oscar Browning of Eton, Dr. Vaughan, headmaster of Harrow, and G. H. Shorting of Rugby, were all celebrated for their indiscreet propositioning of schoolboys under their care.

In *Every Boy's Annual* of 1863 there is a gruesome picture of the fag's life:

Picture to yourself the wretched 'lower boy' slowly roasted before the living coals—picture him sleeping in his master's bed, to warm it previous to its reception of its proper owner [and not only that], or having to sit in during the play-hours to copy out his master's impositions.

But this is only a prelude to the heartening postlude:

Then remember that these are fables of the past, too dastardly to be allowed, and too cruel to be inflicted during the present generation. Yes, little boys, tremble, and weep to your mammas your contemplated horrors of being subjected to the most brutal tyranny; and then, when you have come home for the holidays, recount laughingly to your younger brother how you had only to make your senior's tea in the morning, only keep up his fire during a certain portion of the day; and not even to black his boots, or to brush his clothes.

No one can say more than a century later whether the writer was a P.R.O. for the public schools, but the younger brothers, chirped up by the eulogy, would have had a rude awakening when they got to their schools. Nineteenth-century compassion never made much impression on the public school.

Besides the systematic cruelty of flogging, and the doubtful privileges of fagging there was a considerable amount of off the cuff brutality. When a new boy arrived at Winchester he was given a pair of 'tin gloves'; one of the older boys took a red-hot brand and burned him down the fingers and around the wrist. This was his inculcation into fire-lighting. If he let the fag-master's fire go out the tin gloves would be applied anew. Hugh Walpole, clumsy and short-sighted, had a desperately unhappy school life, being in great demand for the 'circus' where the young boys were forced to swing on gas brackets, jump off lockers, and were jabbed with pen nibs. At King's School, Canterbury, the aesthete Walter Pater declared, 'I do not seem to want a black eye', but he had more than this when he was savagely attacked by his fellow pupils, resulting in a permanent limp.

At Harrow in 1853 a monitor gave a boy named Stewart thirty-one strokes which disfigured him and injured him sufficiently to have him removed from the school. *The Times* reported the case in guarded terms, but Vaughan's only response was to increase the number of monitors

The dormitory, Westminster School, notorious for the cruelty practised on youngsters. (*Pictorial Times*)

from ten to fifteen. The keynotes of Harrow at this period were, according to J. A. Symonds in 1866, 'idleness, plethoric wealth, hereditary stupidity and parvenu grossness combining to form a singularly corrupt amalgam.'

In an environment where cruelty was commonplace, comparison and kindliness were dulled. In later life Edward Lyttelton was headmaster of Eton, but as a student his better qualities were swamped by the pressures to conform, 'I was distressed beyond bearing by the vocalisation of one of the cats that used to haunt Neville's Court, and against these quadrupeds we organised a cat hunt and diminished their number somewhat.' Looking back, Lyttelton tried to analyse the springs of such off-hand cruelty:

Some old ancestral strain in the blood asserts itself from days when man in self-defence was at war with the beasts of the world. Nothing else explains the weird hostility we felt to the timid rabbits, hares, and the lovely cock pheasant. If boy's nature is to be refined and uplifted, the instinct is to be guided, not crushed.

When all the accounts of public schools are examined, it is evident that the disciplinary methods failed in their purpose. But jaded traditions do not have the anticipated affect, and the schoolboys accepted the floggings as part of the upper-class pageantry associated with the prestigious public schools.

Brutish behaviour on the part of the masters, and the obvious enjoyment with which they applied the birch to the bare buttocks of generations of schoolboys, encouraged hooliganism as well as cruelty. As traditional as the block was the practice of hurling large pieces of bread at passers-by, and throwing stones and coal at the local workmen. When the evangelists Moody and Sankey arrived in Eton and Windsor to spread the word, the Eton boys bought up all the rotten eggs that were available. A petition by what were termed the 'good boys' to prevent an assault on the evangelists was contemptuously torn up.

The Eton and Harrow ethos was not forgotten when the boys went to university. Many of the 'hearties', who created such havoc between town and gown, and who indulged in rags where it was commonplace for passers-by to be injured, remained psychologically frozen in their schooldays. The passion for horse-play was often taken into the services and into the socially approved professions.

As *Punch* said, the most fondly-remembered relic of schooldays was the flogging ceremony, with or without quasi-sexual connotations. Pinch an advocate of flogging for white slave trafficking, burglary, and sexual assault, and the odds were that one would find an ex-public school boy.

3

The Subjugation of Women

IN MARRIAGE WOMAN was a second-class citizen; adultery by a wife was regarded far more seriously than adultery by a husband, and in the event of a separation the husband as a natural right took the children of the marriage. A girl on her marriage passed from dependence upon parents to submission to a husband; that is, if she belonged to the better-off classes. If she belonged to the lower orders she would go out to work to help support her husband. A woman of twenty-one could inherit and administer her own property but if she married, her personal property and real property passed into her husband's hands. Without his permission she could not make a will concerning her own property.

Married women were legally subjugated. The most ridiculous feature of it all was that a wife had no control over her earnings. The husband had supreme rights over her person, her children and her property. He could lock her up, chastise her, treat her like a dog, seduce the servants, keep a mistress (even in the same house), and if she ran away he could apply for, and usually get, his conjugal rights restored. The only thing she could do was to run up bills—the husband was liable for wifely debts, even those contracted before marriage.

A characteristic victim of the situation was Mrs. Caroline Norton, who left her husband in 1835 after repeated acts of cruelty. He cited her for adultery, naming Lord Melbourne as co-respondent, and kept the three children of the marriage. Norton's suit failed, but so did a counter-suit, for by remaining with him when he had been cruel and unfaithful she had condoned his actions.

If a married woman was a second-class citizen, an unmarried woman looked upon herself as a third-class person. Much of the unhappiness of

Victorian marriage lay in the desperation of single girls; they did not care whom they married provided that they married someone, for throughout the entire period there was a surplus of women over men. In 1841 in London there were 996,720 females against 876,956 males. The men could get the pick while the women, kept in enforced idleness, simmered with repressed hysteria, assuaging their panic with needlework, piano-playing, and empty pastimes. 'Women don't consider themselves as human beings at all,' wrote Florence Nightingale in a private memo in 1851, 'there is absolutely no God, no country, no duty to them at all, except family.'

They took a lead from the top. Even Queen Victoria was uncertain of her pretensions. She wrote that she was convinced that 'we women, if we are to be good women, feminine and amiable and domestic, are not fitted to reign'. Submission, legal, social, and sexual, was their appointed role. The men did not have to enforce it. The women brought it on themselves.

Women were persuaded into taking a resigned pessimistic view of themselves, and in 1868 the phrase 'redundant women' became fashionable. Women who had not succeeded in getting married often looked on themselves as failures. The word spinster carried bleak connotations, and for a woman not to want to get married was considered unnatural, a slap in the face of all that was holy.

Fortunately there were a number of women who did not mind remaining single, who did not see why the men had to get all the plum jobs and why women were forbidden medicine, the law, and all those pursuits sacred to the male. The Society for Promoting the Employment of Women was born in 1859.

Not surprisingly many men turned on them, and the 'old maids' who wanted university education and who had the effrontery to ask to learn to be a doctor were treated with a savagery that makes uneasy reading. The advocates of what became known as women's rights did not share the assumption that woman was naturally self-effacing, willing to be trodden upon by every man with a mind to do it. In 1861 Florence Nightingale complained that 'Women crave for being loved, not for loving. They scream out at you for sympathy all day long, they are incapable of giving any in return for they cannot remember your affairs long enough to do so.' It was a campaign against cabbage-like somnolence, but it needed more than a handful of women's rights supporters to get the message through.

To get good jobs women needed training. They needed to go to university. The men declared that this was out of the question, and drew support from parents who were convinced that 'solid attainments are actually disadvantageous to marriage' and 'accomplishments and what is showy and superficially attractive are really essential'. There was agreement from Mark Pattison, rector of Lincoln College, Oxford. notorious for his complete lack of contact with the outside world. He thought that the average man of the middle class disliked an educated woman, because she made him too conscious of his own want of instruction—man's superiority syndrome in its most naked form.

Pattison and his ilk thought that it was sufficient for girls to do a little needlework, paint the odd water-colour, prattle a bit in schoolgirl French, and assimilate enough simple arithmetic to be able to tot up their account books. They scorned the idea that women could be truly educated, and laughed at the notion that education could be a solace in later life to those women who had not got married. The schoolteacher Miss Shirreff was dismissed as a foolish busybody when she compared the faces of an old man and woman:

He has ripened through the course of years—she has withered; his powers have enlarged and gained in firmness and weight what they may have lost in fire and brilliancy; hers have been smothered under small cares, small pleasures, and small interests.

Miss Shirreff wrote a book outlining a course of subjects including higher mathematics, the natural sciences, literature, and history, which would assist an intelligent woman to get through her declining years with enjoyment rather than in despair.

There cannot be said to be cruelty in dissuading women from entering the areas of life previously debarred to them. But dissuasion is different from forcibly preventing women from entering careers on which they have set their hearts. The imposition of a stronger will due to fear of competition has the requisite elements of cruelty, motivated by sexual rivalry.

At its mildest, this cruelty consisted of unchivalrous sniping by the gentlemen of the press. *Punch*, as ever, was in the van. When Charles Kingsley gave a series of 'Lectures to Ladies' in 1847 under the aegis of the Christian Socialist movement, *Punch* came out with squibs about professors of bead-purse making and degrees in crochet work. The correspondence columns of the daily press puffed and bubbled with the indignation of choleric old men, who would have been indignant had it been suggested that their ungentlemenly behaviour was due to fear, the fear of the novel, the fear that their roles and those of their sons would be taken over by women.

The instructors at Queen's College were amazed by the eagerness with which their fairly simple lessons were greeted, and appalled at the ignorance of even long-established teachers and governesses. The women could not cope with simple algebra let alone trigonometry, and whereas the lecturers at Queen's College would have dearly liked to have discussed the momentous events then happening in Europe—after all, 1848 was 'the year of revolutions'—the historical knowledge of the women under instruction was so vague that it was considered advisable to instruct them on mundane topics of the 1066-and-all-that order.

It was found that the women were very interested in science, and these lectures were invariably packed. The men closed ranks, and their spokesman, the Bishop of London, excluded women from the lectures on electricity by the scientist Wheatstone (inventor of the electric telegraph) on the grounds that they had 'congregated too abundantly' at the lectures of the geologist Sir Charles Lyell, and had thus prevented more deserving cases—men—from getting places in the lecture room. Wheatstone resigned his professorship at King's College, London, rather than countenance the unfair treatment of women.

Even Queen's College was run exclusively by men and the only female participation in management was the presence in the lecture hall of Lady Visitors, who acted as chaperones. Some balance came with the inauguration of Bedford College in 1849, with a mixed board of management. The success of this pioneer educational establishment for women acted as a goad to all those reactionaries who considered that woman's place was in the home or, to quote Tennyson, 'all else confusion'.

Nevertheless, Bedford College and Queen's College were oases in a wilderness, and in *Thoughts on Self-Culture* Mrs. Maria Grey and her sister Emily Shirreff (who later helped establish Girton College for women at Cambridge) complained that education for women was 'a mere blank, or worse, a tissue of laboured frivolities under a solemn name; a patchwork begun without any aim, fashioned without method, and flung aside, when half-finished, as carelessly as it was begun'.

Whether they liked it or not, the unrepentant men found that the women involved in women's rights were not amenable to mockery, snubs, contempt, facetiousness, or satire, and that they ignored the labels fastened to them—the 'Shrieking Sisterhood' was one. Even the strenuous opposition of Queen Victoria, who was 'most anxious to enlist everyone who can speak or write or join in checking this mad, wicked folly of "Woman's Rights" with all its attendant horrors' was no deterrent.

Women's rights were a threat to male domination. Fear bred anger. It was bruited that the women's rights movement had the backing of Roman Catholic priests and suspicions were not lulled when Annie Besant, later a courageous birth control propagandist, declared that 'if the Bible and Religion stood in the way of women's rights then the Bible and Religion must go'.

The crux of the whole matter was that those most involved in women's rights were well-off. A rich single woman could not be driven into the ground as if she were some feeble mill-girl. Florence Nightingale, her cousin Barbara Leigh Smith (with an income in her own right of £300 a year), Louisa Twining (a pioneer of workhouse reform), and Mary Carpenter (an advocate of 'ragged schools', opening her own in Bristol in 1846)—none of these could be starved into submission. But they and their disciples could be humiliated.

The women who wanted to take up medicine were treated the worst. They were up against not only medical teachers but fellow students who organised rags for the embarrassment and discomfiture of the women. In 1870 a gang of male students lined up to prevent five women entering the Surgeon's Hall, shouting, jostling them, and throwing mud at them. When the women gained entrance a sheep was pushed into the class room. They were followed in the streets by hooligan students who shouted abuse at them 'using medical terms to make the disgusting purport of their language more intelligible'. When the women did well in examinations they were passed over, and scholarships were awarded to the men immediately beneath them.

Examiners deliberately tried to embarrass female students by posing grossly indecent questions.

The sex war also waged in elementary education. In 1867 a deputation of country schoolmasters urged that the authorities should provide them with increased allowances to be paid by reducing the salaries of schoolmistresses. In 1879 the Birmingham Education Authority bowed down to the outcry of male teachers and discontinued the employment of women as teachers of small boys—which was, the men maintained, 'encouragement to immorality'.

Lawyers succeeded in keeping women out of the Inns of Court, the Church of England was closed to women except in the Anglican nunneries (where, it was believed, the most ghastly things went on), but in medicine and education women won the day, simply because the leaders of the women's rights movements had the energy and the money to breach the male bastions.

For the genteel poor, the outlook was bleak. The fashion for educating girls at home produced the phenomenon of the governess. No category was more vulnerable. The governesses' meagre education fitted them for that role and no other, and in the census of 1851 the number of governesses in Britain was reckoned at 21,000.

The keynote of the governess's life was humiliation, and the endurance of psychological cruelty. The definition of a governess, according to the *Quarterly Review*, was a being 'who is our equal in birth, manners and education, but our inferior in worldly wealth . . . there is no other class which so cruelly requires its members to be, in birth, mind, and manners, above their station, in order to fit them for their station'.

According to novelists, daughters of ruined gentlemen commonly became governesses, tragic figures who strived to preserve their independence against all the odds, odd women out, neither fish nor fowl.

The situation of the governess was most pathetic because she did not expect to find herself in such sorry straits. Her wages could be as low as eight pounds a year; in her last situation as governess Charlotte Brontë received twenty pounds a year, actually only sixteen as washing expenses were deducted at source.

The most unenviable governesses were those who were forced to support someone else out of their meagre income, and ended up 'starved, worn out, blind, paralytic, insane, after having educated nephews and nieces, put themselves out of the way of marriage, resisted temptations of which no one but the desolate can comprehend the force, and fought a noble fight'.

Because the supply of governesses was far greater than the demand, many of the more desperate girls would do the job for nothing, just to get a roof over their head. On 27th June 1845 there was an advertisement in *The Times*:

Wanted, a Governess, on Handsome Terms. Governess—a comfortable home, but without salary, is offered to any lady wishing for a situation as governess in a gentleman's family residing in the country, to instruct two little girls in music, drawing, and English; a thorough knowledge of the French language is required.

The duties of a governess, especially one employed by a family of the commercial middle class which delighted in degrading someone of superior breeding, were dreary and disenchanting. As a special treat the governess might be allowed to enter the parlour, but she would take her meals in the schoolroom. The governess heroine of Anne Brontë's *Agnes Grey* was forced to ride to church with her back to the horses, and when she walked with her pupils she was ordered to keep a few steps behind them.

The children of the house and servants soon realised that the governess was fair game. To almost any gentleman she was 'a tabooed woman, to whom he is interdicted from granting the usual privileges of the sex'. Tradesmen, smarting from the snubs they had received from their superiors, took revenge on governesses, a species from the superior classes provided by a divine providence for their spite. The ritual Sunday church service was, to most governesses, social agony.

The governess was tormented by her charges refusing to do their lessons, throwing her work-bag in the fire, or forcing her to go out in the garden and play with them knowing that her lonely meal was getting cold. The larger children would assault their governesses, and the more ambitious of the boys would try them out sexually.

Charlotte Brontë's years as a governess embittered her throughout her life:

None but those who had been in the position of a governess could ever realise the dark side of 'respectable' human nature; under no great temptation to crime, but daily giving way to selfishness and ill-temper, till its conduct toward those dependent on it sometimes amounts to a tyranny of which one would rather be the victim than the inflicter.

When she was famous and invited to a tea-party at Thackeray's house, she was so socially ill at ease that she took refuge with the governess there.

Not all employers were tyrants, not all of them burdened the governess with sewing, housework, and errands, refused to allow relatives to visit her, or discouraged unattached young men from making approaches. And governesses were not necessarily meek and lady-like. They could terrorise their charges if the parents were amenable. Lucy Lyttelton, later Lady Frederick Cavendish, had a governess named Miss Nicholson who, she wrote in her diary, 'was over-severe and apt to whip me for obstinacy when I was only dense'. Miss Nicholson used to parade the young girl along the Brighton sea front with her hands tied behind the back.

Cruelty on the part of the governess was often self-protection, for a churlish child reflected badly on her. It was also revenge for the accident of fate that had put her in the role. Imaginative parents were wise to treat their governesses with kindness, for cruelty could rebound on their own children. A sharp word to an outwardly uncomplaining governess could result in four hours in a dark cupboard for a small sobbing child.

The isolation of the governess bred loneliness and neurosis; Harriet Martineau suggested that there should be an inquiry into the proportion of governesses among inmates of lunatic asylums (there was, and the proportion was high). Peculiar relationships could be built up between governess and pupil, explored by Henry James in *The Turn of the Screw*, and these could have a tragic outcome for both instructor and instructed.

Where there is an awareness of the subjugation of oneself, then there is an additional cross to bear. The tortured sensibilities of governesses made the callousness and cruelty with which they were treated seem far worse than they were. On a pro rata basis, the profession was never treated with the gross brutality suffered by factory girls, apprentices, or workers in the mines. Even the most obnoxious employer would have thought twice about striking a governess.

There were moves during the nineteenth century to make the lot of the governess easier—the age was not short on good intentions. But with a surplus of half-educated women and the absence of equivalent occupations, the governess profession was always overcrowded. The aim of the governess was to start a school of her own; but very few, except in fiction, managed it.

The first step to help the governess was the formation of the Governesses' Benevolent Association in 1841, and in 1846 a home was opened in Harley Street for governesses out of work. An annuity system was started for governesses too old to work, and by the end of 1847 four annuities of fifteen pounds had been secured, for which there were ninety candidates. As the century drew on, there were more opportunities for well-bred girls in other occupations, and some of the pressures were relieved.

But being a governess was never a sinecure. A starving old age was a spectre always present. It may be argued that governesses went into subjugation willingly, that they could have earned a living making shirts or hats. But many grasped at the simulacrum of well-bred living, and accepted the indignities. And few could blame them. Education without opportunity still has its victims today.

4

Social One-Upmanship

THE CLASS STRUCTURE in Britain was never so strong as its supporters believed, and when money rather than birth became the criterion for entrance into good society the upper classes assimilated a grotesque assortment of men and women who would once have been considered outsiders. The Prince of Wales was largely responsible for opening the doors to the parvenu, for introducing actresses and other lowly species into the 'top ten thousand' and making Jewish participation in society respectable. The Prince of Wales worshipped wealth, and it was through him that the Rothschilds became 'a race of social potentates'.

London society was a chaotic collection of sets. Some were more exclusive than others, and the old aristocracy preserved an aloofness that was icy in its rejection of change. There were certain houses and hosts round which the social atoms rallied; there were a few genuine social leaders, and a mass of pretenders. The aristocratic sets revolved around Lady Sefton, Lady Cowper, Lady Marian Alford, Lady Northampton and Lady Pembroke, and woe-betide any intruders who tried to gate-crash on their gatherings.

The newly-ennobled middle classes tried to emulate the aristocracy, and used the same means to crush interlopers—rudeness. But the natural hauteur of the high flyers was replaced by arrogance, polite snub by gratuitous insult, and social uncertainty gave their parties an air of the battlefield, with minefields laid out for the imperceptive and unwary. Typical of the middle classes who had bought themselves into London society were the Brasseys, Sir Thomas and Lady Brassey. Sir Thomas Brassey (1836–1918) was never allowed to forget that his

The Prince of Wales made Jewish participation in society respectable, but Jews were still the butt of cartoonists. (*Picture Magazine*)

father, the railway builder, had been a farmer's son, and was treated with disdain by contemporary commentators on the social scene. Sir Thomas (made Earl Brassey in 1911) was, 'A Foreign Resident' (alias T. H. S. Escott) tells us, 'reputed a good fellow. His manner is phlegmatic and fishlike. Perhaps the latter quality is the result of his extensive maritime experience.'

The Brasseys had made themselves vulnerable not by being rich, but by being ostentatious. 'The simplest journey is converted by Lady Brassey into a royal progress. There must be equipages and outriders, the paraphernalia of a *cortège*. She would like that her arrival at any given point should be announced by a peal of bells from the neighbouring spire or a *feu de joie*.'

The more fastidious sets were determined to preserve their status.

Typical of the middle classes who bought themselves into society was Sir Thomas Brassey. This was his home at Norman Hurst. (*Graphic*)

Their members were intolerant of an obtrusive personality, and there were unwritten rules for newcomers who were on the verge of being accepted: never attempt to be amusing; never venture into an anecdote; watch how anecdotes are received. It was all very confusing, because there were a number of licensed fools who could get away with anything. Seemingly cold and indifferent to anything, a set could be thrown into paroxysms of laughter by practical jokes, a propensity taken over from royalty. When Prince Albert was alive, Lord Granville stated that he would never tell the royal couple his best stories when pretending to pinch his fingers in the door would be much more acceptable.

Those who had fought their way into the inner circles were often shocked by the cynicism that they found, the delight in cruel and malicious gossip, the fondness for trivia, and the preoccupation with putting people in their places, frequently accompanied by a savagery that was the more acceptable if it could be made amusing. There was guerrilla warfare between the sets, the laying of plots, the hunting down of those who had betrayed their class, all conducted with immense sang-froid. Society had the logic of *Alice in Wonderland*. No wonder that many people were permanently bruised by their experiences. The crushing snub and the ceremony of cutting in the street were brought to a peak of perfection, made more damning by the insouciance of the practitioners.

These were all symptoms of cracks in the edifice of society, as revealing as the hysterical cries of the old gentry against the intrusion of Germans and Jews into the sacred purlieus of privilege. Another threat to the status quo was American women; they were marrying by the score into the aristocracy, and brought a breezy commonsense into the gas-lit salons of Mayfair. To some sensible hostesses the American woman was a civilising influence. To others they were brash, and, worst of all, they were warm. English society flourished on cold disdain, an observation of the laws of polite behaviour, and a rigid adherence to an absurd protocol. An example of the way in which common decency was pushed overboard in the cause of good form came in 1885.

The eldest son of an estate owner died, and his funeral was fixed for the same day that a party of fashionable guests was to assemble at the house which he would have inherited. There was no question of putting the party off, and the corpse of the young man came up on the same train as the guests, a subject of idle speculation. The visitors hoped that the funeral would not throw a cloud over their enjoyment.

This kind of detached inhumanity was abhorred by many of the new members of the upper classes who had come from humbler but better-hearted backgrounds, and the social outsiders who had been taken up to relieve the ennui were dropped as soon as their novelty began to pall. On their part, the love affair with the upper classes was sometimes abruptly discontinued when it was discovered what they were really like, though many of them took a long time to realise that they were being treated like animals in a cage, prodded to see what tricks they could do.

The members of society were bound together by an identity of sentiment or pursuit that came from associations at school, college, regiment, club, or in official or diplomatic life. Youngsters of the privileged classes caught on to their special place in the universe quickly.

The privileged could get away with a good deal if their credentials were good, but if they let the side down they would be pitilessly punished. They could cross the narrow line not by doing anything wrong, but by being found out by their inferiors. A short paragraph in a newspaper, indicating that a man had committed fraud, or a woman had been detected in adultery, was social death. The same man, known to be skating on thin ice and dabbling in the unlawful, was wined and dined, and perhaps ribbed about his activities. But as soon as these actions became public knowledge then, whether or not he got off, he was finished. This happened to Whitaker Wright, who broke dramatically into the London scene in 1889, made a fortune, and spent a million pounds on improving his home, Lea Park, near Godalming, bought for £250,000 in 1896. In 1899 his aristocratic patron, the Marquis of Dufferin, stated that there was half a million pounds in the kitty of Wright's front organisation, the London and Globe Finance Corporation. There was only £29,300. Wright crashed, his social connections were cut, and later he committed suicide. He had made the cardinal error of being found out, and being seen to be found out. So far as society was concerned, there was no appeal court.

To some observers, such as the barrister William Johnston writing in 1851, the outward mien of the upper class man dated back to his schooldays and to those outposts of bullying and barbarism, the public school.

If this is true it can explain much of the peculiarities of the attitude of the male members of society, and also their mob mentality. They were gregarious, but off-hand. They were clubmen but not chummy. Not all were intellectually or emotionally stunted, but many were, and when they were nonplussed they took refuge in acerbity. As Lord

Critical 'old Boys.'

Ex-public schoolboys were gregarious but off-hand, and 'were generally cross to one another'. These elderly men were watching the annual Eton and Harrow cricket match at Lord's. (*Windsor Magazine*)

Ribblesdale wrote in his autobiography, 'In my youth people were frequently—almost generally—cross to one another.' A simple sentence that reveals much.

This crossness could be construed as wit, as it was by Lady St. Helier. Bernal Osborne was one of the approved parasites of the aristocracy: 'He was very amusing and witty, but sometimes very brutal, and many people lived in a state of terror of his sharp tongue and cruel criticisms.'

The outspokenness of those with a regular place in society encouraged those on the fringe to join in. But, Escott warns:

Do not suppose that the conversational licence, which society in London sanctions and stimulates, is indiscriminately allowed to anyone who chooses to claim it. You must be a chartered libertine in the possession of a certificate duly given to you by society first.

The joker must know the idiosyncrasies of the company he was keeping, and how he himself was rated. In one of the few outspoken stage plays of the mid-Victorian period, T. W. Robertson in *Caste* (1867) put a commonly-held point of view into the mouths of one of his characters:

> 'Oh, caste's all right, caste is a good thing if it's not carried too far. It shuts the door on the pretentious and the vulgar; but it should open the door very wide for exceptional merit.'

There was a degree of social mobility, for there was ambiguity about the newer professions. In marking out their rungs on the social ladder, groups of the same profession could be at each other's throats. Brassey bought himself into society successfully, but his contemporary Sir Samuel Peto (1809–89) was not so fortunate. The railway boom made a fortune for Peto, and he laid out railways in England, Russia, Norway, Algeria, and Australia. He was created a baronet in 1855 midway between a parliamentary career that spanned more than twenty years (1847–68). In 1866 during the financial panic the firm of Peto and Betts had to suspend payment (the fact that there were assets of £5,000,000 and liabilities of only £4,000,000 was neither here nor there to the true blues anxious to see Peto returned to his proper station in life).

The mockery that Peto was forced to undergo when financial embarrassment curbed his pretentions was gleeful and sustained, and the extent to which the sport of deflating the *nouveaux riches* reached can be demonstrated by flicking over the pages of *Punch* and seeing how George du Maurier fells the interlopers (invariably depicted as fat, coarse, bovine, ill-dressed and ugly):

> Angelina: Look, Edwin! Mr. and Mrs. Dedleigh Boreham! I'm quite ashamed to meet them! They're always asking us to dinner, and we've never even asked them inside our house! We really *must* make *some* return!
>
> Edwin: Some *return*? Why, confound it! Once we actually *did* dine with them! What *more* can they expect?

A more subtle form of deflation occurs in an 1883 du Maurier cartoon:

Mrs. Ponsonby de Tomkyns: And how about your dinner-party, Lady Midas? Who's coming?

Lady Midas: Well, it's *small*, but precious *select*, I can tell you. The Marquis and Marchioness of Chepe, Viscount and Viscountess Silverlacke, the Hon. Oleo and Lady Margarine Delarde, Sir Pullman and Lady Carr, and the Cholmondeley-Mainwaring-Carshaltons.

Mrs. P. de T.: My *dear* Lady Midas, you don't mean to say you've asked all these fine people to meet nobody but *each other*? Why, they'll be bored to death, and never forgive you! It's not as if you were already *one of themselves*, you know! You must wire to Grigsby at once to come and dine and bring his banjo, and I'll get you Nellie Micklemash and her husband from the Jollity. She's not acting now.

Lady M.: But, my dear, she's not respectable, I'm told!

Mrs. P. de T.: No, but she's amusing and that's *everything*! And look here, I'll throw over the Botherby Joneses, and come *myself*!

It may be that society is passably civilised if its members resort to insults rather than fists. There were grades of insult from the gentle innuendo which the thick-skinned would not understand to the untrammelled psychological cruelty that was a speciality of Fanny Kemble (1809–93), the actress, who although never admitted to the more select circles had been granted a provisional licence. One of her victims was Mrs. Lynn Linton, who herself was no respecter of liberties, and was a castigator of the 'new woman'. Mrs. Linton wrote in her autobiography:

> The way in which she levelled her big black eyes at me, and calmly put her foot on me, was an experience never to be forgotten. The pitiless brutality of her contradictions, her scathing sarcasm, her contemptuous taunts, knowing that I was unable to answer her, the way in which she used her matured powers to wound and hurt my even then immature nature, gave me a certain shuddering horror for her.

The temerity of the dragons of Victorian high society is almost incomprehensible when one realises that they were not getting paid for gratuitous insults or insolent behaviour. Naturally, one did not verbally belabour a social superior, but there does not seem any difference in quality between the snubbing of an equal or the snubbing of an inferior. Men and women of mature years and of a high station in life could be treated by their betters as if they were small girls or boys, and humiliated, in private or before guests, servants, or, indeed, anyone who happened to be about at the time.

"WHAT ARE YOUR VIEWS, MR. JONES, ON THE THERMAL EQUIVALENT OF OXIDE OF CHLORINE?"

The art of deflation was assiduously practised by the upper classes and those with aspirations towards membership. (*Graphic*)

One of those who suffered was the society preacher, Mr. Brookfield, the friend of Thackeray, whose wife ran a popular salon. He was visiting Lord Crewe at Crewe Hall. Lord Crewe was a licensed eccentric. He had a penchant for wearing orchids in his button-hole, and his detachment from his environment was exemplified in a comment he made to his sister when Crewe Hall was burning down. She had previously complained that it was a cold house; he told her that she could not say that now.

During his stay, Brookfield went down in the conservatory to smoke his pipe. The following evening he was intercepted by Lord Crewe, who said to him, 'The Groom of the Chambers will show you to your room, Mr. Brookfield. I fear you had some difficulty in finding it last night. Please permit him to accompany you.' To prevent Brookfield going down again into the conservatory to smoke, the Groom of the Chambers was ordered to lock the offending guest in his room.

Being a guest did not debar a visitor from being insulted, and many dreaded the requisite journeys to the haunts of the Dowager Duchess of Cleveland or Lady Derby. At Battle, Sussex, the home of the Duchess of Cleveland, there was an austerity in the hospitality that made good trenchermen blanch, and 'From Battle, murder and sudden death, Good Lord deliver us' was often quoted by the victims. One visitor was Lord Henry Lennox, who was heard by his hostess to use slang. 'May I inquire, Lord Henry,' she asked, 'whether, when you have completely mastered the language of the servants' hall, you mean to adopt its manners as well?'

Lady Holland (1770–1845) was the daughter of a Jamaican planter, a class notorious for cruelty. Her first marriage was dissolved in 1797 on account of her adultery, and this prevented her from being presented at Court, a fact that deeply embittered her. Her acid tongue and rude behaviour were known throughout the kingdom. She was at dinner, and her neighbour was a shy young man. She plunged her hand into his pocket and drew out a handkerchief, which she handed to a servant with the instructions 'Take that to the wash!' Occasionally, very occasionally, Lady Holland was deflated. Count d'Orsay, the consort of Lady Blessington, gigolo and a leader of men's fashions, was a highly desirable component of the fashionable party. At a dinner, Lady Holland continually dropped her napkin so that d'Orsay could do the gentlemanly thing of picking it up. Eventually he tired of the charade, and asked, 'Should I not do better, Madam, to sit under the table in order to keep passing up your napkin more quickly?'

As they had more time to work out their bon mots and their

repartee, women were more assiduous in the art of insult than their men-folk. They were also more conscious of their dignity and the necessity of constantly drawing attention to their own superior station in life. Lady Suffield could not think of mixing with inferiors, and at an assembly (a dance) at Aylsham there were present the sons of a successful local miller and merchant. 'It is most unpleasant here,' she complained. 'I can hardly see across the room for the flour dust.' Many thought that her airs and graces were a reaction against her unappreciative father, who, when told of her birth by the butler, told him that he had 'better go and drag the baby through the horse-pond'.

Because of her ancestry—her father was a singer—Frances, Lady Waldegrave, one of the premier hostesses during the early part of the period, used double bluff to divert the attention of her guests. Of 'curious' or 'unknown' guests who turned up at her home at Strawberry Hill, Twickenham, she would say 'I am sure every one will say they are some of my vulgar relatives', cleverly defusing any situation.

As daughters grew up, they were introduced into their mothers' circles, and acquired the same tone. The second and third generation of Victorian snob could be even more tiresome than the first, and after their apprenticeship of being patronised they learned to give as good as they got.

Lady Emily Lytton was perhaps typical of a kind of person, pleasant and amiable in herself, but obliged to go through the ritual of social snubbing. The South African novelist Olive Schreiner 'speaks with a strong Cape accent which perhaps made her seem rather vulgar, but I think she is decidedly common.' Hardly more than having an overbearing sense of self-importance, perhaps, but such mannerisms could grow, divert a personality into a crabbed narrow path in which the denigration of others became the prime purpose of life. The result was a consumption of the spirit, an empty existence, knowing that somewhere someone would be making fun of one as one was making fun of them. The hard lines of malice came early to the faces of the Victorian matriarchs.

Insults and diatribes that a century earlier would have sent the recipient scurrying for his duelling pistol were received with a calmness and surprising imperviousness by men of note. Spencer Lyttelton said to Arthur Balfour: 'Balfour, I don't know whether it is the vulgarity of your manners, or the ugliness of your appearance which is attracting public notice, but we are the centre of attraction for all observers.'

Balfour did not apparently do anything, and went on to become a remarkably inactive prime minister. To turn the other cheek was the way to get on in politics.

Occasionally the worm turned. One disenchanted sufferer at the hands of Mrs. Dudley Carleton felt that 'a short residence in Lucknow under the late circumstances [i.e. the Indian Mutiny and the siege of Lucknow] would have been a very good thing for her'. And no doubt this was true of many of the fashionable hostesses, society tyrants, and salon mistresses who ran roughshod over the feelings of their equals and inferiors. But never their superiors. This would have broken the sacred law of social primogeniture, and this would have never done.

5

Religious Cruelty

RELIGIOUS PERSECUTION AND cruelty greatly diminished
during the nineteenth century. Nobody was burned or tortured for
heresy, though there was continuous warfare between the various
sects. The occasional violence could rarely be called cruel, and cases of
injustice, such as when dissenters were sent to prison for refusing to pay
church rates, were instances of muddle and the existence of archaic
laws rather than deliberate harassment.

The conflict between the high church and the low church within the
established religion created confusion and disgust, the deplorable state
of many churches made worship uncomfortable or even dangerous, and
there were far too many members of the clergy who did not deserve to
hold down their jobs and who were mad, eccentric, overbearing and
cruel.

In 1850 anti-Papal riots did seem to herald a return to the old days
of religious persecution. 'Catholic England (was) restored to its orbit
in the ecclesiastical firmament, from which its light had long vanished.'
The Queen, the government, the press, and the overwhelming mass of
the people operated as an entity to destroy what they imagined was a
threat from Rome.

It was a rare manifestation of corporate cruelty. Had the same
circumstances occurred two hundred years earlier, one dreads to think
of what would have happened. There would not have been guys
burning on bonfires but live Catholics. The circumstances of what was
known as the Papal Aggression demonstrate not a change of attitude—
anti-Catholicism was as widespread as it had been during the days of
Elizabeth I—but a change of action. A stone through a window had

replaced a stone through a skull, the Guy Fawkes day smell was compounded of burning brushwood instead of singeing flesh.

Dissenters, like Catholics, had their problems. The Primitive Methodists, who had broken from the main body in 1811, held their meetings in the open air, and were vulnerable to hooligans. Gradually the Primitive Methodists won respect from the gentry and the middle classes, and as the century went on the adherents had only to cope with the austerities and cruelties administered by their preachers and themselves.

Of all the varieties of Victorian cruelty, Victorian religious cruelty presents the most ambiguity. Cruelty for pleasure, cruelty for profit, cruelty by proxy, all these can be understood in simple terms, but cruelty for the good of one's soul carries certain problems. The novelist Henry Nevinson expressed the situation of the dissenter well when he wrote in his autobiography: 'We all lived tremulously in a Valley of Shadows.'

The Particular and Strict Baptists were threatened by damnation and hell-fire. The Methodist children were subjected to the hymns of their sage, Isaac Watts:

> Have you not heard what dreadful plagues
> Are threatened by the Lord,
> To him that breaks his father's laws,
> Or mocks his mother's word?
>
> What heavy guilt upon him lies!
> How cursed is his name!
> The ravens shall pick out his eyes,
> And eagles eat the same.

Children were often whipped, frequently punished by confinement in dark cupboards, and treated with psychological cruelty. The stern regimen of Victorian dissenters often had a disastrous effect on family life, and the children of such parents either succumbed to systematic brain-washing or threw off their shackles as soon as they had the opportunity.

Mostly dissenters were left alone but the more flamboyant groups, such as the Salvation Army, were fair game. In its first year, 1882, 642 members of the Salvation Army were knocked down and assaulted,

a third of them women. Hooligans banded together and called themselves the Skeleton Army, and there were clashes between them and the
Salvationists. They were often paid by owners of beer-houses and gin
palaces, made angry by the Salvation Army's successful fight against
drink.

An outsider ceases to be an outsider when the reason for his attitude
is understood. Dissenters won respect by their stubborn adherence to
their principles. They were never considered the threat to the state and
the established religion that the Catholics were.

II THE UNDERDOGS

6

The Mad and the Sick

THE VICTORIAN TREATMENT of the insane was more enlightened than that prevailing in previous centuries, and that there was a good deal of cruelty shown to lunatics during the age was due to flaws in the system, apathy on the part of the public, and human weaknesses on the part of those engaged in administrating hospitals, workhouses, and asylums. There was little official intent to punish people for being insane, and the days had long gone when insanity was regarded as demoniacal possession and where the main aim was to drive the demons out by scourging, torture, or burning at the stake. Nevertheless some of this archaic thought still lingered on, and there were two notable *causes célèbres* where women were certified for professing in the one case spiritualism and in the other Swedenborgism.

There remained a temptation to blame people for being insane, and the usual reason assigned was drink. The mind-bending effects of certain drugs, such as chloral hydrate and laudanum, were rarely appreciated, nor was general paralysis of the insane, the frequent culmination of syphilis. Amongst many doctors there was considerable reluctance to view insanity as a disease rather than a visitation, in the same way that today alcoholism is still not fully regarded as a disease and not just a vicious habit that can be overcome by self-control and getting a grip on oneself.

The effect of insanity upon responsibility and civil capacity had been recognised by the Romans, and their jurisprudence took cognisance of the inability of the insane to control their own affairs. During the middle ages the insane were little protected, and during the reign of Edward II laws were passed enabling the monarch to exercise control over their lands and estates. There was a good deal of doubt about what constituted idiocy, and criteria of capacity such as counting twenty pence, naming mother and father or the days in week, were introduced. The term lunatic, deriving from the belief that the moon had an influence on mental disorders, does not make an appearance in the statute-book until the time of Henry VIII; the legal luminary Coke defined a lunatic as a 'person who has sometimes his understanding and sometimes not'.

The Victorians were hardly more advanced in their views than this. In their treatment of those occasional harbingers of insanity, hysteria and anxiety, they took a step backwards. The eighteenth century had been more enlightened. Cheyne, in *The English Malady* (1733) had referred to the 'apprehension and remorse . . . a perpetual anxiety and inquietude . . . a melancholy fright and panick' and Whytt in his *Observations on the Nature, Causes, and Cure of Those Disorders Which Have Commonly Been Called Nervous, Hypochondriac, and Hysteric* (1764) observed the 'fearfulness . . . uneasiness not to be described' of those afflicted by anxiety. Victorians who were 'hypped and vapoured with imaginary or trifling evils' often found themselves inside lunatic asylums, put there by baffled doctors who had in many cases exacerbated the original conditions by prescribing the vast range of new drugs that had appeared on the scene—morphine, strychnine, narcotine, and the elixir laudanum. The pathologically anxious could be turned into drug addicts overnight.

The people who found themselves relegated to the lunatic asylum were not necessarily what we would call insane. Patients included epileptics and neurotics as well as the amiably senile. Their presence within the escape-proof walls of Colney Hatch or Hanwell depended largely on whether anyone wanted them put away. It is clear from reports of Royal Commissions formed to inquire into the whole question of lunacy that anyone could certify anyone else if he or she had a mind to it, always supposing that one could find two complaissant doctors and a magistrate. Not that a magistrate was necessary; a clergyman could officiate. This was a provision for remote country places where magistrates were few and far between, but for husbands or wives who, for a variety of reasons ranging between suspected adultery and greed, wanted their spouses incarcerated, a clergyman was more easily induced to sign a committal form than a justice of the peace.

The neurotic, the senile and the epileptic were often confined with the raving mad in Victorian asylums. This 1854 engraving purports to depict a contemporary scene. (*Magazine of Art*)

Much of the blame for rash committals lies at the door of the medical profession. Many doctors professed to be experts in the field of insanity whereas they knew nothing, and specialists who did know

were shocked by this. One of these experts was Dr. H. Tuke, proprietor
and resident physician of an asylum in Chiswick, and visiting physician
of Northumberland House asylum. He also had fourteen patients
dotted about in what were known as 'single houses' (houses where rich
patients were treated, one to a house, looked after by as many as three
or four attendants).

In 1877 as an expert witness in one of the periodical reviews of
the lunacy laws he told how he had once been asked to sign a certificate
of lunacy to remove a young lady from Charing Cross Hospital to an
asylum. To his astonishment he found that the woman was suffering
from typhoid fever, and rousted from his bed the doctor who
wished her certified. This doctor retorted rudely that he ought
to know typhoid fever, and Tuke countered by saying that *he* ought
to know acute mania. In the end the President of the College of
Physicians and the physician of the Fever Hospital were called in to
arbitrate: Tuke was right. The girl had typhoid and recovered in
fourteen days.

The willingness of doctors to sign certificates of lunacy willy-nilly
was sometimes prompted by greed. One man who had wrongfully been
committed and who had managed to get the order quashed was the
Reverend W. A. O'Conor. He afterwards asked a doctor, 'How is it
possible that respectable men could do such a thing?' The doctor
replied, 'Well, the fact is this; we are so much in the habit of getting
a couple of guineas for doing a certain work and considering it the
right thing that when we get the couple of guineas, we consider the
thing which we do for it to be the right thing.' O'Conor accused the
two doctors who had certificated him, Drs. Wilkinson and Roberts of
Manchester, of simple cupidity; they were 'wealthy men, and they made
their money by marrying rich wives; I believe they would rank very
low in the profession'.

There was a suggestion that the law should be changed by substituting a solicitor or other professional man for the second certifying
doctor, for it was clear that there was often complicity between two
medical men getting their two guineas apiece for adding their signatures
to a scrap of paper. There was a great temptation to do this when the
person committed was unlikely to cause much fuss—when he or she
was a pauper and was certified from the workhouse. As William
Parkinson, the Master of Bermondsey Workhouse, said, 'In a great many
parishes it is the rule for young medical men to become parish officers,

and I think, without imputing motives to them, they are of course young and inexperienced, and are more likely to send cases to an asylum from an error of judgment than from other causes.'

The fact that young and inexperienced medical officers were invested with the power to send sane people to an asylum reflects not only on the law, but on their medical training. A certification was not provisional, but definitive; it was a good deal easier getting into an asylum than out of one, and a visiting magistrate or Commissioner in Lunacy was very willing to assume that a person in an asylum was insane because that was where one expected to find insane people. No matter how logically a patient behaved or talked, officials were reluctant to set the wheels in motion to have the case re-examined once the stigma had been applied.

The Victorian medical profession was a closed circle, and almost wholly masculine. Male doctors fought tooth and nail to have women excluded from the profession, and for a long time they succeeded. They had a contempt for women, did not know and did not want to know anything about female psychology, were phlegmatic or fatalistic about women's ailments, and either under-reacted or over-reacted to phenomena such as hysteria. A woman subject to hysteria had an even chance of being certified or of having a bucket of cold water thrown over her. Doctors were not sympathetic towards the sufferers, who were considered to be members of the idle class. Hysteria, wrote Dr. Spencer Thomson, was rare 'among the moderately-fed and hard-working population' and was the product of too much introspection. It was 'a disease to a considerable extent under the control of the will, a disease which lives and grows on superabundant sympathy, and whilst all kindness and consideration is shewn, it is wonderful how much good may be derived from a little wholesome neglect'. And neglect, it was implied, was something the state asylums were noticeably good at.

Many hysterics were sent to asylums because it was believed that the state led naturally into madness. Henry Maudsley wrote in his *The Physiology and Pathology of Mind* (1868):

The ordinary hysterical symptoms may pass by degrees into a chronic insanity; the patient losing more and more self-control, becoming more fanciful about her health, and more indifferent to what is going on around her; the body becomes anaemic and emaciated, and there are usually irregularities of menstruation. An erotic element is sometimes evinced in the manner and thoughts; and occasionally ecstatic states occur.

When one considers the possibilities of getting rid of unwelcome relatives the numbers of patients locked up was surprisingly small. In 1844 there was a total of 20,893, including 2,399 private patients. In 1858 this number had risen to 35,597, distributed in 33 county asylums, 4 borough asylums, 15 hospitals, 37 metropolitan licensed houses, 77 provincial licensed houses, 124 'single houses', and 645 workhouses. There were Commissioners in Lunacy who theoretically paid yearly visits, but their trips were well-known in advance via the asylum grape-vine. The commissioners had no power to enter army and navy hospitals where lunatics were kept. Even at the time it was realised that 124 single houses was a grotesque underestimate.

Without adequate supervision, many of the asylums and private homes were run on disgraceful lines. The fees in the private homes could be as much as £500 per year (Dr. Tuke's averaged £280 p.a.) There was an interest on the part of the proprietors in keeping their patients there. This was forcibly put by Dr. William Balfour in 1877:

Private asylums are the property of individuals who derive large incomes from keeping them; it is the interest of the proprietor to have as many good paying patients as possible in his house; it is not his interest to get rid of patients who pay well; as the law now is, it is as nearly as possible impossible for any person to get out of a private asylum without the sanction of the person who signed the application, should the person who signed the application be unwilling to apply for the discharge.

Many people suffering from stress or what we would now describe as anxiety neurosis were decoyed into asylums by rapacious friends. They were told that they would be going for a few weeks into a rest home, only to find that once the committal order had been signed there was no way back to the outside world. Not surprisingly, many of these people were driven mad by the conditions prevailing in the asylums.

In many of the private asylums old traditions lingered on. In 1844 conditions in an asylum in Wales were discovered. Patients had been kept in damp cellars for up to twenty years without ever having seen the light of day, some of them chained by the leg, and wallowing in their own filth. In isolated asylums, as the Earl of Shaftesbury declared to a select committee in 1859, 'even when they are not hardly treated, [the insane] see no one but the attendant; they never hear any voice but the voice of the attendant, and many of them fall into a low irrecoverable melancholy, which would oftentimes have been entirely obviated if they had been placed in more favourable circumstances'.

Referring to some of the conditions in private homes and asylums, the Earl of Shaftesbury mentioned a relation who had had an attack of brain fever in the early 1850s, and who had been under the care of a doctor in London. The doctor had farmed him out to an attendant, who had kept him strapped down in his bed for as long as twenty-four hours at a time. The attendant brought into the room whores and drinking companions. On his release the patient showed the Earl of Shaftesbury the scars on his legs, where the ropes had cut into his flesh, and on his ankles. There was a racket in attendants to rich patients. Several of the London physicians practising in lunacy supplied attendants to other doctors, paying them a yearly stipend, supporting them when they were not employed, and taking between two-thirds and three-quarters of the attendant's fees for their own profit. The attendants carried their own gear from job to job—manacles, ropes, and straitjackets. One London doctor had as many as thirty houses for imprisoning private patients.

Not all the men and women who signed committal papers for their spouses or relatives were evil; some thought it was for the best, and put their reliance on the doctor. When he told them that they should not visit the patient as it would agitate him or her and worsen the affliction they obediently agreed. Occasionally they got to hear of the actual conditions. One case occurred in 1846, and the Commissioners in Lunacy were called to visit a single house. They found a young man chained, sitting on his bed; both his feet were leg-locked and he was wearing a leather apron up to his chin. His hands were fastened before him and he was fed at the end of a stick. There was one attendant and a doctor who visited the man every day. The family communicated with the proprietor of a long-established asylum and on their behalf he went to see the man and ordered, 'Take off his chains, take off his apron, take off everything.' One of the men present said, 'Good God, if you do that, he will murder the whole of us.' The asylum proprietor said, 'I will take the whole responsibility for it; he will murder nobody, take off everything.' This was done, and the patient, who had been cursing and using obscene language, was released, washed, and in two days was dining with his family and hunting with the beagles.

One of those who looked askance at the way ordinary general practitioners dealt with the insane was Dr. Conolly:

> It is astonishing to witness humane English physicians daily contemplating helpless insane patients bound hand and foot, and neck and waist in illness, in pain, and in the agonies of death, without one single touch of compunction, or the slightest approach to a feeling of acting either cruelly or unwisely; they thought it impossible to manage insane people in any other way.

These doctors were aided and abetted by the attendants and nurses. One lady who had been in an asylum was visited by her relatives constantly, but at night she was strapped down for twelve to fourteen hours. When the relatives came the next day and the woman complained the nurse said that it was all hallucination. The patients were entirely subject to the whims of the attendants. The Earl of Shaftesbury said that 'in 99 cases out of 100, you will find that the happiness or the unhappiness, the comfort or the discomfort, the cure or the perpetuation of the malady, depend upon the character and conduct of the attendants'.

Conditions in the asylums varied enormously, and depended largely on how well the attendants were paid and on their supervision. In the large asylums there was usually one attendant to thirteen or fourteen patients; at one of the largest asylums, Hanwell, there was a ratio of one to ten or eleven. At Hanwell, the pay of the male attendants was 20 guineas a year, female attendants 15 guineas. The new model lunatic asylum at Colney Hatch paid better—£25 rising to £30 for men. But these were hardly incentives to attract the better type of attendant, and with an average of one doctor to 300 patients there was every opportunity for a vicious attendant to torment an inmate.

It is often supposed that the worst excesses of Bedlam were in the past when Victoria came to the throne, but there are some nineteenth-century accounts of life in the lunatic asylums that vie with anything that happened previously. The Earl of Shaftesbury was diligent in his attempts to reform the asylums and harked back to his early experiences:

When we began our visitations, one of the first rooms that we went into contained nearly 150 patients, in every form of madness; a large proportion of them chained to the wall, some melancholy, some furious, but the noise and din and roar were such that we positively could not hear each other; every form of disease and every form of madness were there; I never beheld anything so horrible and so miserable. Turning from that room, we went into a court appropriated to the women. In that court there were from 15 to 20 women, whose sole dress was a piece of red cloth tied round the waist with a rope; many of them with long beards covered with filth; they were crawling on their knees, and that was the only place where they could be.

At another asylum there were concealed rooms, unknown to the governor, where inmates were kept. In a room 12 feet by 7 feet 10 inches were kept thirteen women. The keepers had access to the women patients, several of whom became pregnant; one male patient disappeared completely, four patients were burned to death in a mysterious manner, and one inmate was kept naked in a dark filthy room, and could only obtain a shirt by promising a bribe of five shillings to the attendant. In Bethnal Green asylum several of the pauper women patients were chained to their bedsteads stark naked (in December), and dirty patients were rubbed down with a mop dipped in cold water. For 170 male pauper inmates at Bethnal Green there was only one towel allowed per week, and no soap. The wage scale at this asylum was £16–£20 for male attendants.

Conditions at the great metropolitan asylum, Bethlehem ('Bedlam'), were hardly any better. In 1853 an inquiry was made into the state of Bethlehem Hospital, and it was found the female inmates were forced to sleep without any night clothes, on loose straw, with perhaps a rug to cover them. In the morning they were taken to the galleries (as the floors there were of slate) and sluiced down with buckets of water. In the circumstances prevailing at Bethlehem Hospital (now taken over by the Imperial War Museum) the occasional death was accepted with composure; one of the doctors, Dr. Sutherland, admitted that he had caused the death of a patient by over-bleeding.

Many of the investigations were carried out at the behest of private individuals who had themselves been acquainted with people who had been wrongfully committed, and there was one energetic society, the

Bethlehem Hospital ('Bedlam'). (*Old and New London*)

Alleged Lunatics' Friends Society, formed in 1845, which did a good deal to uncover abuses, and which had a list of twenty-six persons who had been unjustly confined. One of the leading figures in this society was J. T. Perceval, and although he did not dispute the occasional necessity of using violence to subdue violence he did draw attention to the misuse of physical force. He declared:

> What I call cruelty in an asylum is where the patients are very often, not from any fault of their own, provoked and tantalised, and worked up, as it is called, by an allusion to their own infirmities, and where they are all of a sudden seized and thrown with any amount of reckless violence on a stone floor, or across an iron bedstead, and they are then kneaded with the knee on the chest, at the risk of breaking their ribs; then they are seized by the throat until the eyes start out of their sockets, and the blood comes out of the mouth. They are also taken by the neckcloth and their heads thumped against the floor or banged against the wall.

Perceval revealed that in most asylums there were refractory wards, screened from normal visitors, where sadistic attendants were given their heads.

The Medical Superintendent of the Devon Asylum (606 patients), Dr. John Bucknill, would have agreed with Perceval that occasionally attendants went too far: the best of asylum governors were often at a loss to discover whether complaints of unjustified cruelty were valid, for the observing patients themselves were 'frequently guided by delusions, and by malicious motives'. There were, said Bucknill, patients who seemed to take a malicious delight in causing annoyance and contention to the attendants. Their testimony was disregarded, and, any way, good attendants who could keep order for £20 a year were not dismissed for an outburst of temper nor, indeed, for behaviour that in other establishments, such as the prisons, would call for instant dismissal. Between 1854 and 1859 only forty-nine male attendants were dismissed from county and borough asylums for ill-treatment of patients.

The most cruel abuses occurred not in the asylums but in the workhouses, where the insane poor were kept in barbaric conditions. The reason they were retained there rather than the asylum was financial, for although it was laid down in government regulations that fourteen days was the maximum stay in the workhouse for the insane this was openly flouted, and known by all to be flouted. It was in the interest of the parish to keep the insane poor in workhouses, for it cost only half as much as in the asylums (averaging five shillings a week against ten shillings).

The workhouses were a dumping ground for the unwanted, and although, strictly speaking, only the insane poor should have been incarcerated, many wealthy insane were deposited there, their friends and relatives not wishing to have to pay for their upkeep in state or private asylums—there was no middle way between the fee-paying and the pauper.

In July 1857 there were 628 workhouses in England and Wales, with 103,409 inmates of whom 6,629 were insane, a percentage of 6·41. For these poor neglected creatures conditions had not altered for fifty years, and their only hope was that a spot-check by Commissioners in Lunacy would uncover their plight. Workhouses did not possess the asylum grape-vine; there was no way for workhouse masters to discover when a government investigator was in the district.

In June 1857 Dewsbury workhouse was visited by the commissioners, and they found three men and one women 'in restraint' by means of chains, wristlocks, and hobbles. As in most other workhouses, the attendants were not responsible paid men and women but other paupers, who were quite willing to admit that the reason they had put these four inmates in chains was not that they were violent but that they were a nuisance. One of them wanted to get out of bed, while another was put in chains because it was thought that he might run away. There were also what were described as two 'coercion chairs' in the lunatic wards.

Dewsbury workhouse was typical rather than exceptional. At the workhouse of St. George the Martyr in Southwark the same means of restraint were used on other nuisance inmates by paupers who had been instructed to look after the insane and the idiotic. Dursley Union workhouse was reported on in November 1858. The only furniture in the male day rooms was a low bench, in the women's room two benches. The yards, ostensibly for exercise, were filthy and were used to dry the bedding. Two paupers looked after the insane, a man, old, feeble and lame, and a woman, who was once capitally convicted and imprisoned for arson. She was put to look after the insane because she was in the habit of pilfering in the workhouse itself, and the master and matron of the workhouse asserted that she was the only person who could bear the loneliness of the idiot ward. She, too, was infirm and walked on crutches, and yet she and the man had to control a violent man who ate candles and who had not been out of the ward for two years. The total of the insane and the idiots under the control of this pathetic couple was eighteen. To add to the misery of the insane and the idiots they were fed on boiled swedes, the outdoor privies had no doors, and the female dormitory was without windows.

It was common for idiot women in the workhouses to have children by attendants or by other paupers. In Walsall workhouse the commissioners found a young idiot woman who had had four illegitimate children there; in Monmouth there were two who had had three children each, and in Mortley and Tamworth there were other cases. All these instances came to light by accident.

In many workhouses the bad conditions arose from neglect and disinterest rather than systematic cruelty, and provided that the insane and the idiots were kept reasonably quiet no one bothered too much about the methods employed by the paupers assigned to them to keep them so. A more ominous note was introduced at Camberwell workhouse, where there were two padded rooms in addition to the usual hobbles, wrist and leg locks, chains and straitjackets.

Paupers were persuaded to look after their insane companions by being given beer or extra food. It was known for some of these attendants to be themselves deranged; this was noted at St. Alban's workhouse, and the attention of the workhouse master was drawn to this anomaly. However, it was not acted upon. Occasions when the insane attacked their pauper attendants were legion. At St. Martin's workhouse a violent lunatic was entrusted to a feeble seventy-year-old man. He attacked him with a poker and killed him.

In some workhouses the sane and the insane were mixed up together, and idiot men with dirty habits were often put two in a bed, the reasoning being that it was less trouble to look after them there. Sometimes the sane and the insane slept together. In December 1856 there was a damning indictment of Huddersfield workhouse by Samuel Gaskell, a Commissioner in Lunacy:

These unfortunate persons are still crowded together in rooms of insufficient size, poorly furnished, and badly ventilated. There is still no classification of the inmates; the insane and weak-minded women being compelled to associate with low prostitutes, wet and dirty patients are still placed to sleep together in the same bed; the bedding is still scanty, and the dormitory floors are still saturated with urine. The means of washing and drying are still lamentably defective; large quantities of filthy bedding and clothing, as well as all other articles of wearing apparel, are still washed in the small room below the infirmary, which is only about 18 feet by 24 feet, and serves the purposes of washhouse, kitchen, bakehouse and brewhouse. The sick and the infirm are still placed in apartments, the atmosphere of which is overheated and impregnated with noxious vapours.

As has been stated, there were 6,629 pauper lunatics in the workhouses in 1857. By 1876 this number had increased to 15,000. In the same period the number of insane had risen from 35,597 to 65,161. This could mean that diagnosis was more sure or that the statistics were more reliable, but it was certainly depressing reading to those who believed that they had got the problem solved. The experts were not surprised. With rates of cure varying between 28 per cent and 50 per cent in the state asylums they were fighting a losing battle (though the national insanity rate was still only 2·68 per 1,000).

Reformers were most upset by the large numbers of insane and idiot inmates still in workhouses; recommendations that these people should immediately be sent to asylums when their condition was discovered had been openly ignored. In 1876 parliament passed a law granting four shillings a week from government funds for the maintenance of pauper lunatics. This induced parochial authorities to categorise as lunatics weak-minded paupers and to force them into asylums so as to obtain these grants and thus relieve the rates. Senile but sane paupers found themselves hustled into the asylums with all their respect-destroying humiliations.

Strenuous efforts were made to improve the treatment of the insane, and the Lunacy Act of 1890 helped to remedy some of the worst abuses. But there still remained insufficient supervision. By the close of the century there were only ten Commissioners in Lunacy to watch the interests of 106,611 inmates scattered throughout England and Wales in state asylums, private asylums, workhouses, and private homes. The commissioners were forced to rely on information received and newspaper reports of abuses.

Compassionate people with feeble-minded or insane relatives preferred to look after them themselves rather than entrust them to the dubious mercies of the specialists, and many borderline neurotics were obliged to live a life of enforced isolation, often being drugged on patent medicines and a roll-call of killer drugs, none of which had been properly tested. These included the 'non-addictive' drug heroin, formulated towards the close of the nineteenth century. There was no sedative to reduce a patient to, as one present authority graphically puts it, 'cold rice-pudding'.

Just as with prisons, there was a conspiracy of silence about what exactly took place in lunatic asylums. The reports of the Commissioners in Lunacy to the Lord Chancellor were lucid and complete so far as they could be, and make interesting reading. Some of the asylums were bright and cheery, but many of them were bleak and harsh, with an absence of reading matter and lack of diversion. At one asylum in 1882 the insane dead were buried in unmarked graves, the final humiliation. There were few asylums where the commissioners did not make a complaint about the drains, about the smells, about the standards of hygiene. At Macclesfield they arrived to find a ward of thirty-five patients without an attendant, and one of the inmates in a fit. It was clear that in one instance at least the grape-vine had been severed.

In the nineteenth century, the fear of being put in an asylum was not at all uncommon; it is still not uncommon. The layman does not understand the processes of law, though he knows that the strait-

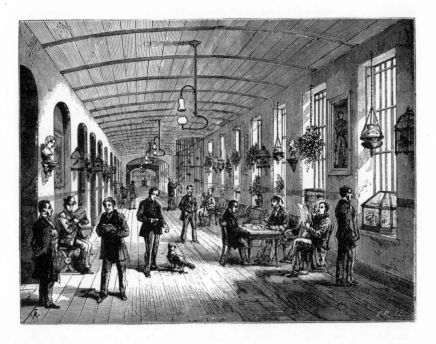

A somewhat idealised view of a ward in Bethlehem Hospital in 1874. (*Old and New London*)

jacket has been superseded by barbiturates and is more alarmed by the prospects of electric shock therapy than cruelty by underpaid attendants. Today there is considerably less chance of being picked up off the streets, certified, and carried off to the county asylum, as happened to the Reverend William O'Conor in 1869 at the instigation of the Chief Constable of Manchester after a mild fracas in a shop. Despite the forceful objections of Mrs. O'Conor, the clergyman was whisked away and placed in Prestwich Asylum:

I was placed in a cell that I can only compare to a large coffin in perfect darkness, extremely small, without any kind of window or opening whatever; and during the entire night the whole air was filled with the most terrific yells and howlings I ever heard in my life; no wild beast I ever heard came near it.

The superintendent had been at a dinner party the night before and so had not seen the new patient, but in the morning he met O'Conor, realised that a mistake had been made, and O'Conor was discharged three days later.

In 1870 Mrs. Louisa Lowe was put into Brislington asylum. She was a spiritualist who indulged in the fashionable pastime of automatic writing; it was said that 'for the last 20 years (she) has been subject to what is termed hysteria'. She married in 1842, had six children; ran into difficulties with her husband and left him. He urged her to return home, and she barricaded her door against him. He therefore had her certified.

Unquestionably Mrs. Lowe was neurotic, but the ground for her committal would have been ground for almost any active spiritualist of the period. Dr. Maudsley, to whose private asylum she was sent and who had milched her husband of £420 for treatment of Mrs. Lowe, complained that her spirit communications were 'all direct communications with the Almighty. Many of them were of a very puerile character, some of them read very blasphemously, and others rather tend to the obscene.' Naturally these spirit writings would not have commended themselves to her clergyman husband, and there is little doubt that Mrs. Lowe was committed because of her religious or pseudo-religious beliefs. There is also little doubt that without the intervention of her sister Mrs. Lowe would have had great difficulty in getting out of the asylums, especially if the superintendents had recognised the sexual connotations of her writings ('Father, thou saidst Satan helped him to slip in and out like an eel. Who, my friend and comforter, doubles him up like an opera hat; but how can a great big six-feet man get in and out of a chimney like this?').

Certain ambiguities do exist about the case of Mrs. Lowe, and it is understandable that magistrates and doctors unacquainted with the world of spiritualism should see something odd in her pronouncements. These do not exist in the case of Mrs. Petschler, who was committed by her sister for business reasons. Mrs. Petschler was the widow of a merchant turned photographer; after his death she had taken over the business, and her sister had objected to her being in trade in the town where she herself lived. Although Mrs. Petschler was self-supporting she had been committed as a pauper lunatic into Altrincham workhouse. A clergyman had signed the committal papers, though there were dozens of magistrates within easy reach.

Although Mrs. Petschler was a Swedenborgian it was clear to everyone, not least the medical officer of the workhouse, that there were no grounds for keeping her locked up. When she was released she found that her home had been broken up and her property sold; the money had gone to pay for Mrs. Petschler's treatment as a lunatic in Macclesfield asylum where she had been moved from Altrincham.

Mrs. Petschler had no money to sue for damages, and the clergyman could not be prosecuted under the law, but the newspapers took up the case and their exposé brought to light other cases of wrongful committal.

Wealth could often keep a man out of prison; but not out of an asylum. In May 1876 two doctors called at the home of Walter Marshall in Thurloe Square and at the behest of his wife certified him. Marshall was, as he admitted himself, of a nervous disposition, and had suffered from depression between 1870 and 1874. He had married in 1866 and been given a clean bill of health by his doctor.

Marshall and many other well-heeled men were not physically ill-treated in the private asylums such as Ticehurst, but the threat was always there; cruelty was always waiting in the wings. Intimidation was often as cruel as physical violence, and when practised by unintelligent and underpaid attendants could overthrow a mind that was nervous or anxious. There were many people wrongfully detained in asylums who wondered whether, after all, they were as sane as they thought they were.

The proprietors of private asylums had more power than almost any head of any institution. Even when well-meaning they had little means of finding out the truth of incidents that were reported to them. If they came across a man in a straitjacket the attendants merely had to say that the patient had been violent, and there was no one to deny it. The testimony of other patients could not be relied upon. There were occasional deaths; these were covered up by attendants. There were cases known where the suffocation of patients by attendants had been disguised by cramming the patients' mouths with poisonous berries.

Inquests on lunatics were not carried out with any great enthusiasm; coroners expected to find bruises, cuts, and scars on the bodies of the mad. Whether they had done it themselves or whether it was the result of restraints was not of much consequence.

No doubt there were nurses and attendants who behaved kindly to the insane, but there were many who found their charges to be born victims, easily broken. The mad were even more vulnerable than the poor; when they were both, then the most brutal, sadistic and callous of actions could be carried out with little chance of a reprimand. The Victorians were ashamed of their mad folk, and this shame was capitalised on by a host of parasites, from disinterested doctors scribbling their names on committal forms for an easy two guineas, through money-grabbing asylum proprietors anxious to keep their patients as long as possible, workhouse masters urged to retain the pauper insane within their own walls to keep down the rates, time-serving state asylum governors desirous of an easy life and waiting for the telegraph to tap out its message that a Commissioner in Lunacy was on the way, on to the mercenaries, the professional attendants with their cases full of manacles, hobbles, chains and straitjackets.

It was a seamy side of Victorian life. But considering the circumstances it is surprising that it was not worse than it was. The insane and the mentally disturbed received treatment depending on their ability to pay, and this was true of the physically sick. Great advances were made in medicine, the stethoscope revolutionised treatment of the heart and lungs, the science of bacteriology was started, and the correlation between hygiene and health brought forth the rise of preventative medicine. During the latter half of the nineteenth century the death rate in some towns was reduced by as much as fifty per cent, and by the end of the century typhus and enteric fever had been almost banished.

But for many doctors all was in vain. Confused by the speed at which theoretic medicine was proceeding, they dug in their heels and isolated themselves, and although laziness and apathy can hardly be construed as cruelty, adherence to old methods and aversion to employing pain-preventing devices resulted in agony to patients that was totally unnecessary. In 1848 the use of anaesthetics in child-birth was attacked by the obstetrician Dr. Ashwell in *The Lancet*. He believed that 'unnecessary interference with the providentially arranged process of healthy labour is sure, sooner or later, to be followed by injurious and fatal consequences. I think chloroform will be no exception to these precepts.'

Victorian doctors awarded blame for certain illnesses or disorders, and treatment of venereal disease and women's diseases could be excessively brutal. Pueperal fever ('child-bed fever') was considered by many to be a just reward for a lascivious or immoral life. There was no control on doctors trying out untried drugs or methods, and one of those who suffered was Edmund Gosse's mother, dying in agony from cancer. 'Her sufferings', wrote Gosse in *Father and Son*, 'were principally caused by the violence of the medicaments to which her doctor, who was trying a new and fantastic "cure", thought it proper to subject her.'

A guide to medical mentality is furnished by Victorian issues of the *British Medical Journal* and *The Lancet*. Enshrined in their pages are atavistic doctrines, outmoded folk remedies, and in the correspondence columns prejudice and advocacy of the knife run riot. During the controversy about the causes of menstruation, women were actually blamed for having periods. Most doctors were ignorant as late as 1878 of what menstruation was, though the explanation had been given in 1863 by Dr. Pflüger.

The equipment of doctors when they made their rounds should have been consigned to museums or dustbins. The instruments were often art objects—forceps with intricately detailed handles, ideal for the concealment and succour of germs (in which many doctors refused to believe). The surgical instruments could have been comfortably accommodated in a butcher's shop. Dr. Stekel in his *Sadism and Masochism* found another analogy: 'Once in visiting a torture chamber I was struck with the similarity between instruments of torture and various medical apparatuses.'

If the standard of medical care was not what one would expect in a progressive civilised country, how much truer this was of the hospitals. Hospitals were dependent on charity, or voluntary contributions as it was put. The doctors in the hospitals were not appointed in consequence of their skill or experience but according to the whims of the administrators or the supporters. Hospitals were bleak, draughty, and often terrifying. Sometimes, when there was not enough money to go round for competent cleaning staff, they were dirty. Interior comforts and convenience were sacrificed to an imposing façade. Until Florence Nightingale launched into her campaign for improving the standards of nursing, the nurses were of a low quality, frequently drunk, often cruel to those patients who were in a state of terror, off-hand towards the dying and sceptical of those who thought that they were dying.

Except for the rich, hospitals were bleak and inhospitable. This is a ward in Hampstead Smallpox Hospital in 1871. (*Illustrated London News*)

Of course there were hospitals where standards were high, hospitals that were provided for privileged groups such as freemasons, but in most cases there was simply not enough money to go round to offer a satisfactory service. New military hospitals, not supported by charity but by government funds, were built which were improvements on the older hospitals. One of these was Herbert Hospital. Lord Dalhousie thought it too good for soldiers; it was, he declared, 'all glass and glare' and that he was against 'unnecessary knick-knacks [amenities to relieve the bleak impersonality] in hospitals'.

Indifference shading into cruelty marked the behaviour of the staff of hospitals for ordinary people, but these inmates were vastly more fortunate than the paupers in the workhouse infirmaries. Dickens was not exaggerating when he described the admission of Oliver Twist's mother to the workhouse infirmary: 'There being nobody, however, but a pauper old woman who was rendered rather misty by an unwonted allowance of beer, and a parish surgeon who did such matters by contract.'

Medical attention was sparse almost to the point of invisibility in the workhouse infirmaries. The parish doctors were young, inexperienced men who were not expected to do more than prescribe emetics, workhouse gardians did not relish having to pay for proper nurses from parish funds and preferred to use paupers who would carry out nursing duties for an allowance of beer, and the matrons were the outcasts of the profession. In 1871 visitors to Poplar Sick Asylum found the matron in a 'low dress with short sleeves, being merry' and drink, indeed, was the common denominator of the workhouse infirmary for patients and staff.

As most of the inmates in infirmaries were old as well as ill, recovery was neither expected nor welcomed; in modern parlance, the infirmaries were terminal wards. There were few attempts to make the last days of the pauper poor comfortable. They slept on stinking straw mattresses, there were frequently no windows, there was nowhere to sit if they were not bed-ridden, and all visitors remarked upon the effluvia. The workhouse guardians took the opportunity to cut down on the dietary of the sick, and the lack of nourishment helped the patients on the way to the grave.

The contrasts between the run-of-the-mill doctors and the experimentalists, between the situations that prevailed in the workhouse infirmaries and those in the luxury hospitals and nursing homes for the rich, illustrate the truth of Disraeli's concept of the two nations. Without state aid the deplorable conditions of the establishments for the poor are understandable, and although these conditions did improve as the nineteenth century wore on—the poor were protected against the worst excesses by acts of parliament—life in infirmaries remained inhuman well into the opening decade of the twentieth century. Only when the Liberal Party brought in the welfare state did matters drastically improve.

For the rich, there were a variety of therapeutic methods available. Gymnastics (advanced by Ling, 1776–1839), hydropathy (V. Priessnitz was a key figure, and there were rich pickings for society doctors such as the notorious Dr. Gully), massage (Weir Mitchell), while hypnotism proved a panacea to hypochondriacal patients such as Harriet Martineau, writer and economist.

At a time when doctors were scrabbling around amidst the exploded relics of antediluvian medicine, modern concepts were being worked up by Dr. Beard in *Mental Exhaustion* (1880), Janet (born 1859), and Freud. In *Erewhon* (1872) by Samuel Butler illness was a crime and the sick were treated like criminals. This kind of thinking underlay a good deal of nineteenth-century medical thought and only when this is realised does the indifference, the contempt, and the casual cruelty of doctor towards patient, make any kind of sense.

7

The Nether World

IT WAS REALISED by many perceptive minds of the nineteenth century that without vast changes in environment cruelty and squalor would continue unabated. Realisation was different from accomplishment; without an overall authority for rehousing the London slum-dwellers there was no chance to do anything but nibble at the problem, even when the London County Council superseded the corrupt Metropolitan Board of Works. Municipal reform was a delicate issue; in 1887 a parliamentary committee was formed to look into allegations that corporation funds were used to fight such reform. The vision of Eastminster, the new London suburb, was never realised; Wandsworth New Town did partly materialise in the form of barrack-like blocks; the garden cities, when they came in the Edwardian era, were populated by the middle and not the lower classes.

Journalists and novelists succeeded in breaking through the self-protective devices that the better-off had rigged up to prevent themselves from knowing the full miseries of the very poor. There were waves of philanthropy. Often, in the opinion of experts, these did more harm than good, though few went to the extent of the *Westminster Review* which, in 1853, dismissed the age as 'foolishly soft, weakly tender, irrationally maudlin, unwisely and mischievously charitable'. Walter Bagehot, one of the acutest minds of the time, believed that philanthropy 'augments so much vice, it multiplies so much suffering, it brings to life such great populations to suffer and be vicious', and Thomas Carlyle thought little of 'blind loquacious pruriency'.

In this curious context, philanthropy was considered to be cruel.

It was believed to subsidise idleness, and also introduce the recipient of charity to a standard of living that could not be continued. The implications of Bagehot's comment is clear : indiscriminate philanthropy would help those to survive who by nature did not deserve to—the old, the sick, and the weakly young. The doctrine of the survival of the fittest was being wrecked by empty-headed charity.

Unquestionably the habit of giving money to the poor relieved the consciences of the rich. Richard Potter, the father of the pioneer Socialist Beatrice Webb, declared, 'What luxury it is to do good!' The statistics produced by Charles Booth were considered by manufacturers and industrialists to be positively dangerous. His statement that the overall poverty level in London was 30·7 per cent in 1891 was deplored but not often disputed. The proprietor of Simmons's perambulator manufactury asked, 'Do not these statistics tend to foster discontent among the poor, and instead of directing them to exercise the discipline, industry, and thrift by which their condition might be bettered, rather suggest that while such multitudes are poor, and so few are rich, the many might plunder the rich?'

These views were shared by the establishment, which regarded with suspicion 'the Perishing and Dangerous classes' (Mary Carpenter, 1851) and 'the Aborigines of the East End' and officialdom was willing to leave the task of rehabilitation to private bodies such as the Metropolitan Visiting and Relief Association, formed in 1843, which aimed to remove 'the moral causes which create and aggravate want; to encourage prudence, industry and cleanliness'. Unfortunately many of these associations and societies had no idea of the immensity of the task awaiting them, or the wiliness of those whom they were helping. Money given for food—and the Metropolitan Visiting and Relief Association had £20,000 to disperse in their first year—was spent on drink or rubbishy trinkets. When the Asylum for the Houseless Poor was opened, there were 200 inmates within six hours of the news getting around; many of these people were not necessarily houseless, but were orientated to grab whatever was going free. There was official blessing for this venture; the London Gas Company was providing, out of the goodness of its heart, free light and heat, and the New River Company was offering water. The Asylum for the Houseless Poor, overwhelmed by the demand for accommodation, cut its losses and provided for winter charity only, shutting down in summer.

Although the Metropolitan Visiting and Relief Association declared

Money given to the poor for food was often spent on drink. (*Leisure Hour*)

that 'there was a willingness of the highest classes of society to mingle with and take an active part in the improvement of the London poor' this compliance was by no means universal. Many of the 'highest classes' gave their money and hoped that they would not be pestered again. As for going amongst the poor, this was what they were paying someone else to do (though they had no objection to having the occasional free dinner organised for table-thumping—*The Times* said of the Duke of Cambridge that 'his heart and mouth are always open to the call of charity'.)

What would the rich have expected to find had they penetrated the fastnesses of the East End?

Perhaps the 'wasp-nest or beehive' of Carlyle, or the ghastly vision of Charles Kingsley in 1850:

> Blood and sewer-water crawled from under doors and out of spouts, and reeked down the gutters among offal, animal and vegetable, in every stage of putrefaction. Foul vapours rose from cow-sheds and slaughter-houses, and the doorways of undrained alleys, where the inhabitants carried the filth out of their shoes from the backyard into the court; and from the court up into the main street; while above, hanging like cliffs over the streets—those narrow, brawling torrents of filth and poverty, and sin,—the houses with their teeming load of life were piled up into the dingy, choking night. A ghastly, deafening, sickening sight it was.

Kingsley was rubbing his readers' noses in the misery, and his more sensitive public turned away with a shudder, preferring the easy didacticism of those who divided the poor into two sharp classes, the respectable working man and his wife who were all that was good, and the drunkard, who thrashed his wife and children, and who, in popular temperance fiction, was redeemed, usually by a goody-goody daughter.

Novelists could get at their readers' sensibilities by harping on slum children, the 'little darlings that toddle about the pavements, sit on the doorsteps, and play on the narrow stairs of their comfortless houses', ignoring the fact that few slum children had a house of their own to play about in and a child on the stairs of a 'building' or a house divided remorselessly into tiny apartments would almost certainly have been brutally booted down them by the first man who came by.

The account by William Barry in his novel *The New Antigone* (1887) was more attuned to reality; the slum child 'was ugly, deformed, ailing, accustomed to stripes and blows, full of premature greed, a thing of rags and disease, old in sin, and steeped in impurity'.

Barry penned in his experience of slumdom with even more verve than Kingsley; 'Rags, hunger, nakedness, tears, filth, incest, squalor, decay, disease, the human lazar-house, the black death eating its victims piecemeal,—that is three fourths of the London lying at these doors.'

By far the most damning evidence of the conditions under which the poor lived was provided by journalists. Charles Dickens was never averse to reminding middle-class readers in his weekly journal *Household Words* of what they had escaped, and ironically led his audience into 'Slaughterhouse Court', situated in 'Low Lane, Saint Crapulens', fictitious locations that served to embody a way of life. The woodwork, brickwork, and stonework of the houses are all rotten. The entrance passages shelve down like the entrances to public-house cellars. The window frames have shrivelled and left gaps, and every dingy pane of glass has been replaced by foul rags, tattered great-coats, impossible flannel petticoats, brown paper, and scraps of the Newgate school of publications (gaudy blood-and-thunder novelettes). The tenants have long torn away every bit of piping and guttering. Each floor is sub-let, and every sub-let is sub-let again.

In such environments, violence is only to be expected. The narrator here is George Gissing:

Here a group are wrangling over a disputed toss or bet, here two are coming to blows, there are half a dozen young men and women, all half drunk, mauling each other with vile caresses; and all the time, from the lips of the youngest and the oldest, foams forth such a torrent of inanity, abomination, and horrible blasphemy which bespeaks the very depth of human—aye, or of bestial—degradation.

Some of Gissing's descriptions have a Doré-like precision. The girls sitting on doorsteps nursing 'bald, red-eyed, doughy-limbed abortions in every stage of babyhood, hapless spawn of diseased humanity', and sweatshop girls with 'that dolorous kind of prettiness', or the really vicious women, 'a rank evilly-fostered growth'.

Gissing did not share the philanthropist's view that knocking down

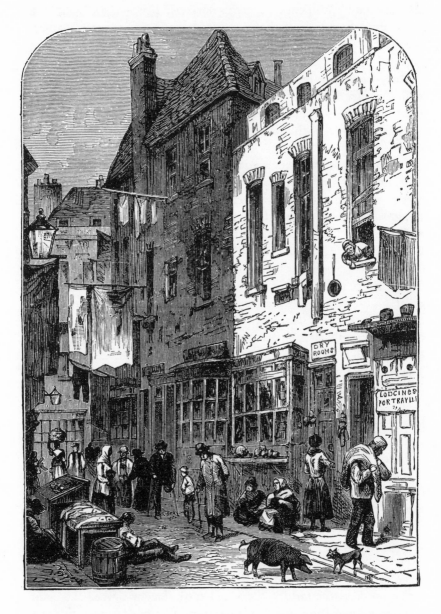

In the slums violence was only to be expected. (*Old and New London*)

the slums and putting the inhabitants into working men's dwellings would solve the problem of the squalid poor :

> What terrible barracks, those Farringdon Road Buildings! Vast, sheer walls, unbroken by even an attempt at ornament; row above row of windows in the mud-coloured surface, upwards, upwards, lifeless eyes, murky openings that tell of bareness, disorder, comfortlessness within.

Arthur Morrison, the author of three East End novels in the 1890s, had been born in Poplar, and he assigned the problems of the poor not to poverty but to monotony. Enforced idleness, a dreary round of nothing, with sex and drink the only antidotes to utter hopelessness—what was to be done? Morrison did not go along with optimists who thought that things would improve. The poor were hopeless 'and must not be allowed to rear a numerous and equally hopeless race. Light the streets better, certainly; but what use in building better houses for these poor creatures to render as foul as those that stand?'

Unlike many of the popular novelists who jumped on the bandwaggon of class war and maintained that because people were poor they were also frightful, Morrison maintained that civilised life was possible in the East End, though he was not sure how.

If the East End was bad, what can one say about the slum districts of northern industrial towns? In London, at least, there were people honestly trying to do something about the conditions, and although there is not much difference between the scenes etched by Kingsley in 1850 and William Barry in 1887 there were great improvements in living and sanitary conditions that alleviated the conditions of the poor. The erection of public baths and wash-houses began in 1844, model lodging houses were being built in 1845, a clean-up of the Thames started in 1858, the first block of Peabody dwellings was opened in Spitalfields in 1864, and Lord Rowton and the Salvation Army with their 'working men's hotels' and hostels provided for the vagrants who for the first time did not have to endure the degradation or brutalities of the 'spikes' or workhouses.

True, the working-class areas of London were a trap, but it was a trap from which there was an escape. This could not be said of the slum districts of Manchester, Liverpool, Glasgow, Edinburgh, or Dublin.

The difference between the proletariat of London and that of the cotton, wool, or other industrial towns, was that the former were not regimented. They may have been workshop and sweatshop victims but were not factory fodder, shuttled from unhygienic and savage mill to pestilential cellar or garret like counters on a ludo board, and with about as much chance of being diverted from their imprisoning squares.

The nightly refuge for the houseless poor, Edgware Road, an attempt to bring some succour to the homeless. (*Illustrated London News*)

The situation of the workers in the large towns was well-described by Frederick Engels in 1845.

Everywhere barbarous indifference, hard egotism on one hand, and nameless misery on the other, everywhere social warfare, every man's house in a state of siege, everywhere reciprocal plundering under the protection of the law, and all so shameless, so openly avowed that one shrinks before the consequences of our social state as they manifest themselves here undisguised, and can only wonder that the whole crazy fabric still hangs together.

Some authorities maintained that the poor in Edinburgh and Glasgow were worse off than in any other region in the United Kingdom. An Edinburgh clergyman had visited seven houses in a day in which there was not a single bed, not even a heap of straw. In one cellar lived two families, plus a donkey; it was so dark in the cellar, even at midday, that it was impossible to tell one from the other.

The old buildings in Edinburgh, in the wynds off the High Street, were built after the Paris fashion, in five or six storeys. The wynds were so narrow that a person could step from the window of one house into that of its opposite neighbour, and light rarely penetrated into the alleys, depositories of refuse and excrement thrown from the windows, for there were no drains or privies. Water was only obtainable from public pumps, and naturally those who lived near the tops of the buildings preferred to do without.

Glasgow also had its wynds and tall buildings. In 1844 the population was 300,000, and of this the working class accounted for 78 per cent. The dilapidated buildings, once the homes of the cream of society, swarmed with people, and as many as twenty people were contained in a single room. When epidemics struck in Glasgow the mortality rate was tremendous. In these buildings, where the occupants stretched out naked on the floor on straw or rags and where gross brutality, incest, and theft were unremarkable, in which there was no furniture other than the ubiquitous tea chest which served as stool, table, or privy, civilised behaviour was impossible, and no one cared.

Technically the 30,000 or so men, women and children who existed in this squalor were squatters. The buildings had been condemned as unfit for habitation, and according to the law no rent could be demanded of the occupants.

In Liverpool, a fifth of the population lived in narrow, dark, damp, unventilated cellar dwellings, of which there were 7,862 in the city. Liverpool was also rich in the notorious courts, small areas built up on all four sides, with a single entrance, a narrow covered passageway. Like the wynds of Scotland, these passageways were used as places to deposit offal, refuse and excreta, and also as places of assignation for the child prostitutes who were a feature of the Liverpool scene. The yards themselves were usually heaped high with ashes and filth.

Courts were also a prominent factor in Birmingham low life. They were narrow, muddy, and ill-drained, and lined with between eight and twenty houses. Although there were upwards of four hundred common lodging houses of a sordid character, there was less overcrowding in Birmingham than in the Scottish cities or Liverpool simply because it had been a smaller city, there was less old property to be taken over by the very poor, and as the thousands flocked in a rush building programme had been pushed through to accommodate the new arrivals. There was little cellar dwelling in Birmingham, and this city was one of the few to cope with the demands of Victorian industry and progress. This could not be said of Nottingham, and of its 11,000 houses between 7,000 and 8,000 were back-to-back properties. Nottingham was an unhealthy place, given to virulent outbreaks of scarlet fever, and on investigation it was found that many of these back-to-backs were built immediately over shallow drains, only the floorboards of the houses separating the dwellers from the effluent beneath them.

Leeds periodically suffered from the overflow of the noxious River Aire, and in some houses the cellars were never dry, and the houses themselves full of 'miasmatic vapours strongly impregnated with sulphuretted hydrogen'. The average working-man's cottage in Leeds took up no more than five square yards, and comprised a cellar, a living room and a bedroom. In Bradford the older part of the town taken over by the working classes was built upon steep hillsides, and the ground floors of many of the houses had to be abandoned because of the action of the river and subsidence. Huddersfield, unique in that it was virtually owned by a single family, the Ramsdens, enjoyed a spurious reputation as a model town, but in 1844 a citizens' committee reported: 'It is notorious that in Huddersfield whole streets and many lanes and courts are neither paved nor supplied with sewers nor other drains; that in them refuse, debris, and filth of every sort lies accumulating, festers and rots, and that, nearly everywhere, stagnant water accumulates in pools.'

In Manchester, the working population not only had to contend with too many indigenous people crammed into too few buildings for the benefit of the mill-owners but also with the immigration of the Irish. In many towns there was an overlap between the areas occupied by the poor and those occupied by the middle classes; in Manchester there was none of this nonsense. The ghettoes were well defined, and of all the ghettoes the most appalling was Little Ireland.

The Irish came over for fourpence each, packed in cattle-boats like sardines. 'He is the sorest evil this country has to strive with,' said Thomas Carlyle.

The occupants of many of the industrial slums had to contend not only with vermin and overcrowding, but with Nature. A scene in Salford during one of the periodic floodings. (*Illustrated London News*)

> In his rags and laughing savagery, he is there to undertake all work that can be done by mere strength of hand and back—for wages that will purchase him potatoes. He needs only salt for condiment, he lodges to his mind in any pig-hutch or dog-hutch, roosts in outhouses, and wears a suit of tatters, the getting on and off of which is said to be a difficult operation, transacted only in festivals and the high tides of the calendar.

No one attempted to cope with the problems of slum overcrowding. In the cotton towns production and profit were all. The wives and daughters of the industrialists were sequestered from the sight and stench of this nether world. They lived in mansions and trim villas in still salubrious areas fronting the countryside. Occasionally some wide-eyed skivvy would be wrenched from her slum to serve her betters for five pounds a year. The two nations did not interact, and an early version of apartheid was evolved.

It is not surprising that violence underlay the surface, that the industrial towns were powder kegs, with smouldering hostility between capital and labour, natives and immigrants. The fuse was kept lit by large infusions of drink.

In 1875, alcohol consumption per head of population reached an all time high. In that year each individual drank 1·30 gallons of spirits; in 1876 34·4 gallons of beer per head were consumed. Wine was not a factor in drunkenness—average consumption per head was about four bottles a year, and between 1801 and 1881 consumption per head had only altered by 0·01 of a gallon, though over this same period duty had gone down from ten shillings to one shilling a gallon. Among the great powers, only Russia drank less wine. The French drank fifty times as much.

Of course, the poor did not drink wine at all, but they more than made up for it in spirits and beer. Consumption of spirits rose steadily from 0·45 gallon in 1800 to the 1875 figure. In 1881 the Scots drank three times more spirits per head than the English, with the Irish somewhere between. Astonishingly the British were not the drunkards of Europe, for the Scandinavians drank twice as much spirits as the Scots, and even the sober Prussians drank a third more than the inhabitants of the United Kingdom. In 1897 the United Kingdom spent £152,281,723 on drink, almost twice as much as in 1860.

Spirits were cheap (gin 4½d–5d a quarter of a pint) and within the pocket of all but the very poor. There were innumerable outlets. Licensed premises (public houses, beer shops, gin palaces) were everywhere—1 per 186 of the English and Welsh population in 1861. In addition there were other sources—illicit stills, impure spirits smuggled in from Europe, and even hardware and general stores (methylated spirits was highly favoured by the cognoscenti of Edinburgh and Glasgow).

Drunkenness in the slums poses the chicken and the egg question. Which came first, squalor, putative feeble-mindedness, lack of moral fibre, or drink, leading to the sorry conditions?

Dr. James Kay put his point of view:

Having been subjected to the prolonged labour of an animal—his physical energy wasted, his mind in supine inaction—the artisan has neither moral dignity, nor intellectual nor organic strength, to resist the seductions of appetite. His wife and children, too frequently subjected to the same process, are unable to cheer his remaining moments of leisure. Domestic economy is neglected—domestic comforts are unknown. A meal of the coarsest food is prepared with heedless haste and devoured with equal precipitation. Home has no other relation to him than that of shelter—few pleasures are there—it chiefly presents to him a scene of physical exhaustion from which he is glad to escape. Himself impotent of all the distinguishing aims of his species, he sinks into sensual sloth, or revels in more degrading licentiousness.

Who was to blame for what Engels called the barbarous indifference, and how is it that the crazy fabric did hang together? Who was most cruel; the mill-owner concerned only with cheap labour and keeping the mills going day and night, the government, hastily washing its hands of anything that would disrupt economic progress, local government, for lamentably failing to keep up with the demand for housing, water, and drainage, or the self-appointed experts (such as Dr. Kay) who were more upset by the moral degradation of the proletariat than their living conditions, and almost blamed them for their plight? Callous all these people and agencies certainly were, but it is doubtful if they could have coped even if they had cared.

Many preferred to treat the matter as a debating issue, such as Alison in his *England in 1815 and 1845:*

What we say is unparalleled in the history of the world is the *co-existence* of so much suffering in one portion of the people, with so much prosperity in another; . . . with a degree of discontent which keeps the nation constantly on the verge of insurrection.

The prospect of never working could result in the overthrow of all moral restraint, and the bitterness and frustration of the unemployed and unemployable found their outlets in acts of rage and cruelty directed against wives and families, whom the men blamed for their plight. This fury was on an instinctive level, a blind lashing-out, only dimly anticipated by the victims except when the man had managed to get hold of drink. At such times violence was predictable.

In the 1860s the average pauperism of London was 96,752. In unusually severe weather, as in the winter of 1860-1, this total could go up 50 per cent. At these times the Poor Law system broke down completely, and it was left to private charity to prevent wholesale starvation. Certain areas of London were more susceptible to chaos than others, particularly the City of London, Bethnal Green, Lambeth,

In unusually severe weather the Poor Law system broke down completely. It is interesting to see that the men distributing soup at the Strangers' Home, Limehouse, were, besides the philanthropic gentlemen in top hats, Lascar and Chinese seamen. (*Illustrated London News*)

Poplar and Greenwich. For the starving poor in these districts there was no other recourse but the pawnshop.

Uncomprehending anger vied with dull depression in the minds of the healthy unemployed, and any new arrivals in the family were seen as added trials sent by a malicious Almighty. Infanticide was widely practised, infant deaths were not registered, and as even the cheapest undertakers charged between 7s 6d and 10s 6d (37½p–52½p) babies were unceremoniously disposed of, a favourite way being to throw them in the River Thames or in the various tributaries. No one enquired too strenuously into the causes of death of new-born babies, and mothers who were convicted of infanticide were extremely unlucky, exceptionally stupid, or misguidedly ingenious.

A favourite way to get rid of unwanted babies was to throw them into the Fleet Ditch. (*Old and New London*)

In 1845 a case was brought to court in which the mother had killed her baby by stuffing mud down its throat, a mother in 1855 used dough down the throat, and in 1863 the mother used a plug of flax to achieve the same result. Poison, because of the expense, was rare amongst the poor, though cases were known of arsenic, sulphuric acid and phosphorous being employed to finish off a baby. The most often used method was strangling, a method of infanticide which could not often be proved, as few doctors would sign their reputation away when encountering a dead child that might conceivably have been suffocated by its own umbilical cord—and the mothers knew it. Other methods included suffocating by using a pillow or a cushion, drowning, or just leaving the baby in the street to die. In 1870 276 infants were left on the streets of London, in 1895 231. Reliable statistics are hard to come by, as most of the infanticide cases were never known (not surprisingly, as infanticide carried the death penalty and the Victorians were avid supporters of capital punishment), but it was stated authoritatively that every year 1,550 infants were smothered in bed.

As late as 1900 infant mortality in Liverpool for those under a year old was 260 per 1,000, and in twelve families rigorously investigated 117 children were born, of which 98 died in infancy. It was impossible to find out what proportion of these 98 were deliberately murdered, were passively allowed to die, or died of natural causes. It is interesting that in a quarter of these unfortunate families the parents were devoted to drink.

Infants were not only killed because their appearance on the scene was unwelcome from the point of view of the family budget. There could also be an incentive to infanticide—insurance. In 1852 there were 33,232 burial clubs and societies with a capital of £11,360,000. The insurance companies were aware that mothers were anxious for their children to die, especially if they had insured them more than once. The insurance pay-out for an insured child varied between 5s (25p.) and £3 10s (£3·50), with the average being £1 9s 3d (£1·46).

It was suggested at a government level that the amount should be lowered to a pound to reduce temptation, but this was scorned by Benjamin Waugh, who declared, 'No. £1 would be a fortune to a gin-drinking woman who has already pawned her husband's tools and clothes, the babies' cot and the babies' clothes.' The doctors were also aware that the vision of insurance money could spell a swift quietus to the baby in the cot. One declared: 'Things are made very difficult for us if we don't give a death certificate, it entails a lot of bother. We get no support, but the father usually engages a clever lawyer to bully us, the verdict is given in his favour, and we are threatened with an action for our pains.'

Sometimes cupidity had its comeuppance. Of 110 burial societies investigated in the Birmingham area, only one was found to be sound. 103 of them held their meetings in public houses, and in 97 of these the public house owners had a direct interest. In 73 of them the funds were shared annually, so woe betide any child who died after the yearly share-out and subsequent celebration. Life insurance was big business; in 1874 premium income was £11,000,000 per annum.

There was a chasm between the attitudes of the poor and the law-makers towards infanticide. The legislators regarded it as murder, the poor hardly more than a misdemeanour, analogous to a deliberately-induced miscarriage. In the mixed agricultural labour gangs, where sexual behaviour was notoriously lax, the rate of infant mortality was so incredibly high that a report was ordered on it. That the government could be sufficiently interested to send a man to see them about their bastard children struck the women members of the agricultural gangs as hilarious. They openly speculated about their companions to Dr. Julian Hunter—'so and so has another baby; you'll see it won't live'.

The doctors were nonplussed. Mothers complained that their children would not eat and were dying, but when the doctor offered food the children were ravenous and 'fit to tear the spoon to pieces'. On the few occasions where a post-mortem examination was carried out, the stomach and the bowels were found to be quite empty. Few charges of neglect were brought against the agricultural workers, and medical practitioners were happy to wash their hands of the uncouth and healthy women gangers, signing their certificates 'debility from birth, no medical attendant' or 'premature birth' or simply 'overlying' (i.e. smothering). Infanticide might interest magistrates but not the country doctor.

Mothers of a less determined disposition contented themselves with keeping their babies quiet by using Godfrey's Cordial, known as 'Quietness', which was cheap, effective, and sometimes fatal. A pennyworth of aniseed, a pennyworth of laudanum, and a quarter of a pound of treacle all mixed up together would make a quart of Godfrey's Cordial. Every village shop had its Godfrey's Cordial in one form or another. Other mothers contented their children with laudanum drops on a sugar lump, while the more adventurous made their own elixirs. The small town of Clitheroe in Lancashire, population 6,725, used 4,000 poppy heads a year. The 'sleepy stuff', as it was called, was astonishingly effective, being a form of opium.

Godfrey's Cordial was used by nurses to keep their charges quiet.

It has not unfrequently happened that a nurse has substituted her own Godfrey for her client's and, frightened at its effects, has summoned the surgeon, who finds half a dozen babies, some snoring, some squinting, all pallid and eye-sunken, lying about the room, all poisoned. . . .

Those women who could afford it surreptitiously got rid of their unwanted children via a baby-farm, refusing to face up to the consequences of this action. Like life insurance on children, baby-farming was big business, and there was a certain connection between the two. The baby-farmers could hardly go wrong; if the child they took died they collected insurance money, if the child grew up it could be sold.

The Sunday newspapers were full of cleverly worded advertisements by baby-farmers. In one week the *People* contained thirty-five advertisements; one woman put twenty-seven advertisements in one newspaper using different names. The baby-farming business was financed by the mother paying either a small sum a week (in Disraeli's novel *Sybil* the going rate was 3d a day) or a lump sum on the undertaking that she would hear nothing more of the child.

A sensational court case brought the whole question of baby-farming before the general public. In 1870 Margaret Waters and Sarah Ellis put an advertisement in *Lloyd's Newspaper*. They were operating from 4 Frederick Terrace, Gordon Grove, Brixton; the premium they were asking was £4. A policeman in the guise of a solicitous father answered the advertisement, and found at the address a number of children. One was very emaciated, and very dirty 'in fact, filthy', another was a mere skeleton, skin and bone, and when the policeman got the parish doctor to come the smell of laudanum was everywhere. There were nine children in all. Seventy-nine pawnbrokers slips were found, many of them relating to baby clothes, and there was some doubt as to how many children had passed through the women's hands since they had started in business four years earlier. There was certain knowledge that four children between the ages of three weeks and three months had died, and Waters was duly hanged, but her accomplice, Sarah Ellis, was found not guilty, though later she was imprisoned for false pretences. Baby-farming was unquestionably profitable but was no sinecure.

Nevertheless, the conditions in the baby-farms were probably no worse than in the London slums. In Church Lane, St. Giles's, thirty-seven men, women and children were squashed into a room 14 feet 6 inches square. A London cellar in 1883 housed father, mother, three children and four pigs. In one room a widow and three children had with them a dead child; the child had been dead for thirteen days.

A lodging house in St. Giles's (where Charing Cross Road and New Oxford Street meet). (*Graphic*)

It is indicative of the climate of the time that investigators were less appalled by the filth and the squalor than by the morality of it all. The absence of privacy was more important than the fact that many of the houses actually had the cesspools beneath the house, sometimes merely boarded over.

Cruelty under these conditions was not memorable; it was not even noted. Nor was it in the common lodging houses. In 1876 there were 4,219 unregistered low lodging houses, with four families to a room, each family occupying a corner. Beds could contain six or more people of different sexes and ages. Incest was unremarkable, and the eleven-

and twelve-year-olds engaged in sexual intercourse without interference. Those involved in the Royal Commission on the housing of the working classes in 1884 did pull one boy up who was indulging himself. Somewhat indignantly he said, 'Why do you take hold of me? There are a dozen of them at it down there.'

The poor existed in layers of hopelessness rather than degrees of filth. Where there was complete apathy, as in the worst of the slums and lodging houses, there was insufficient energy to indulge in acts of brutality. Starvation, as the governing classes realised, was a powerful weapon of repression, though this realisation was hardly ever on a conscious level. The half-employed were more likely to vent their spite in cruel acts against children.

Drink was a vital element in the life of the poor, and cruelty towards children was a frequent corollary. In Edinburgh in the 1850s there were 1,000 whisky shops, 160 in one street, and in Glasgow every Saturday night ten thousand people got drunk. In the prevailing climate of opinion, temperance societies, despite their grandiloquent claims, could make little headway.

The National Society for the Prevention of Cruelty to Children (formed in 1884) realised the close connection between drink and cruelty to children, and estimated that at least half of the cases they were called out to owed their genesis to drink. Such cruelty was not necessarily continuous or systematic; there was a passive cruelty, which involved spending all the available money on drink so that the children would go hungry or even starve, or pawning the furniture and bed-linen so that the children would have to sleep on straw or naked boards. This kind of unthinking behaviour had long-term repercussions, for the children would go out to steal and being inexperienced would soon find their way into a House of Correction where scant regard was paid to the backgrounds of such unfortunates.

The more astute children went out begging, or would join up with adult beggars who knew the ropes, and would pay them threepence a day (1p) or more if the child was a cripple. The higher grade of adult beggars would pay even more—a shilling a pair (5p). The children themselves soon got the hang of the system, and in 1848 *The Times* carried a news item of two girls of eleven and thirteen begging in the streets with a baby, into whom they stuck pins. A crying baby was always worth a copper or two extra.

Whether the maxim 'if you can't beat them, join them' can be construed in this context as cruelty may be in some doubt. It was usual for children to go to the public houses to get the drink in jugs, and many publicans placed steps or raised platforms at the counter for the benefit of the children. A loop-hole in the law enabled children to fetch drink though not to consume it on the premises. It is not surprising that the juvenile carriers consumed it off the premises, dipping into their parents' booze. Parliamentary attempts were made to eliminate this anomaly, but with the opposition of the brewers these attempts made little headway.

On many occasions doctors were called to children who became paralytically drunk in the street. Parents were amused by the addiction of their children to drink; in many cases addiction set in young, for it was common to keep babies quiet by giving them gin. In 1901 there was an inquiry mentioning the case of an eighteen-month-old baby dying from cirrhosis of the liver, and in 1897 there were reports of a girl of two and a half in hospital who continually asked for porter, and a boy of eight with delirium tremens.

Few of the poor indulged in sadistic cruelty. The neglect of children of the labouring classes was the result of indifference and the inability to cope with circumstances, and physical cruelty was usually off the cuff, the result of an explosion of anger and frustration when the panacea of drink had failed to work. Children were proxies for 'them', the unfeeling and mysterious creatures in all the strata of society that boxed them in, kept them under, and used them with a callousness that made the brutality of the poor seem very pallid indeed.

8

The Workhouse

When the Poor Law Amendment Act was passed in 1834 there was very little opposition in parliament. It has been said that for the first time a legislative problem was thoroughly and scientifically tackled, and when the diligent Edwin Chadwick spent two years introducing the new system into the rural districts no rancour was shown to him.

The main point of the act was that relief should not be offered to able-bodied persons and their families otherwise than in a well-regulated workhouse. Until then relief was given to men and families in their homes; those men who were not earning a living wage had their money made up to a subsistence level. This fact was artfully worked on by employers, who paid very low wages knowing that their workers would not starve. Abuses were common. Parishes often fell into the hands of tradesmen, property owners, manufacturers and public house keepers. They had control of the parish funds, and were frequently the employers of those very workmen whose wages had to be supplemented from the parish. They had every right to dip into the till.

The new law was neat and systematic; it was a step towards centralised government. The old parish authorities did not like it, nor did industrial workers when professional agitators got amongst them and warned them of the consequences, telling them that the new workhouses would be nothing short of prisons, that wife would be parted from husband, and mother from child. 'The hatred of the Poor Law was well founded', wrote the agitator Holyoake. 'Its dreary punishment would fall, it was believed, not upon the idle merely, but upon the working people who by no thrift could save, nor by any industry provide for the future.'

Unquestionably the new law was too neat, and the operation of it revealed startling injustices, especially to handloom weavers in Lancashire, Yorkshire and Cheshire. In times of economic recession their earnings went down, and were made up by outdoor relief. Now, under the 1834 law, their wages went down and stayed down. They either had to manage as best as they could on the reduced income, or give up in despair and go into the workhouse. The employers were also not happy about the new order, for they were no longer being subsidised out of the rates. In one town, Carlisle, there was one big firm, Peter Dixon's; no doubt the owner was pleased to see the riots and turbulence in Carlisle when news of the act was brought there.

One of the leading opponents of the law was William Cobbett, who since 1832 had been M.P. for Oldham. In his *Legacy to Labourers* he sketched out its implications. The 'neighbourly' system of relief was gone, no longer would the friendly parish officials bring round the dole. Now the English labourer would be screwed down to Irish wages and Irish diet—the Irish immigrants made good scapegoats. In 1836 an industrial depression occurred, and Cobbett could have said, 'I told you so,' (had he not died in 1835). The Anti-Poor Law Movement sparked off by the depression, by fear, and by the remoteness of the controllers of the system, was eventually to be incorporated into the Chartist Movement.

A number of firebrands contributed their faggots to the Anti-Poor Law Movement, including Joseph Stephens (1805–79), a freelance Wesleyan minister with his own custom-built chapel at Ashton. His oratory had a revivalist flavour:

And if this damnable law, which violated all the laws of God, was continued, and all means of peaceably putting an end to it had been made in vain, then, in the words of their banner, 'For children and wife we'll war to the knife.'

Unfortunately for Stephens and his colleagues, the middle classes liked the new laws. It seemed, at last, as though there was a solution to the problem of the poor. The politicians as a whole liked them; they looked at them as a means of tidying up a messy situation and curbing the medieval powers of local government. They did not see that many of the fears of the agitators were justified, that the guardians of the workhouse would be as unscrupulous as the old parish bosses and furthermore were a long way from London, the hub of workhouse organisation. Men and their wives *were* separated (though in 1847 a husband and wife above the age of sixty were not compelled to live separate and apart from each other, and in 1876 this provision was extended to cover infirm, disabled, or sick husbands and wives). Mothers *were* parted from their children, causing distress and anguish. And the workhouses were not the palaces that the reformers had hoped for; they were fortresses for the subjugation of the poor.

Workhouses were fortresses for the subjugation of the poor, and those who would not or could not work, starved. (*Illustrated London News*)

Not that all workhouses were terrible. There were show-places and apologists could mention Haslingden Workhouse where inmates received, for Christmas 1867, tobacco, oranges and apples from two local doctors and a barrel of ale from local brewers. Christmas 1852 was a time to remember for inmates of Durham Workhouse, with cakes, free beer, and tobacco provided by the workhouse officials. The children in Bolton Workhouse were sent on periodical visits to the wonders of Blackpool.

Charles Dickens was resolutely anti-Poor Law:

> The members of this board were very sage, deep, philosophical men; and when they came to turn their attention to the workhouse, they found out at once, what ordinary folk would never have discovered,—the poor people liked it! It was a regular place of public entertainment for the poorer classes,—a tavern where there was nothing to pay,—a public breakfast, dinner, tea, and supper, all the year round,—a brick and mortar elysium, where it was all play and no work. 'Oho!' said the board, looking very knowing; 'we are the fellows to set this to rights; we'll stop it all in no time.' So they established the rule, that all poor people should have the alternative (for they would compel nobody, not they,) of being starved by a gradual process in the house, or by a quick one out of it.

The irony of Charles Dickens in *Oliver Twist* had its effect; the public would never see the workhouse in the same way, as a beneficial outcome of the 1834 Poor Law. But viewing what went on in the workhouse was very different from doing something about it, and distasteful as workhouse guardians were, they were at least doing something about the poor and keeping them out of sight. The poor were popularly supposed to be shiftless ne'er-do-wells, though few would have gone so far as Thomas Carlyle who said, 'Whosoever will not work ought not to live.'

The picture was muddled because those who would not work were less numerous than those who could not work, or could not get work, but because the law was slanted towards the first group, in fact, if not in intention, the workhouse, or 'work'us' as it was known to its inmates, was geared to austerity. The inmates were made to work, picking oakum or breaking rock being the favoured tasks. Oakum was a preparation of tarred fibre used in shipbuilding, for caulking or packing joints in wooden ships or the deck planking of iron and steel ships. It was made from old tarry ropes, the strands of which were unravelled by the oakum pickers. It was a painful and tedious operation, but it could be done by men, women and children without instruction and but a modicum of supervision. 'These tasks are expected from all comers', wrote the son of the Salvation Army leader William

Booth, 'starved, ill-clad, half-fed creatures from the streets, foot-sore and worn-out, and yet unless it is done, the alternative is the magistrate and the gaol.'

Each parish had a workhouse, under the control of several guardians, who were under the orders of a distant Board of Commissioners sitting at London. The workhouse, or the union (i.e. a union of parishes), was the last stopping place before the grave.

Upkeep of the workhouses was a call on the rates, and the parish guardians did their best to keep the costs down, except when they were taking commissions from providers of food. The very existence of the workhouse system guaranteed pauperism, for the fear that the poor living in their parish would become a burden on the rates made the parish officials reluctant to permit a labourer to move in and rent a house and possibly make something of himself. Even the most robust and hard-working labourer was pushed on to the road, not able to root himself where he wanted, the victim of the parish fear of chargeability.

In the early days of the reign, conditions were extraordinarily harsh, though they did ease up slightly as the century wore on. Journalists damning the hard-heartedness of the system drew parallels 'among those savage tribes who kill their aged and infirm brethren to save trouble and expense'. It was thanks to the efforts of novelists and journalists like Dickens that some amelioration took place in the condition of the workhouse poor—certainly few politicians can have looked proudly at their record.

Inmates were not allowed to follow the religion of their choice, but were saddled with disinterested Church of England clergymen of the middling order of assistant curates. They were not allowed visits by friends or relations. Until 1842 meals were taken in silence, and smoking was not allowed. The food consisted of half a pound of gruel and half a pound of bread a day, with a little meat and cheese. For able-bodied inmates, their bed was a plank; they were in bed at seven, up at five forty-five, ready to start picking oakum or breaking rock, (women were put at the wash-tub or oakum-picking).

At some workhouses water was strictly rationed out; at one, three people had to wash in the same water, and at the workhouse at Mile End there was no water at all. St. George's, Whitechapel, was notorious for the fact that it was always dirty, and a breeding ground for scarlet fever and cholera. At St. Giles's workhouse, in the rookery near Seven Dials, just to the west of what is now the north end of Charing Cross

Road, supper was boiled up for breakfast. St. Giles's was described by the Salvation Army as 'a perfect quagmire of Human Sludge'.

Conditions in the workhouses rarely came to light, but a suicide at St. Pancras workhouse opened up the hideous corners of that establishment. A girl drowned herself rather than face the discipline of the 'shed', a place of confinement for refractory paupers. The shed was thirty-five feet by fifteen, and accommodated between twenty and twenty-four inmates, instead of the six that were allowed by hospital regulations. The damp of an adjoining cess-pool oozed through the walls.

One of the workhouse women was there for throwing her clothes over a wall, another for getting drunk and losing her pail and brush, another because she was weak-minded. One woman had been in the shed for three years. The guardian of the St. Pancras workhouse, W. Lee, had no knowledge of conditions inside the shed, and put the blame on the matron; he 'had no doubt that persons have been confined without his orders'. The matron admitted that she had ordered the suicide into the shed for refusing to do some domestic service.

At Warwick workhouse a two-and-a-half-year-old child dirtied itself, and had its own excrement thrust into his mouth. At Andover the inmates used to fight for gristle and marrow bones because they were starving. At the Hoo workhouse, the master was a sadist who regularly flogged girl inmates. In 1864 a pauper, Timothy Daly, died in Holborn workhouse, and an inquest brought in a verdict of filthiness caused by gross neglect.

The workhouse infirmaries were often as bad as the workhouse itself; they were staffed largely by paupers and by nurses of the old school, who could not get work in the hospitals that had been cleaned up and revitalised by Florence Nightingale and her helpers.

Liverpool workhouse infirmary revealed the system at its worst. The wards were an inferno, and thirty-five pauper nurses had been dismissed in one month for being drunk. Meals were cooked in the wards, which were awash with urine and excreta. Lice and bugs were everywhere, and inmates had worn the same shirts for seven weeks. The conditions were blamed on the practice of letting pauper nurses do the bulk of the work, and on corrupt officials who siphoned away any money given to run the workhouse infirmary into their own pockets. With inmates in Liverpool numbering between 1,350 and 1,500, those few who were trying to do a civilised job were overwhelmed by the odds stacked against them.

It was not surprising that many of the poor would do anything rather than allow themselves to be committed to a workhouse, would rather starve in the street than undergo the humiliation and slow death of workhouse life. In 1873 there were reckoned to be 100,000 paupers in London, 107 of whom died of starvation. *Vanity Fair* was righteously indignant about this—'A hundred human beings slowly tortured out of this world'.

Able-bodied inmates were sent out to do menial work, such as scavenging, wearing a kind of smock marked with the name of the workhouse. Such men, women and children were paid a few coppers for

The able-bodied were let out of the workhouse to do menial work, and with the few coppers earned supplemented their diet. (*London Society*)

their work, and were thus able to supplement the starvation diet. They were consequently better off than those inmates not allowed outside the gates but were still expected to work at oakum picking and stone breaking.

Long-staying guests were not wanted in the workhouse, and the ill were allowed to die without much pretence at keeping them alive.

There was an understanding between coffin-makers and workhouse masters, and the cheapest possible boxes were provided for the dead, with the master getting a cut of the profit. When no one was concerned whether a dead inmate was getting a decent funeral or not, there were few restraints on the perquisites of workhouse masters.

The young were apprenticed out as soon as possible. They were bound till they were twenty-one, and if the master died before the apprenticeship was completed, the apprentice formed part of the deceased man's goods and chattels. An apprentice was not paid, though occasionally received when he was eighteen or nineteen pocket money of twopence or threepence a week. It was usual for a master to be paid £10 for taking an apprentice, and then:

> You may make them into sausages, for anything the constitution will do to prevent you. If it should be proved that you kill even one of them, you will be hanged; but you may half-starve them, beat them, torture them, any thing short of killing them, with perfect security; and using a little circumspection, you may kill them too, without much danger. Suppose they die, who cares?

Who cared indeed?

III INDUSTRIAL CRUELTY

9

What About the Workers?

WHAT SEEMS TO us to be the systematic cruelty practised on employees and workers was regarded by the Victorians with unconcern. They would have accused us of being sentimental, and would have been amused to learn that this characteristic is unequivocally acknowledged as being the prerogative of their own age. The treatment of the workforce was logical in view of the conditions that prevailed.

The first factor to be considered is that there was a surplus of labour, and that a worker who did not fit in or kicked against the traces was out of work, whereupon he or she would starve or go into the workhouse. A known rebel was a liability no one wanted. Unions, despite their pretensions, were weak, and individual members sabotaged militant movements if it seemed as though personally they would suffer. The workers who could dictate terms were those in small closely-knit cliques or those whose skills were sufficient to cause industrial or social discomfiture.

Instrument-makers and cabinet-makers, jewellery-makers and watch-makers, and all those in the higher wage bracket (earning more than thirty shillings a week) would feel reasonably safe, but the unskilled and semi-skilled who made less than a pound a week, such as glove-makers, straw-workers, and silk-workers, were always in peril, aware that they could be replaced at any time. There was contempt on the part of the employers, and for workers like dustmen and sewer cleaners it was customary for them to provide their own tools of the trade, or rent them from the employer. A steel puddler in Wales had sixpence a month stopped from his wages 'for clay to repair the furnaces'.

Clerks hung on to their jobs with grim despair, knowing that if their copper-plate handwriting faltered or accuracy in adding columns of figures dimmed there might be nothing for them outside. The clerks of a Burnley mill in 1852 were 'recommended' to bring in four pounds of coal a day each during cold weather, though the owners supplied brushes, brooms, scrubbers and soap for the clerks to clean their offices. It was an axiom that clerks and similar low life did not strike.

Employers felt a mild distaste for strikes, but employees feared the counter-stroke—the lock-out. Sometimes a lock-out occurred when it seemed that workmen were getting above themselves. In 1872 there was a lock-out in Wales for excessive wage demands. A couple of months later the same men went on strike when told that their wages would be cut by 10 per cent, a strike that lasted three months.

The miners were in the forefront of the militants. In 1875, Earl Fitzwilliam ordered the compulsory use of safety lamps in his mines, but the miners refused to comply and went on strike. Without further ado Earl Fitzwilliam closed down his mines.

From 1799 to 1824 trade unions were illegal, but when the Combination Acts were repealed there was a fervour of activity, and Robert Owen's genteel Utopian Socialism was thought to be the answer to the absolute domination of the masters. In 1834 the Grand National Consolidated Trades Union was evolved for 'the purpose of the more effectually enabling the working classes to secure, protect, and establish the rights of industry', a union that failed miserably within a few weeks, though some of the more energetic practitioners went into the Chartist movement, which itself was languidly suppressed.

The unions that came up in the 1840s were not inclined to revolution, and were prepared, indeed sycophantically eager, to work within the framework of the capitalist system. Prominent amongst these unions were the Amalgamated Society of Engineers, the Amalgamated Society of Carpenters, the Ironfounders, and the London Bricklayers. They were aided and abetted, except with money, by middle-class do-gooders including Tom Hughes, the author of *Tom Brown's Schooldays*, and the Christian Socialist F. D. Maurice, a leading light in the formation of the Working Men's College.

These unions alarmed only the most tremulous of industrialists, and it was considered that the extra-mural activities of the workers could be assimilated by starting brass bands and Mechanics' Institutes. When one considers the weak position of the unions and the workers it is surprising that there were strikes at all. In 1834 there was a strike of

London tailors, followed by strikes by the Glasgow calico printers and Staffordshire potters in the same year. The Amalgamated Society of Engineers struck in 1852, the London cabmen in 1853, the builders in 1859, the silk-workers of Coventry in 1860, the iron puddlers in 1865. None of these demonstrated the capacity of labour to do anything more than inconvenience.

Union members were not surprisingly irked by the lack of effect, and blamed it on fellow workers who were not union members, and the consequence of the great hostility between union and non-union workers was a series of outrages in Sheffield in 1866 directed by unionists against non-unionists resulting in injury and death. The leaders of the unions hastily disassociated themselves from these happenings and added their voices to the demand for a government inquiry.

The inquiry made it clear that not only was there complete confusion about the numbers of trades unionists in existence, but also about the role of the union and its operations, and the extent to which unionists bullied and terrorised non-unionists. It was apparent that a power structure was being evolved within an industrial unit, and that the cruelty and self-interest of employer *vis-à-vis* the employee was being recapitulated within the factory, under the name of 'rattening'.

Rattening could take various forms, from merely sending a non-unionist to Coventry, hiding or stealing a man's tools, to violence, including vitriol-throwing. The more timid non-unionists were intimidated by the strong action of pickets when unions went on strike. The word 'black-leg' was used as early as 1862. Those men who continued to work in defiance of the union call were beaten or threatened, and so were their wives and children. Their lives could be made a misery long after a strike was technically over.

In 1867 Ellen Meade was convicted of threatening and molesting a non-unionist workwoman, Mrs. Mills. Mrs. Meade had accused Mrs. Mills of doing the dirty work. When Mrs. Mills had asked what business it was of hers, Mrs. Meade had retorted, 'Yes, it's all to do with me; it's all such stinking hussies as you who are keeping men out of their work, you stinking cow, and when the strike is over you'll be off, and there will be no work for you. You are a . . . When the strike is over I will do for you.' Most of such cases never approached a court of law; the non-unionists knew that appearance as a prosecutrix was simply not on.

Many strikers took their cue from the United States where strike methods were often violent. As early as 1740–41 journeymen bakers had struck in New York City, and although they were indicted for conspiracy no action was taken. Where labour was in demand, as it was in America, strikes could be more than inconvenient, but many British trades unionists did not realise that parallel conditions did not exist their side of the Atlantic, and that the only people hurt by strikes were the strikers themselves.

Nevertheless, as the organisation of trades unions improved towards the end of the nineteenth century, strikes did damage the economy. In 1893 there were 615 disputes, involving more than half a million workers and causing total stoppages of thirty million days. In 1889 a prolonged strike by dock and waterside labourers in London was successful; their sixpence an hour was raised to eightpence, The success was partly due to the general public which contributed £50,000 to the strike fund, and Australian workers who sent £30,000. Because of the support of the public, the violence and intimidation that went with the strike were largely ignored.

Punch ran a cartoon of a capitalist being completely unconcerned by a strike, while the worker was in desperation, knowing that starvation would inexorably follow. Not unnaturally strikes caused a good deal of ill-feeling, and with the growth of union membership even the small family firms, where the masters and the men were on amicable terms, had its quota of union militants, forcing a gap between worker and management where a genuine friendliness had existed before.

The surplus of labour guaranteed that in any dispute not involving key workers those at the bottom of the social scale would suffer. In almost intolerable conditions the workers slogged on. A factor that weighed against strike was the long hours that the men and women worked. They were too tired to be militant. In the cotton towns of Lancashire they were hard at it from early in the morning until late at night, and moralists never failed to point out the quietness and lack of crime in the cotton towns compared with Liverpool. Small wonder that the middle classes saw a disciplined labour force as a desirable component of the civilised society.

The conflict between capital and labour was exploited by fiction writers, and violent incidents in industrial novels served to increase the uneasiness of the reading public. In Mrs. Gaskell's *Mary Barton* (1848) the son of an employer is murdered by a Chartist. The boot is on the other foot in Mrs. Frances Trollope's *Michael Armstrong: The Factory Boy* (1840) where a boy is systematically tortured by a ruthless industrialist. The scene in Mrs. Tonna's *Helen Fleetwood* (1841) where an overseer cripples a young girl had many parallels in real life in the mills and factories.

Most of the novelists put the blame on the employers, many of whom were not aware of the intolerable conditions under which their

Mill-workers in the cotton towns were too tired to be militant, and the quietness of Manchester compared with Liverpool was often remarked upon. (*Graphic*)

workers slaved. No doubt many of the readers were moved by the passionate tirades of the novelists, but, able as they were, they did not have the charisma of a Dickens. Dickens, by writing about workhouse brutality in *Oliver Twist* and school cruelty in *Nicholas Nickleby*, did succeed in raising indignation strong enough to slip into action. His contemporary novelists made their points, and they were taken—for just as long as it took to read the novel.

Crusading journalists, too, looked askance at the situations existing in industry, at the rat-race, at the lack of scruple and the pursuit of the main chance right along the line, from financiers who floated companies to the small shopkeeper who fleeced his customer. In 1892 *Chambers's Journal* joined in:

> 'Every man for himself,' says the phoenix financier, rising from the ruins of companies, heedless of the sobs of the women, the execrations of the men, he has helped to ruin, in their ignorance; to recall and ponder over them, perhaps, in the silent night-watches of a sleepless old age. 'Every man for himself'—it is the quintessence of smartness and wide-awakeness to the ignorant egotist hurrying to grow rich, who, without knowing it, has entered a *cul-de-sac* whence there is no egress, and where he will one day awake to find himself— as in a prison—alone.

However, it needed more than a courteous well-bred article in a respectable weekly paper to encourage an industrialist to make working conditions in his factory less intolerable.

When one talks of almost intolerable conditions, one must not forget that this term is subjective, and that although some aspects of Victorian life are not so different from those today, the conditions in which manual workers operated do not bear comparison. Nor do the attitudes of manual workers; certain classes of labourers were treated as beasts of burden, and often this was justified. The navvies, the navigators or canal builders, were violent, savage, and dangerous, and iron discipline that could be construed in our own easy-going times as cruelty was necessary to stop them running completely amok. An engineer told the select committee on railway labourers in 1846 that it was dangerous to approach them when they were not at work, and even the gang bosses, who dominated them when they were working, were afraid to penetrate their vile sordid encampments.

On Saturday nights after they had been paid the navvies took over like an army of occupation, throwing stones at passers-by, overturning carriages, and 'put at defiance any local constabulary force; consequently crimes of the most atrocious character are common, and robbery without attempt at concealment an everyday occurrence'. It was common practice for the inhabitants of villages and country towns anywhere near where the navvies were working to lock and bolt their doors and windows and remain indoors, and woe betide any woman, young or old, who ventured out alone. Rape was an unconsidered misdemeanour.

Townships of up to two thousand sprang up, totally outside the law, and the only way to cope with the navvies was by using troops. This was done reluctantly and only as a last resort, for the building of the railway network was considered a national priority, though troops were brought in when pitched battles were fought between gangs of Irish and English navvies working on the Chester–Holyhead railway using as weapons the tool of their calling, the short sharp-bladed excavating spades. Navvies 'on the randy' served as an awful example to the middle classes of what would happen if the labouring classes were not kept resolutely under. When navvies were taken to the Crimea in 1855 to build the Balaclava railway line they were kept in order by flogging, a form of army discipline heartily approved by the timid middle classes who had seen, or more likely heard of, the navvies on the rampage.

Physical force was the only way of keeping the navvies under control and at their work. Not that the navvies were underprivileged. They were paid twice as much as ordinary labourers, and although they may occasionally have maimed or even killed a ganger they did not whine about their condition. Accidents were frequent, and explosives necessary in blasting out cuttings were handled casually. That they did their job well is clear from the quality of railway works such as viaducts and tunnels still used after a hundred and twenty years. The discipline was consistent with the need for it. But in other industries the same type of discipline was used, without the justification. It was all very well to beat and berate the tough hardy navvy, but these sort of actions were not necessary in factories where the work force was suppliant, half-fed and included women and children.

With a few honourable exceptions, industrialists were indifferent to the conditions prevailing in their works and factories. Their only concern was profit, and for this profit the well-being and the comfort of employees were insouciantly sacrificed. It must be remembered that most Victorian industries were owned by one man or one family, and that joint stock companies were not common until the century was well under way (an act for limiting the liability of joint stock companies was passed in 1855, but by 1864 only 3,830 joint stock companies had been formed on the limited liability principle). Throughout the period the tone of a factory was given by a hierarchy not an amorphous group of share-holders. The more greedy and rapacious an industrialist was, the less interest would he have in the welfare of his employees. The incentives to get rich were manifold; there was hardly any income tax (up to 1s 4d during the Crimean War, but that was rare) and a wealthy Victorian was wealthy indeed.

Safety measures cut down the work rate and thus the profit margin, and it would not be stretching a point to interpret callous disregard of employees' safety as a kind of cruelty, operating at long range. In Birmingham the principal sources of serious danger were the shafts and bands used for turning lathes and wheels, and a woman killed in a screw factory through becoming entangled in a shaft had been caught in the same way previously at least four times. The long dresses were caught in the revolving parts. The manager of Nettlefold & Chamberlain's patent screw works, Smethwick, near Birmingham, pooh-poohed the idea that something should be done to protect the girls from shafts and bands, considering that if they got caught up in them it was their own fault. 'Still,' he admitted, 'it is a very awkward thing, for the girl sets up a great screaming, and all the rest do the same. I have known three caught in one day, and then perhaps a month without any.' The only way to stop a girl screaming when she was caught up in a machine, and maybe lose a finger or two, was to fine her. And this Nettlefold & Chamberlain did.

Accidents due to the absence of guards from presses and stamps were common throughout industry, but the mutilation or loss of a finger were not reckoned of any consequence. The sub-humans who operated the presses and stamps were not likely to want to play the piano. Misadventures with presses not only arose from the absence of guards; in many factories there was very little light. A commission on the metal manufacturers of Birmingham reported in 1864 that 'the gloominess of some of the work-places is extreme. In some, as casting and many stamping shops, good light is not essential to the work. . . .'

The small employers were probably more indifferent to the dangers of machines than the big industrialists. The proprietor of Shirtcliffe's Ivory, Pearl, and Tortoise-shell Cutter factory in Sheffield let off most of his works to small masters, and how they treated their work force was no concern of his. At this firm a number of children were playing hide-and-seek during the lunch break; the master switched on the machinery. One girl could not get out of the way in time. 'They

Industrialists regarded themselves as gods, though it needed an excess of ego to have oneself 'done' in marble and put on exhibition. (*Magazine of Art*)

had to pick up her bones in a basket as they found them, and that's how they buried her.'

In every aspect of industrial life management held the whip-hand. In 1889 the cotton mills of Lancashire and Cheshire were put on half-time at the behest of speculators to limit the production of cloth and thus raise the prices, throwing tens of thousands out of work. Small wonder that a proposal in 1892 to cut wages by five per cent resulted in a strike. Many workers lived in a state of terror; if they dressed too well there was a good chance that their wages would be reduced to bring them into line and make them realise that they were the lowest of the low. In any litigation the employers always had the edge; in what is known as the Taff Vale judgment of 1901, the unions were sued by the employers for the profits they had lost during a strike. The employers won, and this case set back labour/management relations for many years—indeed, amongst the hard-core of trades unionists this judgment has never been forgotten. Recalcitrant workmen were always in danger of being framed on trumped-up charges; a William Hawkes saw a workman removing a file value 7d. The workman was sentenced to transportation for ten years.

Not surprisingly the attitudes of employers infiltrated into private life, and they treated their servants as they treated their work force, as members of an alien species whose lot was to serve uncomplainingly. It was the destiny of industrial magnates to go into politics, taking with them their contempt for the working classes and incapable of understanding their aspirations. Typical of these was Joseph Chamberlain, whose firm of Nettlefold & Chamberlain was in the forefront of reaction, and who started the Chamberlain political dynasty and whose incomprehension was mirrored in the 1930s by that of his son, Neville. Neville Chamberlain's wing-collar cut him off from the ordinary people as assuredly as Joseph Chamberlain's indifference to the women mangled by his factory's machinery did for him.

10

The Cruel Trades

A WORKING MAN out of employment had the choice of starvation or the workhouse, and this fact of life was mercilessly worked upon by manufacturers. In private life many of them were not necessarily cruel, but they kept their home and their public lives in logic-tight compartments, and when towards the end of the century prying journalists penetrated into factories and workshops, industrialists were indignant by their exposés, an indignation matched by that of city worthies anxious to project favourable images of their towns and their products.

Certain industries are by their nature arduous and hazardous; today the workers in them demand, quite rightly, that they be treated as special cases, saying that they, and only they, have to do these dirty jobs and should be well-paid for it. There were far more of these trades in the nineteenth century, the workers were not helped by labour or health-saving machinery and there was no provision for their welfare. They were not paid any more than their contemporaries in salubrious trades, and their willingness to slave at obnoxious tasks was proof to employers that their workers belonged to an inferior species.

In *The White Slaves of England* published in 1853, John Cobden wrote that 'the subjection of the majority of a nation to an involuntary, hopeless, exhausting, and demoralising servitude, for the benefit of an idle and luxurious few of the same nation, is slavery in its most appalling form. Such a system of slavery, we assert, exists in Great Britain.' For many, matters did not alter for half a century. In the early years of the present century the average working man's wage was just over a pound a week.

There had, of course, been some alleviation in the lot of the poor.

A number of the worst abuses had been stamped out. But at the time of Queen Victoria's 1897 Jubilee there were still areas of industry, far enough away from the centre of government to be overlooked, where conditions had not altered since the black days of the 1830s and 1840s. Widnes and St. Helens in Lancashire were accepted as being dreary places, made so by the alkali and salt works. Widnes, formerly Wood-end, had a population of less than two thousand in 1851; in 1901 it was 28,580.

Widnes was geared to the propagation of a stunted sickly population. The chemical trade was brutal and subtle, and its masters cruel and demanding. Drunkenness was rife; the leading doctor in St. Helens declared that the men involved in the manufacture of salt could not do their work unless they were half-drunk. A 'salt-cake' man expected to get through between twenty and thirty pints of beer a day.

The men on the councils lived in their large Victorian Gothic houses well out of reach of the sulphuretted hydrogen gas that pervaded the two towns. The gas laid metallic blue-green slime on water and mud. Worse than this gas was 'Roger', the curious name given to the chlorine gas which, pumped on to slaked lime, transformed it into bleaching powder. The packers wore goggles over their eyes and twenty thicknesses of flannel around their mouths, for a 'feed' of the gas killed the men in an hour.

'Roger is coming!' was the cry raised when the wind bore the green fog down the alleys and streets, and few escaped the ravages of chlorine gas. A worker was finished by the time he was forty-five, whereupon he spent a year or two 'nobbling' stones (breaking stones to extract the sulphur) before ending his days in the workhouse. The salt-cake men lost their teeth at an early age. The fumes rotted the teeth within twelve months.

The average wage was less than a pound a week, but without any other local industry the men of the district were glad to get it. Considering the horrid conditions, the salt-cake men had little to look forward to but an early death. To make their miseries worse, the leading manufacturers of Widnes and St. Helens had banded together early in the 1890s and dropped their wages, while increasing the prices of their products. Bicarbonate of soda, the prime Victorian antidote to gluttony, had gone up from £5 5s (£5·25) a ton in 1889 to £7 a ton in 1897, salt-cake from 1s (5p) to 2s (10p), and caustic soda had also doubled in price.

There was no guarantee of continued employment. The manufacturers cut down their work force when trade was slack, and when men were desperate there were cases of them throwing themselves into the vats of vitriol. The workers in Widnes and St. Helens had additional expenses not shared by factory workers in Birmingham and Sheffield. They had to wear wool, for the gas rotted cotton in less than forty-eight hours.

The publicity given to conditions in Widnes and St. Helens by the newspaper magnate C. Arthur Pearson created ructions among the town officials and the manufacturers, who successfully 'blacked' the Chemical Workers' Union, which lost its local branch and with it the club houses, which were closed and their furniture auctioned. The town councils were derisive about the unflattering accounts of their twin purgatories which were, they claimed, so healthy that they were thinking of advertising them as spa towns.

The wool-combers of Bradford shared many of the hazards of the alkali workers. In unventilated sheds a hundred feet long men fed wool to as many as sixty machines. 'The noise', one observer wrote, 'is deafening—a grinding screeching noise; the whole place vibrates. The heat is very great, and the air is full of a yellow, noisome dust.' Unlike the alkali workers, the wool-combers were not great drinkers— they were too exhausted, and the thinness of the operatives was notorious. Because there were too many people chasing too many jobs, the Bradford industrialists could do much as they liked with their labour force, laying them off when trade was slack and working them harshly when big orders came in. A deputation of the wool-combers' union went to see an employer, who said: 'I shall not spend my time in discussing the question with you, beyond saying that our hands will have to work when we want them to work; and if they refuse we will get others that will.'

Every evening at five o'clock the unemployed gathered at the gates of the factories to see if there was any work for them on the night shift. They were not too proud to batten on the misfortunes of those workers who had arrived a minute late and were sacked on the spot. Disease was rife amongst the wool-combers, especially anthrax. The wages averaged out at 14s (70p) a week, but the wool-combers preferred the drudgery to the 'grubber' (the workhouse) or 'larking' (being unemployed). Women got less—$2\frac{1}{2}$d per hour instead of $3\frac{1}{2}$d, though they were marginally protected by the Factory Acts which allowed them set times for meals. The men had to eat when they could.

Compared with other industries, the workers in the white-lead factories were well paid, and even women could earn nearly a pound a week. The white-lead industry was a killer, and the factories were surrounded by high walls, with policemen at the gates to stop unauthorised prying. The process of making white-lead was dangerous at every level. The lead is melted, and put into moulds. When it cools it has a blue colour, and is then carried by the blue-bed women, or blueys, to the stack-house. Each woman carries five stone of the lead. The floor of the stack-house is covered with tan, and pots of acetic acid are placed on the tan. After three months the action of the vapour rising from the acid transforms the stacks of lead into subacetate of lead, and the carbonic acid rising from the tan into carbonate of lead, white lead in its first stage. The white-bed women enter the scene; they 'strip' the white bed, and are in peril from the poisonous dust even though they wear respirators, known in the trade as muzzles. The grinders are mainly men, paid up to two pounds a week. They rarely live past forty. One grinder declared that 'the lead gets up under the nails and works up the joints and twists the arms'. Colic was the first sign of the inroads of lead poisoning, followed by wrist-drop. Yet the grinders were safer than those involved in the next stage, where the washed and ground lead was churned into a paste and placed in a stove.

The percentage of deaths amongst lead workers was greater than in any other industry, and employers were watchful over those who looked as though they had caught lead-poisoning—the first outward indication was a blue line on the gums, due to the action of sulphuretted hydrogen upon lead circulating in the blood. It is estimated that 75 per cent of the workers in the more dangerous phases of white-lead production had this tell-tale mark, but only when this was coupled with other signs such as pallor or wrist-drop did the employers take action. Factory doctors were instructed to lay off workers who had clearly begun to succumb, but so desperate was the need for work in Newcastle-on-Tyne, one of the principal centres of the industry, that many of the discharged workers applied for employment under different names, necessary when the masters circulated through the trade the names of those operatives who had been suspended by the doctors' orders. The girls who formed such a large percentage of the labour force asked which was preferable—a quick death by starvation or slow death by poisoning? They chose the latter. This is incredible when one considers the final stages of lead poisoning—blindness and madness.

The Home Office made sporadic attempts to discover the incidence of lead poisoning, which also occurred in the manufacture of pottery, and in 1895 notification of the disease was made compulsory following a scientific inquiry in 1893. The frightening figures encouraged the inquiry to apportion blame not to the employers but the employees, 'that a large part of the mortality from lead poisoning is avoidable; although it must always be borne in mind that no arrangements or rules, with regard to the work itself, can entirely obviate the effects of the poison to which workers are exposed, because so much depends upon the individual and the observance of personal care and cleanliness'.

There was a sanguine hope that lead poisoning was on the decrease, but figures brought out in 1897 proved that this was not so. The pottery manufacturers were aghast when scientific experts recommended in 1899 that the use of raw lead should be abolished. Such a prohibition, the manufacturers declared, would leave the market free for foreigners and jeopardise the jobs of all those who worked in the Potteries. No one was very clear why this should be, but the problem was shelved and reappraisals in 1906 and 1910 did little to alter the situation, and wrist-drop, acute urinary and digestive troubles, blindness and madness were still the lot of those who worked with lead.

The workers were apathetic, the employers were philosophical; some of them provided baths and washing-places, and blamed their employees when they only wanted to get home after a ten- or twelve-hour shift and did not make use of the facilities. The idea of installing machinery and dust-removing apparatus to reduce the dangers of lead poisoning was anathema both to management and shareholders.

Humanitarianism was sacrificed to profit, and it is difficult not to see industrialists of the period as a race of Scrooges only intermittently worried by the spectres of the workpeople who had died under their yoke from lead poisoning, anthrax or poison gas. When the working classes were as incapable of fighting back as they were before the days of strong unions (and even then) there was a powerful incentive to see them as ciphers and nothing more.

There was only one thing for a worker in one of the dangerous trades to do—get out. But it was difficult to do this without hope. And hope was soon crushed amongst the salt-cake men, the wool-combers, and the lead-grinders, and all the others wriggling at the bottom of the social ladder, incapable of grasping the first rung.

11

Sweated Labour

PHYSICAL CRUELTY DOES not form part of the saga of sweated labour, and it might be said that it is sound business practice to get as much done for as little as possible. Villains are not easy to find, and when it is found that some middle-man is pressing too hard for his pound of flesh it is often true that somewhere someone up the line is applying pressure on him. Some of the miseries of the persons involved in sweated labour lie at the door of Victorian progress; the prices of everyday articles were going down, and outworkers had to compete with the machinery of the factories. They also had to contend with immigrants, especially Jews, who managed to live on even lower earnings than the native-born.

If there was not physical cruelty, there was certainly callousness and greed. The government was not free from blame, for not only did it fail to pass legislation protecting the sweated labour force from exploitation but undercut the rates themselves. Much of the clothing for the navy, the army, and for convicts, was done by sweated labour. The clothiers put in bids and the lowest tender was accepted. The money paid by the government departments to the clothiers bore no resemblance to the cash laid aside in the estimates for clothing purposes. In one typical year there were 105 battalions of infantry, and £255,000 was paid for clothing them. The colonels of the battalions first of all took their cut—£63,000, £600 a year each.

Competition was keen among the clothiers to get the contracts, and many of them went bankrupt by putting in absurdly low bids. In these instances, the outworkers suffered twofold, by undertaking to do the work at starvation prices, and by not being paid when they had carried it out. Outworkers received 2s 6d for a navy jacket that took eighteen hours to make. A private's coat took between thirteen and fifteen hours to make; the worker received between 1s 1d and 1s 4d and the worker had to buy his own thread.

The hands worked for the piece-masters who in turn got the material from the warehouses. The piece-master received a penny for each garment he returned to the warehouse made up, and although the hands envied the piece-masters they could not hope to become one, for the piece-masters had to give £50 security to the warehouse. One hand who made trousers in 1849 earned sometimes 8s a week, though over the year his wages averaged out at 2s 6d. 'We had better go to bed and starve at once, and that's what most all are doing who are at this kind of work.'

There were others worse off than him. He kept a cat for 'a poor maiden lady, who's starving, brought her to me, and begged me, with almost tears in her eyes, to take of it for her, for she couldn't afford to give it a meal—she hadn't one for herself. She's a teacher of music, and I'm sure she's dying for want of food. She's just out of hospital, and, oh dear, much too proud to go into the house [i.e. the workhouse]. I know she's never had anything but tea—tea—tea, for months. . . .'

A woman making convict clothes earned 2d a day. She had been formerly on better quality convict work and had made 6d a day, but she was now over seventy and the better work was being given to the young.

The inconsistency of the work drove many of the younger women to prostitution. One twenty-year-old woman and her mother made between them 4s 6d to 5s a week, of which they paid 1s rent. 'It is of course impossible for us to live upon it', she said, 'and the consequence is I am obliged to go a bad way . . . I am satisfied that there is not one young girl that works at slop work that is virtuous, and there are some thousands in the trade.'

In 1850 the number of people engaged in needlework and slopwork was 33,529, of whom 28,577 were women under twenty years of age. Some worked at home, some worked in small workshops. One girl was going blind, and her attendance at the Royal London Ophthalmic Hospital caused the assistant surgeon to look into her case. He found out that the girl worked eighteen hours a day, her meals were snatched with an interval of a few minutes from work, and it was clear that she had contracted consumption. Another young woman who had gone blind through 'excessive and continuous application to making mourn-ing' had been compelled to remain without changing her dress for nine days and nights consecutively, any sleep she could get was snatched on a mattress placed on the floor, and her meals had been cut up for her so that as little time as possible should be spent in their consumption. Frequently seamstress apprentices received no money at all; they, polite fiction, were learning a trade.

There were approximately 18,000 sweated tailors in 1850. As with needleworkers, the supply was greater than the demand. The big establishments in the East End put out advertisements for a thousand tailors, and the proprietors picked through the applicants to find out who would do the work the cheapest. The middle-men in tailoring were known as captains, who not only took a profit on each garment but fined the outworkers when they were late in delivering the work. Because much of the tailoring work was carried out in extreme squalor, a fine of fourpence was exerted on each garment where a louse was found.

The average wage for a sweated tailor was about eight shillings a week, but because work came in bits and pieces the average over a year was considerably less. Undercutting by the manufacturers was blamed for the low rate paid; the aristocracy and middle classes wished to get West End quality at East End prices. It was customary for sweated tailors to use the clothing they were working on as bed covering, and there was scarcely one that did not have come clothing of his employers in pawn. One article was continually substituted for another to prevent inquiries.

Sweated labour covered a wide variety of trades. The match-box makers of the East End could earn up to 1s 3d a day. They received 2¼d a gross, but had to supply their own flour for making the paste. Until the 1890s no machinery had been invented to make match-boxes cheaper than that, and the great match-making factories such as Bryant and May openly used sweated labour for their boxes. Because of foreign competition, especially from Sweden, the rates had been going down steadily, and match-box makers in 1889 recalled the days when they were getting 4d a gross.

A curious trade practised in Hackney was the mending of bad nut-megs. Worm-eaten nutmegs were brought from the factory, and re-paired with nutmeg dust. The nutmeg menders were paid 2d a gross. In Tower Hamlets necklaces were made for China and Japan at 2s 3d a gross; a good outworker could turn out half a gross a day. The neck-laces consisted of four rows of beads, twisted, and fastened with a metal clasp. In Holborn there was a trade in relining muffs and jackets. A journalist from the *British Weekly* called at a hovel near Red Lion Square and found a woman sweeping the floor, and emptying the contents of her dust-pan into a basket. She was short of wadding, and was using the sweepings from the floor to fill in a seal-skin jacket that had been sent to a shop for repair.

Brush-making was largely carried out by sweated labour. The wooden part of a hearth brush had 109 holes punched in it, then threaded with fibre. The workers received $\frac{1}{2}$d a brush. There were certain small brushes measuring four inches by two inches made from india-rubber; each of these contained four hundred pins. The outworkers were paid 2d a dozen for sticking the pins in.

One of the most unhealthy of sweated trades was fur-pulling, centred on Bermondsey. This involved removing the hairs from rabbit skins, and the fur-pullers worked in the stench of dried unclean skins, the filth of fluff, and heat that in summer was almost unbearable —if the windows were open the air would force the smaller hairs into the noses, eyes, and lungs of the workers. They could 'pull a turn and a half' a twelve-hour day, a turn being sixty skins. The rate of pay was elevenpence ($4\frac{1}{2}$p) a turn for English skins, rather more for 'furriners'— Australian and New Zealand skins. 'Furriners' took considerably longer to do, even considering the extra pay, and the fur-pullers pre-ferred English skins though they were given to them in a filthy un-washed condition whereas the Australasian skins were parchment white.

The women and girls who made up the work force had to buy their own tools. The knives cost eightpence, and sharpening them cost twopence a week, and the handshields threepence, though these wore out quickly. One woman who with her child made 7s 6d ($37\frac{1}{2}$p) a week had been promised a place working in the shop, 'for the shop was a beautiful place, more like the 'orspital than a shop'.

Other jobs carried out by sweated labour included the making of 'snaps' for crackers for one and ninepence (9p) a day, and paper bags at three-farthings (less than $\frac{1}{2}$p) a gross. A woman with four chil-dren helping her averaged two and fourpence a day (11p). The manu-facturer employed sixty hands 'inside' making these bags and more than a hundred outworkers. This gives some idea of the extent of sweated labour.

Another indication of the wide variety of jobs suited to sweated labour was furnished by the small advertisements of the *Clerkenwell News* in 1872. Small businessmen were looking for, among others, floss vulture hands, steelers (for making crinolines, though crinolines had been out of fashion for years), leaf hands (for floristry), Garibaldi hands, knickerbocker hands, regatta hands (for shirt-making), Pall Mall hands, Beaufort hands, Regent hands, Brother Sam hands, eureka hands, and tippers and bracers (for making umbrellas).

Many young people who allowed themselves to be apprenticed had no idea what they were letting themselves in for. There was sweated labour behind the shop counter as well as in the squalid back rooms, and the children of working-class parents were urged to become shop assistants as it was a step up the social ladder. As with governesses, there were always too many aspiring shop assistants to go round. In 1886 *Chambers's Journal* put its collective finger on the reasons for this:

> Much of this over-supply is due to ignorance on the part of parents and guardians, who, finding a 'genteel' employment for the boy or girl, do not stop to inquire what goes on behind the curtain of gentility . . . a master who, through thoughtlessness or greed, overworks, under-pays, badly houses and badly feeds his employees, or dismisses them without a character, is at perfect liberty to do so, and is in no danger of being called to account for his actions.

In 1849–50 the *Morning Chronicle* ran a series of letters by Henry Mayhew exposing the sweating system, and these were followed by a pamphlet by 'Parson Lot' alias Charles Kingsley called *Cheap Clothes and Nasty*. Kingsley returned to the theme in his novel *Alton Locke*, and he and his friends in the Christian Socialist movement proposed to combat the evils of the system with the formation of co-operative workshops. Well-meaning as the Christian Socialists were their attempts were inept, and the matter was left to lie until 1876 when there was another outcry. This was not on account of the misfortunes of the workers, but because there was fear of infection from garments made up in insanitary surroundings. Obviously the lice, for the presence of which outworkers were fined fourpence apiece, had not been detected at source, or the lining of some lordly jacket had burst open to reveal the sweepings of a Whitechapel floor.

Another flare-up occurred in 1887 when a wave of immigration into the East End created a labour force ready to undercut existing sweated labour. Mr. Coyle, secretary of the Slipper-makers' Union, complained that 'we had always plenty of work until the Russian Jew appeared on the scene'.

A select committee of the House of Lords was called in 1888 to investigate the sweating system. The committee came up with all the right answers, but there matters rested. It needed more than a parliamentary inquiry to overturn the sacred cow of private enterprise, even private enterprise at its most pernicious.

12

Child Labour

THE VICTORIANS EXPLOITED child labour, not because they were peculiarly brutal, but because it never dawned on them that there was anything wrong with such exploitation. The use of child labour in agriculture had been sanctioned by tradition, and the pioneers of the Industrial Revolution had seen no reason why they should not use the cheap labour offered by children. The economics of the time, with the poor existing either just on or just below the poverty line, meant that any jurisdiction to make child labour illegal was greeted with hostility by the parents and it was the impassioned opposition of outsiders who eventually succeeded in curtailing a kind of slavery.

Much of the cruelty that hangs over the entire question of child employment in the nineteenth century was not intentional, and arose from the conditions. The users as well as the used were the victims of the capitalist system at its most naked; they had to provide a product at a realistic price, for otherwise their competitors would steal the market. The easy answer was to employ women and children for long hours at minimal wages, and from this arose the sweating system, in which a middle-man made a profit by taking advantage of unskilled and unorganised labour under the contract system.

Good intentions were, and are, thwarted by the demands of convenience, and nowhere was this demonstrated more clearly than in the case of the climbing-boys. The climbing-boys and, less often, the climbing-girls were apprenticed to chimney-sweeps, and employed by them to force their way through the maze of narrow winding passages that were the domestic chimneys of the well-to-do. The Victorian house made more demands on the ingenuity of the climbing-boys than earlier varieties, for, convoluted in design, it was readily believed

The Victorians exploited child labour because it never dawned on them that there was anything wrong in such exploitation. (*Windsor Magazine*)

that Victorian houses had chimneys that defied anything but the personal touch.

Cruelty towards the climbing-boys was compounded by the attitudes of the three groups of people involved—the chimney-sweeps themselves, the parents of the boys and the householders. The householders did not want to know the means used by the sweeps provided that their chimneys were well and truly swept, and the parents of the boys belonged to the lowest echelons of society, those to whom their children were disposable.

Climbing-boys were not peculiar to the nineteenth century, and had existed ever since a hole in the roof had been replaced by the domestic hearth and a network of passages to carry away the smoke. However, it was the coming of coal that stimulated the demand for chimney-sweeps and their climbing-boys.

One of the first men to interest himself in the fate of the climbing-boys was Jonas Hanway (1712-86), the author of seventy-four books, a navy victualling commissioner, the first man to carry an umbrella in the streets of London, and a violent opponent of the use of tea, in which role he engaged Dr. Johnson in controversy. In 1773 he persuaded other philanthropically-inclined persons to join him in trying to get chimney-sweeps to treat their climbing-boys with a little more consideration. Two years after he died, parliament made a gesture by passing an act forbidding sweeps to take apprentices under the age of eight, though this act was universally ignored, and the sweeps continued to send their apprentices up chimneys, spurring them on by pricking them with knives on their bare soles or by lighting wisps of straw.

A chimney-sweeping machine had been invented in 1805, but few used it and in 1834 an act was passed, regulating the construction of chimney flues and prohibiting sweeps shouting their trade in the streets. No one paid the slightest regard to either of these stipulations. In 1837 Charles Dickens wrote *Oliver Twist*. It is easy to overestimate the effect of Dickens, but certainly in 1840 another act was passed to prevent apprentices under sixteen years of age from going up chimneys. In 1842 the age was put up to twenty-one, but it was an act without teeth, and although in certain towns men and women uneasy about the role of the climbing-boy employed agents to keep an eye on chimney-sweeps, none of these agents managed to do anything about the open disregard of this act. They were handicapped by the refusal of householders to have their chimneys swept by new-fangled machinery.

Few of these people realised the cruelty that went into making a climbing-boy. In the first place, his flesh had to be hardened. This was done by rubbing the elbows and the knees with the strongest brine, obtained from a pork-shop, applied close by a hot fire. This was a painful procedure, and was only accomplished by threats or a bribe. It took a long time for the flesh to harden, and the climbing boys came down the chimneys with their knees and arms pouring with blood, whereupon they were applied again with brine.

The best age for starting a boy off was six, but some children were inculcated in the craft at four and a half, one father saying that he would make 'a nice little climber'. Experienced climbing-boys were in hot demand, and there was a sharp trade in them; many were kidnapped and sold in France for £10 apiece. Their day began at 4 or 4.30 a.m. and lasted for about twelve hours. A sweep and his boy would average out about six shillings a day.

The law against having apprentices under twenty-one years old worked to the advantage of the more avaricious parents, from whom the sweeps would buy a likely lad for a sum of money down. The boys did not go to school, could not read or write, though at one time the chimney-sweeps knocked off work at noon to let their climbing-boys take in a little education, an innovation that was soon dropped.

Many sweeps deplored the attitude of other sweeps to their boys, making exceptions of their own exemplary attitude towards their own 'apprentices'. Some admitted that the idea that only boys could do the work was a fiction, and those who had got on to machines found that they were cheaper. The machines varied in price between £1 5s (£1·25) and £3. But even those who rated the machines highly found that householders refused to have sweeps who used them in preference to the older method.

The attitude of the sweeps towards their helpers was very much on the lines of 'spare the rod and spoil the child'. Richard Stansfield, a chimney-sweep of Manchester, said: 'In learning a child, you can't be soft with him, you must use violence.' He remembered as a child how he had been beaten until he was raw, then thrust into a cellar where soot bags and straw formed the beds. The soot bags were used the following day for work.

The indifference of the sweeps naturally affected the boys themselves. It was customary to 'sleep black', and the sweeps themselves boasted that they only had three washes a year, at Whitsuntide, Goose

Fair (October) and Christmas. Tuberculosis was common among the climbing-boys, as well as 'sooty cancer' which ate off their genital organs and for which there was no cure. This was believed to be because of the practice of 'sleeping black' and the general filthiness that pervaded their lives. One sweep admitted that he wore a shirt until it rotted on him, and one he had on when he was interviewed by members of the Children's Employment Commission in 1863 had never been washed for fifteen months except by the rain. Verminous, ill-kempt, the climbing-boys had no future. If they lasted that long, they grew out of their trade at fifteen or sixteen, and became part of the human debris of the workhouse.

Leading the fight against the maltreatment of the climbing-boys was Lord Shaftesbury, but although he was tireless in his efforts for more than thirty years the liberation of the climbing-boy was due to participants on parliamentary commissions who went to see for themselves the conditions under which the sweeps and the boys operated. Another act in 1864 was hailed as the triumph of right over injustice, but it largely failed through the reluctance of magistrates to act, though sweeps found guilty of ignoring the law could now be sent to prison.

Proof of the widespread evasion of the law was furnished by a series of climbing-boy deaths. In 1872 a climbing-boy was suffocated in a flue in Staffordshire, in 1873 a boy aged seven was killed in a flue at Washington, County Durham, and in 1875 a fourteen-year-old died sweeping a flue in an asylum near Cambridge. The conclusion that in the last case the use of a climbing-boy had official sanction was drawn by *The Times*, which declared that 'whoever deliberately authorised and permitted the employment of this unfortunate boy, are morally guilty of murder'. The sweep got six months' hard labour.

A further act was passed in 1875, but it was not until a later act in 1894 that the climbing-boy passed into history.

An interesting survey was carried out in 1844 in the tailoring business; it was found that in the West End of London there were 676 sweated workers; made up of 179 men, 85 women, 45 boys, 78 girls and 265 young children. These were crowded into 92 small rooms, averaging ten feet by eight feet. Children in the tailoring and associated trades were employed from the age of four, and by the time they were five they could do tasks such as stitching the fingers of gloves, working until eleven or twelve at night, kept at their task by being pinned to their mothers' knees and slapped when they fell asleep.

The use of child labour was rationalised. It was considered good for the child to work, for what would he or she do otherwise? Josiah Wedgwood, the pottery manufacturer, did not wholeheartedly approve of children working. It would be better, he maintained, if they could spend their formative years playing or learning their lessons, but this idyllic condition, he considered, was unattainable. William Sedgwick, a cotton spinner of Skipton, was in favour of child labour, commenting that if children under ten were not allowed to work their parents would be injured by depriving them of the child's wage. Sedgwick was one of many who shelved the prickles of conscience in such a manner.

A needle manufacturer of Redditch considered that eight was a fair age to start children off at work, a printer in Glasgow thought the age should be ten, a tobacco manufacturer started his girls at under nine, claiming that the work was of a light easy nature. The sharks of industry were handicapped by the Factory Act of 1874 which made it necessary for young people to have a doctor's note to certify that they were thirteen if they went to a factory to get a job. This act was widely ignored, but, in agriculture, parliament in its wisdom considered that eight years of age was the minimum for child labour.

In many factories, no doubt, the foremen and overseers were gentle and understanding, but in others brusque treatment was meted out to young children who did not seem to be pulling their weight. In theory, the working of the acts was the responsibility of inspectors, but this whole operation was a farce, for living-rooms were specifically excluded from their briefs, and child workers were thrust out of sight if there were any inspectors about. In many factories and manufacturies child workers slept on the premises, on truckle-beds pushed beneath the work benches. These workers were never seen by Factory Act inspectors, who in addition took care not to pursue their enquiries too far. The local authorities often had vested interests in the factories, and a too assiduous inspector could find himself out of a job.

The ghastly conditions in which many of the children worked would not have been possible but for the tacit co-operation of the parents. In the tailoring and dress-making trades, and all those businesses run on sweated labour, pressures were put on children working on Friday and Saturday to double their usual output. Traditionally their fathers 'shacked' at the beginning of the week; in industrial areas 'Saint Monday' was sacred to pigeon-racing, and without the few pence earned by their young daughters before the weekend this honest pleasure would have been hard to come by.

The willingness of fathers to let their children earn enough coppers to prevent the family starving while they themselves idled was capitalised on by factory owners and the operators of sweat shops. In the textile industry, in which a degree of automation was introduced at a fairly early stage in the Industrial Revolution, a male factory hand could make between 14s and 22s a week (70p and £1·10), a woman employed as a throstle spinner or a power loom weaver between 5s and 10s (25p and 50p), and a child between 2s 6d and 5s (12½p and 25p). A factory hand with four children of workable age could send them out to the factories knowing that between them they could bring in as much money as he could. And he did.

Some industries were worse than others. The cotton mills of Lancashire had an ever-open maw, and as cotton was the only industry in that area available to unskilled labour, the owners of the cotton mills were in an impregnable position, cutting down wages and laying off adult workers when a seasonal slump came along and creating machinery that could be operated by children. The sense of helplessness pervaded the whole family, children aged early, and grotesque hours of labour and malnutrition sent these children, many of them shrivelled and malformed, to premature graves. Their diet was herrings, potatoes, and porridge—there was rarely milk or meat—and they lived with their parents in insanitary cellars, in foul courts or vile alleys, knowing that even this food and accommodation would be denied to them and their parents if they fell ill. These conditions affected not only the natives of Lancashire but the hordes of Irish who flocked over to England after the great potato famine.

Children were worked even harder by their parents if they were doing outwork. Knitting frames were hired out by middle-men at 4s 6d a week (22½p), and woe-betide the child who did not do his or her quota, especially as there were extra coppers to be found for oil and candles.

The number of persons employed in the cotton, wool, silk, and flax manufactures of Great Britain were in the 1850s estimated at about two million, three-quarters of whom were in cotton. The hardships of the mill were put into fictional form by Mrs. Gaskell in *Mary Barton, a Tale of Manchester Life* (1848), but for the most part the cruelties inflicted on young mill-workers were glossed over. The overseers usually carried a strap to beat idle children, and sometimes boys were lashed with the cat-o'-nine-tails. Girls got home black and blue, but the parents rarely complained to magistrates, for they would be labelled trouble-makers and, more to the point, their daughters would be unable to get work as soon as the word got around.

Brutal as the slubbers (overlookers) were, they were not as sadistic as the 'doffers' (female charge-hands). One victim said 'some uses 'em very bad; beats 'em; but only with the hand; and pulls their ears. Some cry but not often.' There was a strict hierarchy within the mills; the drawers were under the control of the weavers, who passed on the beatings and strappings that they themselves had received.

The task of Ellen Ferrier, aged thirteen, was carrying bobbins. She worked from five-thirty in the morning until seven-thirty at night, with two half-hour breaks. She occasionally fell asleep, and the overseer 'licked us very bad, beat our heads with his hand, and kicked us very bad when the ends were down'. At certain mills even the managers struck the children. William Campbell recalled that he had seen the manager 'continually beating the children. The faults were usually very trifling.'

At Trollick mill in Scotland, girls were stripped naked and beaten with the strap. At Lytton mill in Derbyshire there were refinements of cruelty; hand-vices weighing a pound each were screwed to the ears of the child workers. In 1852 Robert Blincoe wrote about the habit of tying twenty-eight-pound weights on the backs of naked children and trussing one leg up.

The overlookers claimed that it was necessary to be cruel. 'There are some children so obstinate and bad they must be punished. A strap is used. Beating is necessary, on account of their being idle.' In many mills the children were directly employed by the workmen, who were paid by the amount of work they produced. These operatives knew how much it was possible to produce, and they used this as their norm. If they were slack, if the proprietors were dissatisfied with the amount of work done, the workmen would be out of a job.

The horrors of the mill were put into verse form by Francis M. Blake:

> The overlooker met her,
>   As to the frame she crept,
> And with the thong he beat her,
>   And cursed her as she wept.
> Alas! what hours of horror

Made up her latest day!
In toil, and pain, and sorrow,
They slowly pass'd away.

It is not to be wondered at that the overall impression one gets from accounts of the mills is hopelessness. No one really reacts to the cruelties, and bouts of righteous indignation soon die out when it is clear that whatever happens the mill-workers' lot can only be alleviated by long processes of legislation.

Harsh as conditions were in the cotton mills of Lancashire, there arose a kind of camaraderie amongst the young workers but there were other industries in which there were no compensations. In the bleaching factories the temperatures rarely fell below 90° F and could rise to 130°. In 1856 the House of Commons rejected a bill that would regulate the hours of labour in the bleaching factories.

The conditions of the bleaching factories fall into insignificance compared with those at the glue factories, at which the 'trotter scrapers' slaved for 2s (10p) a week. Bullocks' and horses' feet were steeped in lime and the hooves were prepared. A glue factory in Blue Anchor Lane, Deptford, was visited by the diarist Munby, who commented that 'the smallness of the wage seemed almost incredible: but each girl stated it thus, out of hearing of the other'.

The match factories employed a large child labour force. The smaller manufacturers kept their workers in atrocious conditions, and the rooms where the sulphur and phosphorous composition were heated were without ventilation, there was nowhere to wash, and a white vapour continually arose from the matches in the course of manufacture. The owners of the small firms defended themselves by saying that they did not make so many matches as the large combines, and therefore the work was less dangerous.

In 1863 a parliamentary commission was formed to look into the match making business, and although the members of the commission were aghast at the conditions that prevailed at the small firms they were persuaded into complacency at the larger manufacturers, such as Bryant and May. 'The mode of manufacture carried on by us is,' claimed Mr. William Bryant, 'I believe, perfectly free from any injurious influence upon the health of those engaged in it.' His partner, Mr. Francis May, interviewed separately, somewhat contradicted him, for while drawing attention to the facilities that were offered to the young children working for them, such as separate privies for boys and girls, commented that the firm's benevolence in letting the children go to school did 'much to counteract the noxious vapours inhaled during the time of work'.

What neither of the two men mentioned was that working in the match trade was a sentence to death or mutilation, for the vapours of phosphorous are a deadly poison and prolonged exposure to them results in necrosis of the jaw-bone ('fossy jaw'). The workers at Bryant and May's were less sanguine than their employers, and a foreman had known many people who had died from the disease ('phosphorous on their inwards'). It was common for people to lose their jaws. Of one victim, 'you could take his chin and shove it all into his mouth'.

Fossy jaw could attack within four or five months, and the children, unaware of the dangers, would eat their meals with the phosphorous still clinging to their hands. The use of red phosphorous instead of yellow or white was said to have reduced the danger, but the scandal of the match industry eventually led to a strike at Bryant and May's, fostered by the energetic Annie Besant, theosophist and promoter of birth control propaganda.

Exploitation of child labour was seen at its most naked in the Midlands. Six-year-olds were employed at Dain, Watts and Manton's, button manufacturers of Regent Street, Birmingham. One of these youngsters was spotted by a member of a commission evolved to investigate the metal manufactures of Birmingham; 'She was a beautiful child, with bright innocent face, but looking lost and bewildered amongst so many workers. Her eldest sister, aged twelve, had a sullen hardened look and manner.' The girls were in a neglected condition, and a member of the firm, seeing the interest shown in them by the man from London, was 'struck and pained' and told the mother that he would not employ them unless she showed more care. The girls earned 1s a week each (5p).

Birmingham was the centre of the steel-pen industry, and many children were employed in it. The machine-made pen was introduced by John Mitchell about 1822, and by the 1830s mass production was in full swing. The making of steel pens involves the immersion of sheet steel in dilute sulphuric acid, the rolling of this sheet into thin ribbons, the stamping out of the blanks, the hardening and tempering of the blanks, a further dip into vitriol, and the cutting of the slit. It was hard cruel work for children, irrespective of the inhaling of the sulphuric acid fumes, but young boys were pushed into the trade by their parents because of the high wages paid—up to 6s (30p) a week.

There is nothing new in the idea of parents wishing to get their children off to work as soon as possible to supplement the family income. The raising of the school leaving age from fourteen to fifteen over the last few decades brought forward the same kind of thinking— what good is 'book learning' to a working-class child when he or she could be earning a few shillings a week? Doubtlessly in future generations the notion that a boy or girl could go out to work at fifteen will evoke the same horror that we feel about six-and-seven-year-olds entering the labour market. The parents did not think that it was cruel. It was part of the nature of things. That others did, even then, consider it cruel is evident from the uncomfortable defensive attitudes adopted by the employers of child labour. They adopted double standards, were guilty of blatant hypocrisy. Thus the philanthropist Wilberforce could rail against the slave trade between Africa and America and yet countenance parallel conditions in his own English factories.

The parents knew no better, the employers did. In the brick trade there was a saying that a moulder's child was born with a brick in its mouth. In the country children hardly more than toddlers were sent out into the fields from four in the morning to seven at night scaring crows for 4d (2p) a day.

The brick and glass industries were particularly harsh on young workers. At a firebrick works in Brierly Hill in the Black Country close to Birmingham ten-year-old girls were employed carrying bricks from the kiln, part of a human chain moving 17,000 bricks weighing $7\frac{1}{4}$ lb each in a day and a half. It is difficult to conceive moving 54 tons of bricks for the princely sum of 9d (4p). It is easy to understand why one of these girls, when interviewed, wanted to be an angel and sit on Jesus' lap.

Near to Brierly Hill was Halesowen, a centre for the making of nails. This was a cottage industry. The nailers operated small forges attached to their homes, and worked for the 'masters' for pittances. It was usual for boys to help their fathers from the age of eight. One nailer proclaimed that his own son, then aged five, would not be a nailer if he could help it when he reached eight, though provided a let-out clause by adding 'unless he was obligated' i.e. had run into debt through drinking or through 'pigeoning'. The nailers were philosophical about the hazards of the trade, the burns and the scars that the young boys suffered. It was part of the pattern of life.

In the cottage industries a child would be cuffed for not pulling his weight, but systematic brutality would only cut down the work-rate. This was true also of the mechanised industries such as cotton or the metal manufacturies. The glass works of the Midlands had a tradition of brutality. One boy told of his experiences:

> The men are not very kind to you in the glass-house; they are rough brutes there. They beat you with iron things, and hit you about the head with them, and kick and cuff and swear at you, and they will do this for such little things. . . . We do not tell the masters, they would beat us worse then. They are awful brutes and would do anything at you. I have seen them knock boys down and kick them terrible when on the ground, so as to make bruises on the body and legs. . . . I saw a man hit a boy of about 12 on the back of his head with the blowing iron, which had some glass on the end of it, and cut his head open and make it bleed.

The owners of heavy industry did not hesitate to use child labour for tasks that were physically injurious. In the iron and steel works of Sheffield boys of under ten were employed to drag red-hot metal from the rollers and wheel it off, and 'holders up' of the same age were used to stand a few feet from the furnace and draw up the furnace doors while the metal was being extracted. The owners of John Brown and Co., Saville Street, Sheffield, were disdainful of criticism that such work was too heavy and dangerous for under-tens. Yes, it was hot, one of them agreed, but the boys could get plenty to drink. No, the boys did not get regular breaks—the peculiar conditions of steel and iron making prevented that. As for danger, what was the loss of the occasional finger? John Brown and Co. provided a written answer to the question of children on night shift, and should it be prohibited: 'It is impossible for us to do so: it would be tantamount to stopping our works.'

This would be the answer of the coal industry if asked why they employed so much young labour. Children were essential down the mine, for many of the passages and galleries were only big enough to take children, many of whom worked from early morning to night at the age of six. In the Scottish mines, boys of ten were expected to carry a hundredweight of coal on their backs as they scuttled backwards and forwards doubled up.

The children were usually the sons and daughters of mine-workers or were taken from the workhouses under apprenticeship schemes. They were sent on trial to the butties, the men who superintended the transport of coal from the face to the pit-shaft, the customary age

Youngsters in the mines were put on 'trapping', opening and closing trapdoors to prevent draughts. (*Pictorial Times*)

being eight or nine. Their apprenticeships ended when they were twenty-one, by which time they were too despairing and beaten-down to do anything else with their lives. They were old men by the time they were forty, and few were able to work past the age of fifty, subject to a wide variety of ailments, usually respiratory.

The youngsters were often put on 'hurrying', drawing or pushing the coal-cars, or 'trapping', opening and closing a trap-door that separated the lengths of passages. Both boys and girls were employed in these jobs; they rapidly became bald at the crown of the head through pushing the coal-cars. Women were also used as beasts of burden, naked from the waist up. Leather belts were strapped around their waists, to which was attached a ring and a four-foot length of chain. They went forward on all fours, with the chain between their legs, pulling the cars which weighed up to five hundredweight.

When the children were thirteen or fourteen they were put on wagoning, drawing the larger wagons that ran on lines. The boys eventually became colliers, at the coal-face. It is characteristic of the 1840s that investigations into the conditions in which young children worked were more concerned with the moral aspects of the business than the sheer physical cruelty of placing children in such conditions. So intense was the heat, so arduous the labour, that the men worked naked. Mary Barrett, aged fourteen, said: 'I work always without stockings, or shoes, or trousers; I wear nothing but my shift; I have to go to the headings with the men; they are all naked there; I am got well used to that, and don't care much about it; I was afraid at first, and did not like it.' In the pits there was casual coupling between the men and women, and girls were broken in by the time they were twelve. Pregnancy did not stop them pulling the coal-cars.

Scotland was perhaps the worst place for children down the mines, for the pit-bottom was reached by winding stairs or a succession of ladders instead of a cage operated by steam power. Ten-year-old children carried creels full of coals up these ladders.

One mine surveyor was underground when a woman came towards him groaning under an excessive weight. She said, 'Oh, sir, this is sore, sore work. I wish to God that the first woman who tried to bear coals had broken her back, and none would have tried it again.' Of course, the first woman who tried to bear coals had not broken her back, and the child labourers had proved that they could stand the work as well as any pit-pony. It was, declared a seventeen-year-old girl, sad sweating and sore fatiguing work, but when women and children were released from their subterranean torture and put to work on the surface many, surprisingly, wished to go back. One Lancashire 'pit-brow lassie' told the diarist Munby that she 'liked it reet well—would like well to work below again—used to draw with belt and chain—liked it better than working up here.' To colliery owners such statements were comforting, proving that they were right and the legislators wrong.

Education was considered totally unnecessary for child workers in the mines. There were Sunday schools where they could go, but 'when boys have been beaten, knocked about, and covered with sludge all the week, they want to be in bed to rest all day on Sunday'. Rupture, heart damage, asthma, and most common of all, the disease known to colliers as 'black spittle', the boys and girls in the mines were prey to all these. They accepted them as part of the order of things. The coal-mining towns were closed communities, the inhabitants having no awareness of what was happening outside the confines. In 1841 there were 110,000 workers in the mines. In 1854 64,661,401 tons of coal were mined, rising in 1897 to a staggering 202,119,116 tons.

An act was passed in 1841 prohibiting women from working down the mines, but it was ignored. An act of 1887 had more teeth, again prohibiting women from working underground, and also children below the age of twelve. As the Victorian age went on, mine-workers became more conscious of their unique position; there was a big strike in Staffordshire in 1864, and one near St. Helens, Lancashire, in 1868. A thousand miners, men, women and children, were killed every year. The mine owners sanguinely accepted these risks, and, furthermore, the strikes were often convenient, giving them an excuse to drop wages at a later date.

The vast profits of Victorian mine owners and industrialists depended on an unending supply of cheap labour. A coal-cutting machine was produced in 1872 which did the work of ten colliers, but why use it? Industrialists did not need to be selective. The Sheffield iron and steel trade could have utilised the inflow of Irishmen, coming to Britain at the rate of 50,000 a year, had the employers bothered to go to Liverpool to recruit them, but they considered that the work could be done cheaper by local children, many of whom were introduced into the factories by their fathers who also worked there. It was an eternal circle. The boys would marry at an early age, and when their children reached workable age they too would be drafted into the industrial bedlam.

There was no way out for the boys, victims who could not escape their fate. The girls could get married, with perhaps a thin chance of avoiding a lifetime in the factory or mill. Young girls in factories were frequently persuaded to give themselves to foremen, managers and owners by being offered a higher wage than was usual. Sometimes these extra-mural activities were written into the conditions of employment, and a Royal Commission on the employment of children in factories asserted that three-quarters of the girls between fourteen and twenty were unchaste. So prevalent was immorality in the cotton trade that the phrase 'cotton mill morality' was understood by all. In the Potteries, the throwing rooms were said to be 'emporiums of profligacy' and the girls there had 'no sense of the sin of whoredom or of the bestiality of uncleanliness'.

Often sex in factories was a way of relieving the boredom and the quiet desperation. It was an escape from the cruel realities of life. Few cared about children in industry, and although Dickens and Kingsley (in *Alton Locke*) drummed up indignation, *laissez faire* operated just as often for cruelty and unabashed barbarism as for individual freedom.

IV CRIME AND
PUNISHMENT

13

The Prison System

THE PRISON SYSTEM of Victorian England shows the age at its most ruthless and most efficient. The prisons of the eighteenth century, barbaric as they were, were at least human. The Victorian aim was soullessness, and this aim was achieved.

In the late eighteenth-century prisons were pest-ridden dens, dark, dirty, and grossly overcrowded with little or no ventilation. Prisoners depended for their food on the whims of the gaolers, whom they had to pay. Prisoners also had to pay 'garnish', a contribution to a central fund to be spent by the whole body of the prisoners, usually on drink. The inmates of eighteenth-century prisons were not necessarily guilty men; many of them were awaiting trial or were in prison through debt.

The cruelty to which Victorian prisoners were subjected had little to do with discipline. Respectable people thought that criminals were a sub-species, easily recognised and impossible to reform, and criminals themselves went along with this concept.

The first prison built in accord with the new thinking was Millbank, begun in 1813 and completed in 1816 at the cost of half a million pounds, but for a considerable time Millbank was merely a token of the future. In London itself there still existed Newgate, with its cells in three rows, one above the other, each measuring eight feet by six and holding three or four prisoners. The furniture consisted of a rope mat and rug, an iron candlestick, a stove, and a privy which was a hole crossed by two frames.

The exploits of Mrs. Fry in rehabilitating the female denizens of Newgate have been grossly exaggerated. In 1817 she turned what was described as a den of wild beasts filled with women unsexed, fighting, swearing, dancing, gaming and yelling into a 'scene where stillness and propriety reigned'. Mrs. Fry is important in that she was an outsider involving herself with prisoners, but she did not achieve a great deal herself, though serving as an example to others who came later.

In 1830 Lord John Russell decided that cellular separation was desirable in all prisons, and in 1840 the first stone of Pentonville was laid. Pentonville, with its 520 cells, was taken as a model, and in half a dozen years fifty-four prisons were built on the Pentonville pattern. In Pentonville, the cells were 13 feet by 7 feet by 9 feet, and contained a W.C. Seclusion was absolute, and talking was rewarded by a spell in the dark penal cells, and prisoners attended chapel with masks over their faces, isolated in individual stalls. A prisoner was allowed a visitor every three months. Between 1842 and 1848 Britain became a land of battlemented Gothic prisons, housing 11,000 inmates. Neat and tidy as was the new regime, and agreeably picturesque to the law-abiding middle classes, the rate of insanity amongst inmates went up eight times. The criminal classes of early Victorian England could cope with filth and squalor but not solitude.

Old prisons existed side by side with the new ones. The Victorians were energetic but lost interest quickly, especially where public money was involved. The new prisons were expensive to run, and the reactionaries were not slow to point this out. Typical of the old prisons was Giltspur Street Compter, which was so crowded in 1850 that prisoners hardly had room to lie down. Newgate, despite the efforts of Mrs. Fry, still had its deplorable women's wing where 'vices undreamt of became familiar', i.e. lesbianism.

In the eighteenth century, prisoners were left very much to their own devices. Nineteenth-century prisoners were certainly not. To keep them occupied there were a large number of amusements, most specifically the treadmill and the crank. The treadmill was an instrument of pure cruelty, whether or not it performed a function such as pumping water or grinding corn. Basically it was a large hollow cylinder of wood on an iron frame. Round the circumference were a series of steps about seven and a half inches apart. Steadying himself by handrails on either side, the criminal trod on these steps causing the wheel to revolve. The criminal did six hours a day, alternating fifteen minutes on the wheel with a five minute rest. In the course of a day's session he climbed 8,640 feet. In the Prison Act of 1865 it was laid down that every male prisoner over sixteen was to spend at least three months in what was described as labour of the first class.

There were perquisites to be obtained by the commercial use of the prison treadmill. At Northallerton the governor hired out the treadmill to the local miller. Whether women should be used on the treadmill was a debatable point; the governor of Coldbath Fields in 1837 thought so: 'With regard to women, I believe tread-wheel labour, if judiciously used, is highly beneficial to health, particularly in cases of disorderly women, prostitutes, etc.'

As late as 1895 there were thirty-nine treadmills in use in English prisons, but this number had dwindled to thirteen by 1901. An alternative to the treadmill was the crank. There were two basic kinds of crank. One consisted of a small wheel, similar to the paddle-wheel of a steamer, revolving in a drum partly filled with gravel and operated by a handle. For obdurate or physically strong prisoners a brake mechanism made the task of turning the wheel more difficult. A prisoner had to make 8,000 to 10,000 revolutions in his six-hour spell. If he idled there were additional punishments.

The other form of crank consisted of a narrow drum on legs with a long handle. Cups or spoons revolved, carrying sand to the top of a wheel, and when this sand dropped to the bottom, to be scooped up again for the next revolution, it operated a dial mechanism.

Another activity was shot-drill. This involved moving cannon-balls from one pyramid to another. For those rendered insufficiently docile by treadmill, crank, and shot-drill, or picking oakum, there was always flogging. No flogging had been carried out on women since 1820, and discipline was enforced among them by confinement in the dark cells. To many women a flogging would have been preferable, and many tried to escape from the punishment cells to the infirmary by self-mutilation, using glass powder inserted into the vagina to counterfeit an internal haemorrhage.

It was not until later that Holloway was used as a women's prison; in Victorian times it was Brixton. The regimen was harsh but nowhere near as cruel as that operating in the men's prisons. The female prisoners were engaged in shirt-making, hemming, stitching and laundry work. Although women's prisons were predominantly run by women warders there were male warders in the offing for the frequent acts of violence that the women indulged in. As in Victorian factories, women prisoners obtained privileges for themselves by sexual intercourse with the male members of the staff.

Although Munby, the diarist who married a serving wench and was obsessively preoccupied with labouring women, believed that women should be treated harshly in prison and visited Tothill Fields prison in the hope of seeing some exciting female flagellation he was forty years too late. Not so for the perverse who got their kicks from seeing children flogged.

Typical of the treatment meted out to young offenders was that suffered by Thomas Miller of Clerkenwell. In 1845 he stole some boxes, and was whipped, and sent to prison for a month. He was then eight. In 1846 he robbed a till, and was sentenced to seven years transportation. He was too young, and spent three months in prison instead. Immediately on discharge he committed larceny again, and spent two further years in prison. In May 1848 he was discharged, but in July he was back again for fourteen days. In April 1849 he was whipped and imprisoned for two days. Thomas Miller was then aged twelve. His height was four feet two inches. Reformers threw up their hands when confronted with the Thomas Millers.

A scene on board the prison hulk *Justitia* in 1845. There were still four prison hulks in use as late as 1862. (*Pictorial Times*)

Notwithstanding the plethora of prisons that existed in the 1850s it seemed to the government that things were becoming uncontrollable. It was no longer possible to keep prisoners in the prison hulks, moored decaying ships rich in cholera and vermin, though in 1862 there were still four of them being used. It was no longer possible simply to despatch prisoners to a colony—the colonies would not have them. Van Diemen's Land (Tasmania) refused to take any more despite a shortage of labour, and the appearance of a convict ship off the Cape of Good Hope nearly produced a riot. Only Western Australia welcomed prisoners. In 1853 the Penal Servitude Act was passed, substituting shorter sentences of penal servitude for transportation. The space of time between the sentence of penal servitude and the years of transportation was regarded as a kind of parole. The prisoner was let out on what was called ticket-of-leave. It was hoped that the short sharp prison sentence would cause the criminal to revise his ways.

This did not happen. Following the reduced transportation quota came a crime wave and the appearance on the crime scene of the garotters, thieves who strangled their victims. The government was blamed for making the criminal's life too soft, despite treadmill, crank, and shot-drill going full tilt. The 1865 Prison Act deliberately made prison life more uncomfortable. The more easy-going prisons were brought sharply into line, talking was punished even more severely, bare wooden boards replaced hammocks, irons and chains were brought out from cupboards and refurbished, and the dark cells, to most prisoners a form of punishment more to be dreaded than a flogging, were brushed out ready for a massive intake. By then, there was hardly any chance of transportation—which many criminals welcomed, knowing that there was a good time to be had in the far-flung Empire— and the last convict ship left for Australia in 1867.

Uniformity amongst prisons could not be guaranteed while control of the prisons was vested in local authorities, and in 1877 the Prison Act was passed. Although many local prisons were closed, including those run as profit-making organisations by the governors, convicts were still treated as a sub-species. In some prisons a system of marks was put into operation; if a prisoner behaved himself he could obtain a degree of concession.

That the Victorian public was not exaggerating the threat of the criminal classes is evident from statistics of 1889. In that year there were:

houseless starving	1,715,500
in workhouses & asylums	190,000
in convict prisons	11,660
in local prisons	20,883
in reformatories	1,270
in industrial schools	21,413

The public took a cold, hard look at the figures for those in re-formatories and industrial schools. These were the pauper young, a threat to the stability of society, the criminals of the future, im-possible to reclaim or send abroad. There was considered to be only one sure deterrent—the birch.

The people who dealt out whippings to the pauper young were the magistrates, most of whom had been at public schools and therefore were aware of the part ritual flagellation played in the curriculum. When cases came to them of children being beaten at school with excessive force or enjoyment, they were inclined to treat the matter coolly.

If teachers were cruel at ordinary schools, they were much worse at reformatories or industrial schools. In 1897 the Reverend Marshall Vine, warden of the Farm School, Redhill, was asked by a parlia-mentary commission if he knew that the maximum number of strokes allowed was eighteen. The answer was typical of an age and of an attitude; there was an insouciance and a contempt for the layman who framed ridiculous regulations:

They lay it down at eighteen. We never have felt ourselves bound by that—it is a very rare case that we should ever exceed it—but there are cases where I would not hesitate, and I have done it, to go beyond that number, where a great big fellow of eighteen or nineteen years of age requires to be thoroughly taken down . . . I should give him three dozen, and I have done it.

The whippings in the reformatory and industrial schools were carried out in the interests of internal order. Police-court whippings were acts of revenge. They were alternatives or preludes to more formal punishments. Many magistrates thought that it was a milder form of punishment than a prison sentence.

A seven-year-old boy was sentenced to four strokes with the birch for stealing a watch. He was examined by a doctor two or three days after this was carried out; 'his little back was covered with wounds which extended right through the skin to the muscles, and not only was his back a mass of rawness, but the wounds had come round to the front of the abdomen, and they had cut down to the muscles on the front of his frame'.

Quite frequently in minor cases an appeal was made to the greed of the parents. They were told that if they flogged their erring child, the fine ordered would be remitted, and the only proviso was that a policeman should be there to see that the court request was carried out (though in law the magistrate had no power to order a policeman witness). Like the flogging teachers at the public schools, the flogging magistrates were a law unto themselves.

There were also wiser men who realised that the whip did not deter young criminals, and that the melodramatic sentences of a judicial flogging were acts of self-indulgence, and maybe nostalgia, by the magistrates. Just as in the public schools, there were floggees who were proud of their record and who considered that their bravery in standing up to a whipping without fear was commendable. The response of the general public when they heard or read of such boasts was predictable: beat them until they did take notice.

There was always a body of public opinion that wished for a return to the old days, with pillory and whipping at the cart's tail. Many members of the public openly regretted that so many statutes had been passed eliminating the death penalty for certain offences. The present gap between public opinion and parliament on the question of capital punishment was mirrored in 1840 when ninety members of parliament voted for the abolition of all capital punishment. Supporters would have been hard put to it to find ninety members of the general public with the same views.

There was little sympathy with the criminal by the public, and the prison governors were at one with laymen. Frequently ex-military men with strong beliefs in the efficacy of iron disciplines, the efforts of the reformers left them scornful. There was no enthusiasm in finding out why a certain criminal was there, whether he should be there rather than in a lunatic asylum, or whether indeed he should be there at all. There was no communication between the upper echelons of the prison service and the convicts, and governors often permitted the introduction of medical officers and prison chaplains into their prisons only because the law said that such people should be on the pay-roll.

It is not surprising that as late as 1899 a twenty-four-year-old labourer sent to prison for exposing himself in public was not found to be raving mad until six weeks had passed by. In the prison hulks in 1841 there were incarcerated three children under ten, and 213 between ten and fifteen. It is doubtful whether anyone on the conveyor belt knew or cared. Even with benevolent governors there was no guarantee that acts of brutality on the part of warders would reach their ears. Prison warders were not generally in the same class as the corrupt eighteenth-century gaolers of Newgate and the old prisons, but they had a narrow way of seeing things and reacted to insubordination and insolence on the part of the convicts with off-hand brutality. They knew their sort and were determined to put them in their place.

Newgate Prison was in use until late in the nineteenth century. (*Old and New London*)

The most vengeful were the lower middle classes; criminals were no better than they should be. Even those who commiserated with the poor, the ill, the unfortunate, found it difficult to find a place in their pantheon for criminals. They were a class, not individuals who committed crimes. They destroyed the image of the Great Society. This view persisted until the end of the century.

The completely irrelevant use of treadmill and crank only makes sense if one realises that the Victorians were bent on revenge. To claim that the treadmill could be used for practical purposes such as pumping water was avoiding the question; there were better ways of pumping water, such as using a steam engine.

Of course there were two publics—those who could not envisage being incarcerated, and those who, only too clearly, could. Similarly there were two public attitudes towards the police. There were people to whom a policeman told the time, helped get across a road, found dogs, and were unpaid ancillary servants. Indeed, on the wage scale the policeman was rated no higher than a servant, or a labourer. There were others for whom the policeman was representative of 'Them'.

As with prison warders, policemen were not paid the salary commensurate with their duties, and the calling did not attract the right kind of person. Only in 1878 did their pay go up to thirty shillings a week (for a first-class constable). Servile to their social superiors, who regarded the policeman's main function as the protection of property, the police cracked down on the working classes, behaving with considerable cruelty when they had the chance. Meetings of the working class in Hyde Park and other places were excellent opportunities for showing their mettle. Truncheons flew, arms and legs were broken, and the more aggressive dissidents were taken away into a side street and beaten up. This dark side of the Metropolitan Police persisted into the Edwardian era. During the Suffragette rioting, women demonstrators were taken from their beats in Parliament Square, beaten, kicked and had their breasts pinched.

The suspicion of the Metropolitan Police shown by the proletariat had existed since 1829 when the new force had been introduced. There were songs that demonstrate a cynical attitude towards the police:

> I'm known to all the prigs in town—
> To learned thieves well known my face is;
> The frail ones, too, my favours own,
> And charge me nought for sweet embraces.
> And if they're going a house to rob,
> Don't I watch (as is my duty?)

But never splits about the job,
For don't myself get half the booty!

In 1886 the commissioner of the Metropolitan Police, Colonel
Edmund Henderson, was forced to resign because of excessive brutality
in putting down riots when a meeting of the unemployed in Trafalgar
Square was joined by left wing agitators, and a mob ran amok between
Pall Mall and Oxford Street.

Cruel actions were justified under the banner of law and order, but
police commissioners and superintendents realised that matters would
not improve until a new pay code was brought in. In 1890 agitation
about pay and conditions led to a strike of policemen at Bow Street
station. A hundred and thirty men refused to go on duty at 10 p.m.
Forty were dismissed and combined with a gang of roughs to cause a
riot. Six months later increased pay was introduced, and a new class
of policeman joined the force, no longer reacting against miserable
wages by taking it out on the poor. The poor were still vulnerable,
were still eyesores to be bustled out of the shopping streets of the West
End, but, like everyone else, they realised that things were changing.
Hostility towards the police began to be replaced by an amiable
jocularity. On the stages of the music hall cynicism was replaced by
'If You Want to Know the Time, Ask a P'liceman'.

14

The Convicts Speak

THE PRISON SYSTEM was a massive attempt at de-humanisation, and because, compared with today, the criminal classes were well-defined and their numbers comparatively small (though the 1867 London figure was put at 100,000), the task could be carried out with the likelihood of success. Prison governors had everything on their side—a reluctance to interfere on the part of the government, a ready cadre of staff drawn from ex-military and naval personnel anxious not to be thrown on the scrap-heap, a band of servile and second-rate medical officers, and gaunt prisons that were almost escape-proof. They could also provide carrots. A`marks system was in operation which could cut down slightly the prison sentence.

When asked, all concerned in running the prisons agreed that things were going swimmingly, that the no-talking rule was everywhere obeyed, and that prisoners taken ill were accorded all the facilities that modern medicine could offer. Governors tried to give the impression of benevolent autocracy, but as with so many noble Victorian projects the façade was not altogether convincing, and when ex-convicts talked no amount of white-washing could wipe out corruption, incompetence and systematic cruelty that had little to do with keeping discipline.

The convicts talked because they were invited to do so by the commissioners appointed to inquire into the working of the Penal Servitude Acts, and governors, medical officers, and warders had the unique experience of having to explain their behaviour and answer accusations by ex-convicts. From the muddled and unconvincing shows many of these officials put up it is clear that not all the ex-convicts were motivated by revenge. Because of the fear of retaliation if or when they returned to prison, several of the convicts hid their identity beneath initials.

One convict who did give his name was Henry Harcourt, who had been convicted and sentenced to penal servitude twice, for seven years in 1864, and for five years in 1872. During this second period he had been imprisoned at Pentonville, Millbank and Portland. His stay at Pentonville was short, for Harcourt declared that he was a Mohammedan, and this was considered a good enough reason for the deputy governor to threaten to flog him if he did not pick on one of the Christian religions. As Harcourt was born in Constantinople, and his father had embraced Islam, there was every evidence that he was telling the truth.

To escape the flogging, Harcourt chose the Roman Catholic faith, and was transferred to the old prison at Millbank, but he refused to take in the Christian books that were compulsory reading for convicts, and was put on bread and water for three days. Harcourt was suffering from piles, and could not pick the oakum that was his prescribed task without standing up. Picking oakum in a standing position was not allowed, and Harcourt was given three more days on bread and water although most doctors agreed that three days was the limit for this penal diet.

Ointment was prescribed for the piles, and they cleared up, but when Harcourt complained of a twitch the medical assistant considered that he was malingering, and, having read the papers relating to Harcourt's previous conviction, declared that he was an outrageous character and would punish him. This he did with the aid of a galvanic apparatus, a popular pseudo-medical instrument that gave electric shocks. Shortly afterwards Harcourt was sent to Portland, and put to work in the quarry hewing stones. A large stone fell upon him, he was kicked by a warder who shouted 'Now then, get up, will you?', and after he regained consciousness he was taken to the infirmary.

The rock had fallen on what Harcourt delicately describes as his 'loins', and Dr. Askham, having read the patient's case history, applied the galvanic apparatus to Harcourt's loins and ordered him to take a dose of medicine which Harcourt refused. Harcourt was then sent to the punishment cell. He complained that his urine was discoloured, with blood he thought, and although Askham called in a local doctor no treatment was proffered.

Harcourt wrote to the Turkish ambassador declaring that the authorities would not let him follow his religion; he was punished for this, and then further punished for using his urinal during the breakfast hour. He had been seized with an attack of cramps and vomiting, and had to use his chamber pot and his wash basin. Convicts were also punished for urinating at night.

Convicts were used for back-breaking labour in quarries, and many succumbed under the harsh regimen. (*Graphic*)

In a sorry physical state, Harcourt was punished for not being able to work, and intermittently the warders took the galvanic apparatus to his cell, used it on him, and 'gloated over his contortions'. Harcourt threatened to tell the authorities of the things that he had seen, of a weak-minded boy named Thomas who had refused to undress himself and been beaten up by warders, subsequently dying, and of a prisoner named Pritchard who had died after being flogged four or five times. Harcourt's bed was taken away, and he was forced to sleep on bare boards. He became so ill that it was thought that he was dying, and he was moved to the infirmary where he had treatment with a hot iron, which ceased when a Dr. Bernard took over from Askham.

Harcourt recovered, and was sentenced to flogging for throwing a cell pot at an infirmary nurse, and also put in an iron guard bed, a bed with loops at the top and bottom in which the prisoner was confined. Harcourt tried to commit suicide by filling his wash basin with water and putting his head in it, brought low by repeated punishment and slow starvation. The bread supplied, the main item of diet, was kept wet and damp so as to take less dough to keep up the weight, and the men on hard labour ate dead mice, dead rats, grass, dogs, and earth-worms. Candles were often eaten by inmates.

Harcourt also gave details of men who had hanged themselves, especially at Dartmoor where the work was exceptionally heavy and the food especially bad, and for the theory that the silent system worked he had nothing but contempt.

Other convicts confirmed much of what Harcourt had said, but most of them had walked a good deal more warily in the hope of getting good marks or an easy job. A.B., in prison for eight years for forgery, landed the post of tailor. In the tailor's shop the warders did not strictly enforce the no-talking rule, and A.B. passed the time tolerably at Brixton prison, though matters were different at Portsmouth, a labour camp, where he was put on brickmaking. He had something wrong with his foot, but despite this he was forced to wear boots and sent out to the kilns. A warder saw him, and exclaimed 'What the devil have they sent this man here for?' and told him to pick up a few brick ends and do what he could. The foot was swollen to twice its usual size, and the day at the brickworks landed A.B. in the infirmary.

The medical officer was aware that A.B. was incapable of working at brickmaking, and mentioned to a colleague that it was absurd to put such a man on hard labour. Nevertheless, he said that he could not 'alter it'; A.B. had been put down for hard labour, and so far as the medical officer was concerned that was that.

A.B. was then sent to the cement manufactory, and at night confined in corrugated iron sleeping cells. He agreed with Harcourt that the food was insufficient, and that the prisoners were often so weak that they could barely walk. He also agreed with Harcourt that the no-talking rule was universally disregarded, and it was easy to pass letters out by using 'liberty men' employed at the cement works. Warders were used to bring tobacco and money in. They charged ten shillings a pound for tobacco, buying it on the outside at four shillings a pound, and distributed it through a man who cleaned the chapel, who hid the tobacco in buckets. Those who wanted to smoke but did not have the money to buy tobacco exchanged their loaves for a pencil-thick piece.

Because of his foot A.B. spent a good deal of time in the prison infirmary where he had the opportunity to see what warders did to lunatic prisoners. Lunatic prisoners had to obey the rules, irrespective of whether or not they understood them or had the ability to obey them, and minor transgressions were punished by removing prisoners bedding and making them lie on bare boards. Lunatic prisoners who were violent were repaid with violence. A Henry Balls was stripped nearly naked, dragged across the gravel, and thrown into his cell. He was also beaten about the head by the warders and flogged so often that the prison doctor called a halt.

Some of the warders were reluctant to beat the man. One of them exclaimed, 'I am sorry for poor Harry; I was told to do it.' Another feeble-minded prisoner, Chambers, was dragged down the steps by his neck collar, and although he was between sixty and seventy he was left in the middle of the yard to recover by himself before being dragged away to the punishment cells. Another old man, Richards, was too sick to walk upstairs to his cell, and was forced to crawl there. In the evening he died. A.B. and the other convicts who had seen the brutalities of warders kept quiet for fear of losing their marks, and did not give evidence at the inquests, considered by inmates as useless and mere exercises in white-washing.

The members of the Parliamentary Commission were especially interested in investigating reports of homosexual behaviour, and were particularly concerned with searches of prisoners and how often prisoners' anuses were examined. They were shocked by the evidence of prisoners, that prisoners were made to stoop and their genitals handled by warders. One of these prisoners was C.D., who had recently served a sentence for forgery. Timid, short-sighted, C.D. wished to get through his term of imprisonment with as little aggravation as possible, and did not report the indecent behaviour of the warder. But no matter how well a prisoner behaved, there was one time when it was impossible to avoid being confined in the punishment cell—just before discharge. It was a saying amongst prisoners that 'if you have never been to choky, you will have to go to choky before you leave'.

C.D. concurred with other prisoners that food was insufficient, especially in fat, and that all prisoners ate as much of their candles as they could, but he himself was more privileged than most for he was working in the map department of the prison, colouring maps, and the warder in charge brought in fruit for him and also allowed him access to the *Daily Telegraph*. News was a marketable commodity in prison, and convicts trafficked in portions of newspapers.

The commission was particularly interested in C.D. Nowadays he would be called a trusty. The warders talked to him, and as he was a freemason he was able to build up contacts with those officials who themselves were masons. It was clear that C.D. was not liked by other prisoners, and he was sent to Coventry by them. He occupied a kind of no-man's-land, and looked with ironic amusement at the wastefulness and incompetence that were about him. He was obviously a clever man, and in the map department he was the only person who knew what he was doing. He drew the attention of the commission to the case of the pint of varnish that cost sixteen shillings. It was originally two shillings, but each time the wrong kind of varnish was sent. It was used for coating War Department maps. The pint of varnish went backwards and forwards for two months, each time incurring a carriage charge of sixpence.

Through one prisoner it was learned that outside officials who were inspecting the prison were shown not the cells in which convicts were punished or kept but 'visitors' cells', which were clean and contained a strip of coconut matting. C.D. also pointed out the difference between the dark cells and the punishment cells. The punishment cells had windows fitted with a perforated plate through which a certain amount of light came, but the dark cells were pitch black.

Recidivists were better treated than newcomers, for they knew the ropes and took care not to afford too much trouble for the warders. They sacrificed their rights for a quiet life. Michael Davitt was a prisoner of a different order. He was sentenced to fifteen years' penal servitude in July 1870 for treason-felony, and released on licence in December 1877. Davitt was a political prisoner, A Fenian, a member of the Irish-American movement devoted to ridding Ireland of the British yoke. He was fair game to sadistic warders, an outcast whose complaints would be ignored, a member of a dreaded secret society.

He was first sent to Millbank, the custom-built prison that stood where the Tate Gallery now stands, was searched in an objectionable manner, and compelled to sit on a bucket every day to carry out his appointed tasks. There was no stool or table in his cell. If he attempted to lean against the wall, or walk about the cell, he was threatened. For ten hours a day he was forced to pick coir and oakum. The winters at Millbank were harsh, and frost-bite amongst the inmates was common.

Davitt had only one arm, and complained about the difficulty of picking oakum, but the warders were not sympathetic, saying that they knew of several disabled prisoners who had managed to pick a fair quantity with their teeth. The fact that he was a Catholic worked to his disadvantage, for Protestants were allowed light literature with a religious cast such as the magazines *Leisure Hour* and *Sunday at Home*, but the Catholic priests objected to their charges reading such corrupting literature, and so Davitt had to do without.

At Millbank prisoners were permitted to wash their feet once a week and have a bath once a fortnight, but the water was not renewed except after thirty prisoners had bathed. Davitt was watched closely at Millbank but not brutally treated, though when he was sent to Dartmoor he was placed in a cell ten feet away from the water-closet which comprised three tubs, over which soil was occasionally thrown. His cell was so dark that he had to lie on the floor to read; the only light getting into the cell was under the door.

Food in Dartmoor was very bad, and the convicts working in the cookhouse got more than their fair share. Beetles were rampant in the cookhouse and bakehouse, and got into the bread. Each convict was supplied with a mess tin, and these were never properly washed. Those convicts working outdoors were the worst hit by inadequate food, and Davitt related the case of a man who used to eat fragments of candles he had salvaged from the cesspool, and who died shortly afterwards.

Davitt was employed hauling and breaking stones, and eventually he was transferred to Portsmouth where conditions were easier. He told of the various fatal accidents that had occurred on Dartmoor, and of the brutal treatment of a boy named Murphy who was struck down with the butt end of a rifle. Five of the men in the working party complained about this, and they each received thirty-six lashes, twenty-eight days bread and water, and six months' confinement in cross-irons, one of the four means of restraint laid down in Standing Order 325 issued in February 1870. Cross-irons were chains forty-two inches in length fitted with rings which were riveted round the ankles; they were also known as leg chains. The other means of restraint were handcuffs, body-belts and canvas dresses. Cross-irons were not often used; in a census taken on 15th January 1878 of a prison population of 8,817 only forty were then in cross-irons.

Initially prepared to dismiss ex-convicts' accounts as so much tittle-tattle, cross-examination of the prison officials cited by the convicts indicated that their statements were justified. Many of the governors, warders, and medical officers were shifty and evasive, forced to admit that there was a deal of unprovoked cruelty and habitual callousness on their parts. The governors blamed this on the poor quality of prison staff, the medical officers on pressure of work and uncertain relations between them and the administration. Many of the warders clearly did not understand what all the fuss was about; yes, they agreed, if feeble-minded prisoners misbehaved they were flogged or put in punishment cells. Mr. Jeremiah Coffey, chief warder of Brixton prison, openly admitted that his men laid about them, but only in self-defence. Lieutenant-Colonel T. H. Colvill, governor of Coldbath Fields Prison for twenty-three years, scorned soft treatment, and was a strong advocate of the birch over the cat-o'-nine-tails (it gave more pain but caused less injury).

The incredible ignorance of many of the men involved in prison administration was clear from the evidence of George Everest, for fifty-five years on the Criminal Department of the Home Office, and for thirty of these chief clerk. He was simply not aware that in complaints against warders prisoners' evidence was inadmissible, and was in favour of keeping prison matters within prison circles. He was resolutely against the open publication of the reports of inspectors of prisons—this might, he claimed, 'be injurious'.

The nineteenth-century British prison system was the archetypal closed society in operation. It was dehumanising rather than methodically cruel. There was considerable cruelty, but it was usually off the cuff. The warder class was not homogeneous, and although there were ex-naval and military men who took pleasure in exerting discipline and hankered after authority there were also men who looked upon their situation as just another job, who wanted nothing more than to get back to their wives and families in the married quarters after their shifts. They were not munificently paid; the minimum salary of a warder was £84 (a chief warder got twice this). No wonder that the convict service did not get the quality of men it should have obtained.

15

Amateurs of Suffering

CHARLES MATURIN (1782–1824) was a curate of St. Peter's, Dublin, and although he was known to his parishioners because of his war against poverty, he had a bizarre side to him which found expression in a large number of horror novels, including *Melmoth the Wanderer* (1820). In it he suggested that:

It is actually possible to become *amateurs in suffering.* I have heard of men who have travelled into countries where horrible executions were to be daily witnessed, for the sake of that excitement which the sight of suffering never fails to give. . . . You will call this cruelty, I call it curiosity,—that curiosity that brings thousands to witness a tragedy, and makes the most delicate female feast on groans and agonies.

Cruelty by proxy was widely spread through all the levels of society during the Victorian age. Someone else was doing the dirty work while the connoisseurs sat back and admired, comparing one plum event with another, basking in their own self-satisfaction. There were watchers who were ashamed of the awed fascination they felt; there were others who claimed that they forced themselves to go, to describe the scenes, so that the legislators would become so sickened that they would pass measures to ensure that such things did not happen again. Too often their words savour of hypocrisy, and the willingness with which they dropped everything to scuttle off to some prestigious execution reveals an aspect of their nature that they themselves would have been horrified to find.

For the amateurs in suffering there was not enough legalised torture
to go round. Public floggings were rare, but when they occurred many
of the most unlikely and respectable people made certain that they
would be there. George Bernard Shaw looked at the phenomenon in the
Saturday Review in August 1897: '

> A public flogging will always draw a crowd; and there will be in that
> crowd plenty of manifestations of a horrible passional ecstasy in
> the spectacle of laceration and suffering from which even the most
> self-restrained and secretive person who can prevail on himself to
> be present will not be wholly free.

The appeal of public cruelty and humiliation can be assigned to
repressed sadism, and much of the raw material that excited the
amateurs in suffering had sexual overtones. Richard Monckton
Milnes, poet, biographer of Keats, friend of Sir Richard Burton and
Swinburne, avidly collected stories of the atrocities that occurred
during the Indian Mutiny. There was Miss Jennings who was raped
before her parents' eyes, Mrs. Macdonald who was murdered in front
of her husband who was strapped to a tree, an anonymous captain
who was castrated and blinded at Meerut, and the lady who was
dragged from her phaeton, covered with straw, and set on fire.

These were then occurrences not often brought to the notice of the
British public, and whereas today there would be horror and incomprehension at an English aristocrat methodically collecting this
data for his own edification—horror because he would be letting down
his class and incomprehension because there is so much of it about—
Monckton Milnes's contemporaries thought there was little odd in
him following his foibles. Similarly no one thought it out of character
when Robert Lucas Pearsall went in search of 'The Virgin Mary' and
Jungfernkiss in Germany, wooden and iron hollow figures in which a
victim is put and mutilated by spikes or knife blades, either fixed
in the interior of the figure or activated by machinery. Being an amateur
in suffering was gentlemanly.

Public executions gave the greatest opportunities to the connoisseurs,
though many regretted that hanging in chains was no longer carried
out. As late as 1874 a correspondent of *Notes and Queries* remembered
'several pirates suspended on the side of the Thames opposite Blackwall'
and recalled that taverns provided spy glasses for the benefit of their

patrons. When the corpses were moved there was an outcry, and the daily papers complained that the people of London were 'being deprived of their amusements in not being able to enjoy the view of these pirates'.

A CORNER FOR THE CURIOUS—NO. 12.

INSTRUMENTS OF TORTURE AND PUNISHMENT.

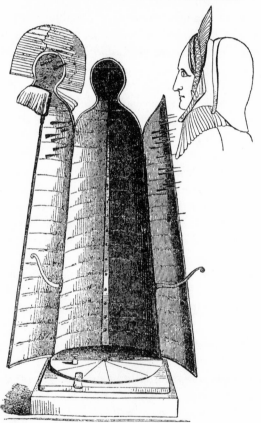

The Victorians had an intense interest in instruments of torture, and in 1856 the *Illustrated Times* included the *Jungfernkiss* in its 'Corner for the Curious'. (*Illustrated Times*)

Nevertheless, there was ample scope in public hangings. The hangmen themselves were racy characters who intuitively sensed the ambience of the situation, and did their best to make a production of the ritual demanded by the law. All the public hangings that occurred during Victoria's reign were carried out by John Calcraft.

Calcraft was born in 1800, and earned his living first as a lady's shoemaker, then as a watchman at Reid's brewery, and then as a butler to a gentleman in Greenwich. He met the current hangman John Foxton when he was hawking pies round the scaffold at Newgate, and Foxton took him on as assistant. His first duties in 1828 involved flogging juveniles at ten shillings (50p) a week, and shortly afterwards he helped Foxton hang two men at Lincoln. When Foxton died Calcraft applied for the job, and was appointed on a retainer of a guinea a week, a guinea per hanging, and £10 for a country execution. There were other perquisites—half a crown (12½p) for a flogging, and out-of-pocket expenses for items such as 'cats' (cat-o'-nine-tails) and birch rods.

Calcraft was 'a short thickset shabby man, with venerable white locks and beard which his sinister face belied'. His methods were rough and ready, and he practised his art on dogs, though he was fond of animals and kept pigeons, rabbits and a pony. After his retirement in 1874 he was awarded a pension of £1 8s a week. During his term as public hangman he received bad publicity when he refused to support his seventy-three-year-old mother incarcerated in Hatfield Peveril workhouse.

Scaffolds varied from place to place. Some were more elaborate than others. There were far more executions outside London than at Newgate, and because of the infrequency of London hangings they enjoyed much more prestige. In the provinces scaffolds were somewhat ramshackle affairs, often consisting of a hinged flap (the death-trap) supported against the prison walls, with a beam overhead to carry the rope. The Newgate scaffold was more elaborate, with uprights and a crossbeam from the centre of which a short chain hung. The trap was operated by a lever similar to the handle of a water-pump which released a horizontal bar beneath the flaps.

Hangings at Newgate usually took place on a Monday morning, and shortly after midnight the scaffold would be brought out of the main gate on a waggon and erected. When the occasion was especially auspicious the crowd would begin to gather at seven or eight o'clock on the Sunday evening, and the refreshment sellers, the pie-hawkers, and the coffee shops would run a brisk trade.

1838 was a lean year for the connoisseurs—there was no Newgate execution, in 1839 there were two, but in 1840 the crowds gathered in their thousands for the most famous hanging for many years. It was the only one of the year, so the mob made the most of it. The condemned man was François Courvoisier, valet to the late Lord William Russell, whose throat he had cut.

At four in the morning Monckton Milnes and Thackeray set out after a repast of fowl, sherry and soda water, and amongst others present were Charles Dickens, reporting for the *Daily News*, the actor Charles Kean, the Earl of Malmesbury, Lord Alfred Paget, and the fashionable painter of historical extravaganzas, Daniel Maclise. An attic storey of Lamb's Coffee House cost £5 admission, windows at a lower level £2. The Earl of Malmesbury and his cronies had got good positions, and in an atmosphere of what they described as 'pleasant festivity' punch was handed around.

The best standing positions were occupied by 'stunted ill grown lads in ragged fustian', and all about were young dandies, tradesmen sipping tea, Mohocks (the bother boys of the day), and tipsy women. It was not surprising that broadsides were already in circulation, for with any spectacular murder these were printed before the murderer was even discovered. Nor was it strange that melodramas were being performed almost before Lord William Russell was cold. As one theatre manager put it, 'if a particularly horrible murder excited the public, we had it dramatised and on the stage before any one knew who had been guilty of the crime'. Yet one article of commerce strikes us as odd —plaster phrenological heads, showing that Courvoisier was 'unhappily organised'.

Both Thackeray and Dickens took the line that the spectacle was disgusting. There was, declaimed Dickens, 'nothing but ribaldry, debauchery, levity, drunkenness, flaunting vice in fifty other shapes'. Hats were raised as 'at a Play—to see the stage the better'. A woman who wanted a better view fell out of a window. High places were in demand because if the hanged man showed a tendency to dangle too long, the trap would open and an assistant would emerge beneath the man like the Demon King in pantomime and tug at his legs.

Like Dickens, Thackeray was distressed by the execution, but later, in his book *Sketches and Travels in London* he wrote that the crowd 'was extraordinarily gentle and good humoured', irrespective of the lewd chanting of hymns reset with new lyrics, the bawdy chat of the whores, and the frenzied copulations taking place in private rooms. For the more progressive amateurs, the scene provoked them sexually, though the more prim English commentators ignored this aspect of public execution, leaving it to their French contemporaries such as the de Goncourt brothers.

The next hanging to excite the mob occurred in 1849, when Mr. and Mrs. George Mannings were hanged outside Horsemonger Gaol. Charles Dickens was present again, together with his biographer and friend, John Forster, and the *Punch* cartoonist John Leech. Prominent amongst the spectators were Irish navvies on the railway termini, the usual ragged boys, and the pickpockets. The navvies were muzzy with beer, and were fair game to the sleight-of-hand artists. There was the customary obscene chanting, and a particular favourite of the Mannings hanging was a parody of Negro melodies such as 'O Susannah'. This vied with established favourites such as the hymn parody 'Oh my!—Think I've got to die'.

Five hundred policemen were called in to control the crowds, and one woman, Catherine Read, was crushed to death. This momentary alleviation in the festivities did not worry Calcraft, who was somewhat the worse for drink and entertained the mob with whimsical asides. It was, said *The Times*, national homicide publicly as well as solemnly done, though there was little solemnity in evidence from eyewitnesses' reports. The ballad-mongers had twinned the Mannings case with the execution of James Rush six months earlier, and 2,500,000 broadsides were sold.

The appeal of the Mannings' execution partly lay in the fact that it was a double event. Husband and wife hangings were rare. Mrs. Mannings was blindfolded by a black silk handkerchief, and observers noted that she and her husband walked over their own graves on the way to the scaffold. The ladies who viewed from windows with their opera glasses saw that Mrs. Manning wore a satin gown, and this sufficed to put satin out of fashion for thirty years.

Although it was not one of Calcraft's most efficient efforts it was one of his most popular, and within three days Madame Tussaud's waxworks exhibition had the Mannings on show, satin gown and all. There were those who deplored Calcraft's demeanour and who thought that the 'disgusting levity' complained of by the press could be laid at his door, that his habit of pandering to the mob was macabre, and that Mrs. Mannings should not have been kept hanging for half an hour after she was dead. Nevertheless, there were far more who gave Calcraft pop-idol status.

The crowds surrounding Horsemonger Gaol may have been eclipsed in size by the mob that gathered the same year in Liverpool for the hanging of John Gleeson. The coming of the railways had brought in a new public, and special trains were run to Liverpool. All the ground in front of Kirkdale Gaol presented 'much the same appearance with respect to numbers as Aintree or Epsom on the Cup or Derby Day', and it was estimated that 100,000 people saw Gleeson go to his doom.

Something went decidedly wrong with the execution of William Bousefield in 1856, condemned for murdering his wife and three children. Bousefield would not go through the trap, and the crowd roared 'He's up again!' He was three times on the platform, and although eventually he went, the awful effect was spoiled by the church bells ringing out the end of the Crimean War.

Liverpool was again the venue in 1863 for the execution of Thomas, Alvarez, Hughes and O'Brien, described as ferocious murderers. Benjamin Thomas, a Welsh sailor, was not intimidated by the occasion and amused the crowd of 100,000 with his ready wit. The railway authorities had laid on excursions from Huddersfield, Blackburn and Bradford. There were thirty carriages alone from Bradford, crammed with respectably dressed 'decent mechanics' with their wives in their Sunday silk. *The Times* declared that 'there is no use in denying the fact that "hanging" has become a public amusement with a great portion of the nation' and compared it with bullfighting and gladiatorial contests.

The amateurs of suffering, the aristocracy who sipped their sherry and seltzer and analysed their feelings as the drop fell, were gradually being replaced by the amateurs of technique, working and middle class. In 1862 Mrs. Catherine Wilson poisoned her friend Mrs. Soames, and was hanged. Being a stout woman she, related a bystander, 'fell beautifully'.

The rich connoisseurs may have been jaded by the ordinary executions, but in 1864 they were all back in force for the hanging of the *Flowery Land* pirates. Five men were being hanged together, the first time since 1828. The windows in a small house were rented out at £75, and even single windows fetched £25. Calcraft was now in his mid-sixties, and was heartily booed by the crowd, while the pirates (who were also murderers) were cheered. One of those present was Police Inspector Thomas Kettle, who recorded the chat of some costermongers. One of them said 'So help me, God, ain't it fine—five of them, and all darkies!'

Time was running out for the devotees of the scaffold, and although Calcraft was selling pieces of the rope he used for sixpence an inch he too would soon tie his last knot. Most people could not remember a time when he had not been the public hangman. It seemed as though he was immortal. More and more he was resented, and when Samuel

The sermon delivered to a condemned man at Newgate was not so exciting as a hanging, but there was no shortage of visitors. (*Old and New London*)

Wright was hanged in 1864 for killing his mistress in a drunken quarrel in a Waterloo Road lodging house there was an ugly situation when the mob decided for no very clear reason that they would like to see Wright freed. 'Take him down! Take him down!' the crowd screamed out, and Wright bowed to the spectators. He was still bowing when the drop fell. Calcraft may have been haphazard and occasionally incompetent, but he never let anyone get away.

In 1868 came the last public hanging, and the old faithfuls turned up to bemoan the passing of an institution. Had he been alive, Doctor

Johnson would have supported them. As he said to Boswell, 'executions are intended to draw spectators; if they do not draw spectators they do not answer their purpose'.

The victim was Michael Barrett, a Fenian, a supporter of the Irish cause, who had been sentenced to death for his part in the blowing up of the Clerkenwell House of Correction. Between the hanging and the cutting-down time, Calcraft was subject to the sneers of the victim's sympathisers: 'Come on, body-snatcher! Take away the man you've killed.' Gradually the crowd drifted away, aware that any future hangings would be in private. *The Times* added its requiem the following day:

> It is said that one sees on the road to Derby such animals as are never seen elsewhere; so on an execution morning one sees faces that are never seen save round the gallows or near a great fire. . . . None could look on the scene, without a thankful feeling that this was to be the last public execution in England.

Calcraft retired in 1874, and was replaced by William Marwood, who rapidly obtained a place in urban legend. Born in Horncastle, Lincolnshire, in 1820, Marwood was a cobbler, and when he applied for the job as public hangman there were a hundred candidates including clerks, doctors, soldiers and sailors and a butcher. Marwood had once been a preacher and was proud of proclaiming that he was doing God's work. He was more of a perfectionist than Calcraft, and was a believer in the theory of the 'long drop'. He retained his shop throughout his term of office, and on the door was inscribed 'Marwood, Crown Office'. He occasionally saw poetry in his work: Charles Peace (executed 1879) 'passed hoff like a summer's heve'. Much better paid than Calcraft, Marwood received £10 a man plus expenses and a £20 retainer by the City of London.

Marwood's tour of duty was cut short after nine years. He died in 1883, and was replaced by Berry, a thirty-one year old boot salesman formerly in the Bradford police force. Competition for the job was much fiercer for Berry than it had been for Marwood, and there were 1,400 applications. He had met Marwood and had inquired into the trade; he had bought from Marwood his rope together with a pair of pinioning straps and a pair of leg straps. Immediately upon his appointment, Berry was sent to Edinburgh to execute a couple of poachers.

The new public hangman—the title held though the public were no longer spectators and had to be content with a notice pinned outside the prison gate—was described as having a 'cool business-like manner'. He evolved tables correlating length of drop with weight of victim, and as a hobby he collected photographs, relics and mementoes of his clients. He continued to live in Bradford, fathered six children, like Calcraft kept pigeons and rabbits, and successfully upgraded the job. He became a salaried worker on £350 a year.

Having no longer the opportunity to see him in action, the public had to be content with the image of Berry. He believed in a life for a life, and although he considered that murderers were fiends he made a point of shaking hands with the men he hanged. He was a hangman to suit the age of Victorian respectability, though two events in 1885 disturbed his supporters. After executing John Hill and John Williams for murder in Hereford, he 'returned to the neighbouring hotel where a smoking concert was in progress, and there held a ghastly levee'. A week later he went to Norwich, and miscalculated his distances and weights. Robert Goodale, who had murdered his wife, had his head severed through a too long drop.

The same kind of happening caused Berry's disappearance from the hanging circuit. In 1891 he had been to Kirkdale Gaol, Liverpool, to hang a man, and he had succeeded in decapitating him, which had led to a disagreement with the prison medical officers. In 1892 Berry retired, but, unlike Calcraft and Marwood, he had time to cash in on his experiences. He went on the music hall, billed as 'The Late Hangman—The Man Who Will Entertain You With Exciting Episodes'. To the music-hall-goer this savoured of funereal meats, and Berry ended his life in some obscurity, becoming successively an innkeeper, a cloth salesman, and a bacon salesman. He also wrote his autobiography, packed with come-ons:

Does the reader think that I have spun out this chapter too much? Does he think that I have unnecessarily harrowed his feelings?

The answer, every time, was yes. None the less he had considerably more presence than his successor, ex-hairdresser James Billington, who carried out his trade in relative obscurity until 1901. By that time, executions had lost their public appeal; there was little nostalgia for the days of yore, when thousands of people were crammed together in the narrow streets of the City of London united in excitement, waiting for Calcraft to climb on to the scaffold and amuse them with gay jests, joining in the choruses of ribald songs, and savouring the last moments of a man ritually done to death on behalf of the Crown.

There were other forms of public punishment that lingered into the Victorian period. Burning at the stake had ended in 1789, and defendants no longer feared being pressed to death, the *peine forte et dure*, for refusing to enter a plea. In 1827 an act was passed which directed the court to enter a plea of 'not guilty' when a prisoner refused to plead. The pillory, the stocks, and the ducking stool, remained in use until Victoria's reign was well under way. In theory the pillory ceased to be used in 1812 except for perjury, and this punishment was formally abolished in 1837, though it needed more than government legislation to spell a definitive end, especially in the country districts where old habits died hard.

In its simplest form a pillory consisted of a horizontal length of wood at shoulder level with three holes cut in it, one for the head, two for the arms. This length of wood was in two sections so that the victim's head and arms could be inserted, and fastened together with a padlock. Stocks were used for minor offences, such as failing to attend church, and were employed in 1853 in Beverley, in 1840 in Market Drayton, in Gretton in 1857, and in Stanningley in 1860. The last recorded use of the stocks occurred in 1872 in Newbury, Berkshire, when a local rag-and-bone man was placed in them for drunkenness and disorderly conduct in the parish church.

The brank or scold's bridle was introduced into England in 1623 from Scotland, and it was often brought out as a threat at petty sessions when magistrates were tiring of garrulous women. There were many on the walls of workhouses, and there is evidence that they were used. Branks were made of metal, or leather and metal, and consisted of a frame that surrounded the head, with a tongue-piece of iron, usually the form of a spoon but sometimes in the nature of a spike. The last recorded use of the brank happened at Bolton-le-Moors in 1856, when a prostitute had one fitted and was forced to parade between the town cross and the church steps. Branks were not intended to be permanently injuring. As with the stocks, the pillory, and the ducking-stool as used for Victorian 'witches', it was judicial embarrassment rather than judicial torture. No one died in the Victorian age from the effects of them, and they were used by local magistrates and officials who had no interest in the governmental desire to systematise punishment. They represent the last fling of penal free enterprise.

The pillory was formally abolished in 1837, but it was still used in country districts and as an amusement in museums. Notice the man trap on the floor, used well into the present century. (*Graphic*)

16

The Armed Forces

IN 1815 THE British Army numbered 300,000. Five years later it was down to 88,100. This was a low point, and a succession of wars pushed this figure up, though during the major part of the nineteenth century only one big war was fought, with Russia in 1854-6. Most of these wars were colonial and bush-fire wars in which disease and incompetence were the main enemies, and although the numbers of the British Army reached 265,466 in 1856 to cope with the Russian threat, the strength usually averaged out at 200,000, a considerable percentage of whom—nearly half between 1876 and 1881—were on permanent service in India.

The colonial wars did not call for great quantities of men, and as therefore the home-based British Army had nothing much to do there was a good deal of mischief the soldiers could get up to. The War Office considered that the only way to keep the common soldier in line was to heavily discipline him. Punishment, indeed, was used as a way of passing the time, and instead of providing soldiers with reading-rooms, games-rooms, canteens, and quarters fit to be lived in, a policy was pursued of keeping the soldier under, to prevent him from thinking for himself and curbing anything that savoured of insubordination. This was not only satisfactory to the Horse Guards, from where the army was governed, but the officer class, an élite which brought itself into power without training, knowledge, or vocation.

There was a chasm between the officers and the men, and those who were promoted to officers from the ranks were regarded as freaks. Men were expected to obey the most ludicrous of orders uncomplainingly, to face death with British phlegm, to do the best they could with equipment and arms that were frequently inefficient and inappropriate. Provided the wars were won it did not matter how many soldiers died unnecessarily, provided that they died in accordance with military etiquette.

During the period of the Boer War there were a large number of stories written in which the plot revolved around a private soldier giving up his life for his officer. It was a comfortable image, but was not reflected in the facts. Officers and men were alien species, and although officers occasionally achieved Godhood, such as Lord Roberts, hero of the Boer War, they were remote enough to the other ranks not to be confused with the all-too-near lieutenants and captains who tended to treat war as like a game of croquet. Lord Kitchener (1850–1916) was more typical of the officer class than Roberts; he was never known to speak to a private soldier, and, furthermore, took pride in this assertion. To far too many commanders in the field, the troops were something they had been lumbered with.

Living conditions for troops, whether at home or overseas, were usually frightful. In India three hundred men per room were generally accommodated, and tubs and basins were allocated at the ratio of one per hundred men. Even in the model barracks at Aldershot men were in hopelessly cramped quarters. Married quarters consisted of large huts divided by thin partitions or curtaining. The cost of housing a soldier was less than that of a convict; a soldier was allocated 400 cubic feet of space, a convict 1,000.

The tuberculosis rate in the army was five times that of civilians, and in 1858 the mortality rate amongst the foot guards and regiments of the line was twice that of civilians. The food was worse than that given to the navy, and cookhouses had only two utensils, one for meat and one for potatoes. Soldiers had to be content with two meals a day, at 7.30 a.m. and 12.30 a.m. Anything else the soldier had to buy from his miserly pay at the canteen. To add insult to injury a private had to pay 1s 10½d a week towards messing, as well as 2¾d towards general maintenance and washing. And this came out of his 7s a week pay. It is sufficient to say that the state made a profit of £50,000 per annum from canteens.

It would perhaps be too much to say that poor quarters, poor food, and no amenities constituted cruelty. Soldiers were the victims of the same sort of closed societies as those that existed in the mining towns, the white-lead works or the mills. But industrial workers did not have to sign on for life, as did soldiers, not were they subject to the ritual cruelty that was part and parcel of the British traditions.

Soldiers were worse off than factory labourers because they were expendable. The army authorities looked with indifference at the effects

Married soldiers were harshly treated, even in the new model barracks at Aldershot. (*Graphic*)

of venereal disease. In India more than a quarter of the soldiers had V.D. The camp followers were not discouraged, for sex was a recognised safety valve, and the squalid brothels that existed around Aldershot Camp were left to flourish unhindered. The officers assumed the men under their command would contract venereal disease; it was all they expected from the common soldier.

The wide latitude given to soldiers in their amorous pursuits contrasted strongly with the discipline imposed on the barrack square. The basic punishment was flogging, but this could be supplemented by shot-drill (moving cannon balls from one pyramid to another in full battle order and at the double—this was still used in detention barracks until after the Second World War). Insubordination on active service could result in a soldier being shot. As drunkenness was as widespread as whoring, insubordination was not uncommon.

A soldier was perpetually walking on thin ice. The most unruly behaviour outside barracks and bloody hand-to-hand engagements with civilians could result in a mere caution, if that. A button off on the barrack square could evoke fury. In May 1848 Private George Riley went insane, but as this was no excuse for unmilitary-like behaviour he was flogged. During the flogging he died. The implement used for flogging was usually the cat-o'-nine-tails, with nine thongs. In the early days it was knotted in three places, which resulted, wrote John Shipp in *Flogging and its Substitute* (1831), in wounds 'as though the talons of a hawk were tearing out great lumps of flesh'. Up to the end of the eighteenth century as many as a thousand lashes could be awarded, and 500, 600, 800 lashes were commonplace.

In 1825 4,708 soldiers were tried by courts martial, 2,280 were sentenced to punishments other than flogging, and 1,737 were flogged. In 1834 10,212 men were tried by courts martial, but only 963 were flogged. This could be analysed in two ways; barbarity was giving way to humanitarianism, or more crime resulted from fewer floggings. In 1838 a regulation was introduced into the British Army directing that a soldier was to be examined by a doctor before being court martialled. The doctor would then issue a certificate declaring whether the soldier was fit or not for corporal punishment, and if the man was injured during the flogging the error of the medical officer would damage his own career. There was thus a brake, though perhaps accidental, on excessive flogging.

By the start of the Victorian period, many of the more bizarre punishments inflicted on the soldiery had been abolished. These included burning and bottling, cobbing (bastinading an offender with a cobbing-stick on the buttocks), booting (flogging a man on the soles of his feet), and blistering (boiling oil or water applied to the backs of habitual drunkards). Painful and degrading, these were not the ritual tortures of flogging.

The reduction in the number of lashes began in 1812 when the Duke of York sent a circular to all commanding officers recommending a maximum of three hundred lashes, though many officers flagrantly disregarded the advice. One officer swore that he could not, or would not, comply, 'for my conscience would not allow me to award a sentence of 300 lashes when I felt convinced that the man *deserved* 600'. Nevertheless, there is no subsequent Victorian record of anything like the number of lashes inflicted on a man of the 67th Regiment in 1807 —1,500 lashes.

The person who actually did the flogging varied with the arm of the service. The infantry appointed their drummers, under the control of the drum-major, the cavalry their trumpeters or shoeing-smiths, under the control of the trumpet-major. If they did not carry out the punishment to the satisfaction of drum and trumpet-majors they themselves were flogged. On occasions, even these exalted personages fell short of expectations, and were lambasted with a cane by the adjutant. For the maximum permitted, three hundred lashes, there would be twelve floggers, each of them dealing out twenty-five lashes. Between each lash there would be a pause, equal to three paces in slow time. A commanding officer was not justified in prolonging the agony, though many did.

By article 102 of Rules and Articles of War the following offences were listed as being punishable by flogging in 1841:

Larceny by clerks or servants; stealing, or severing with intent to steal ore, etc., from a mine; stealing, or destroying plants in a garden; stealing, or cutting trees; hunting, or stealing deer in enclosed places; stealing, or dredging for oysters; larceny by lodgers; embezzlement by clerks, or servants; setting fire to crops; damaging ships with intent, etc.; destroying sea banks, locks, and piles; threatening letter demanding money; threatening to accuse a man of sodomy, or unnatural crime, or threatening to kill, or burn, etc.

However, the usual crimes punishable by flogging were of a more mundane nature—drunkenness, insubordination, late on parade, dirty weapons, abusive language, indecency, or slovenly marching. For such 'crimes' as slovenly marching a drum-head court martial was convened on the spot. This name was derived from the fact that the man's sentence was written on the drum at the head of a marching column.

It was usual to beat the offender across the back, but occasionally flogging on the buttocks was carried out. This often caused an erection, which amused the spectators. When the skin was ulcerated or inflamed from earlier punishments men were flogged on the calves of the legs. Detail varied with regiments; one commanding officer steeped the cat in brine before the punishment, another employed a left-handed drummer and a right-handed drummer so that the flogging would cover both shoulders, and another alternated breech and back flogging.

After the flogging the man would be released from the triangle, his shirt was loosely thrown over his shoulders, and he was led off to hospital where his back was dressed with cloths wetted with a dilute solution of sugar of lead. The dressings were kept in place by a cloth known as a 'saddle' and where the injuries were extensive by a 'wrestling jacket'. At a drum-head court martial where it was important to keep the column on the move improvised triangles were used, consisting of criss-crossed sergeants' halberts (a kind of a pike).

A commanding officer had the power to terminate a flogging when it seemed as if there was a danger of permanently injuring the victim, but he also had the power to make the punishment as terrifying as possible, by prolonging the time between lashes and by refusing to have the thongs of the cat washed during the punishment (the flogging was far more painful when the cat was coagulated with blood). In one case, a flogging was administered by African soldiers. To add insult to injury, those flogged were charged for the use of the cat.

After the Crimean War it was realised that the army authorities were too free with their floggings, and in 1859 measures were adopted to curb them. But although in 1867 flogging was restricted to insubordination with violence and 'indecency' it still went on.

In 1868 flogging was technically abolished in peace time. Edward Cardwell became Secretary of War, and in 1871 the Army Regulation Bill was passed abolishing the purchase system—an officer could not now buy himself into the army. The enforced idleness of soldiers stationed at home was relieved by a vast programme of military manoeuvres at which as many as 50,000 men took part. By 1871 the elementary sanitary reforms instigated by Sidney Herbert had cut the mortality rate in the army from seventeen per thousand to nine.

Matters were much improved for the private soldier, though there was still flogging notwithstanding the 1868 edict. However, it was rare for more than fifty lashes to be inflicted, yet, wrote Lord Roberts, 'even under this restriction the sight was a horrible one to witness'. Easier conditions brought a higher standard of recruits, and although it was hardly a model army the days were gone when the British Army was a refuge for every ne'er-do-well.

The old soldiers were too set in their ways to change. The brutality that they had been subject to in the past was reflected in their attitudes towards those whom they could lord it over, especially when the soldiers were on foreign or colonial service. Many of them were proud of the floggings that they had endured, and had no feeling of degradation. In his *Recollection of a Highland Subaltern* (1898) Colonel Gordon-Alexander told his readers about the man of his company who had been sentenced to fifty lashes for assaulting a non-commissioned officer. He received his fifty lashes with silent contempt, and as he was led away to the hospital he turned round to the colonel in command of the parade and shouted 'Dae ye ca' that a flogging? Hoots! I've got many a warse licking frae ma mither!' For which, of course, he got another flogging.

As with the army, the primary mode of discipline in the navy was flogging. In 1797 two acts were passed for the suppression of mutiny and these were looked on as a floggers' charter, supplementary to the Articles of War of 1749, which laid down severe discipline and summary punishment to keep the riff-raff in order. And riff-raff there was. Crews were impressed into service by the press gang because there were too few volunteers, and the press gang, in fact, operated well into the nineteenth century and only ceased to function when in 1853 a new deal was given to sailors. In 1835 the government openly declared that impressment was still in operation.

Gaol-birds, loafers, drunkards, all were scooped up from the dock areas of Bristol, Plymouth and Liverpool, and it required a strong hand to keep them under. They did not accept the discipline of the navy philosophically, as did the soldiers; the soldiers had vounteered, and were soon inculcated into obedience. Sailors were surly and mutinous, and it is not surprising that sea captains had to beat them into a state of submission.

Although the number of lashes inflicted on sailors were less than those inflicted on soldiers, it is said that twelve lashes at sea were as agonising as a hundred lashes on land. The naval cat-o'-nine-tails was made out of a piece of rope, thicker than a man's wrist, five feet in length. There was three feet of solid rope, two feet ravelled into hard twisted and knotted ends. It was much heavier than the army cat, and was laid on in a different manner; in the army the drummer stood to one side, but in the navy the flogger, usually the bosun's mate, stood two strides away from the victim, combed out the tails, swung it over his head, and delivered the stroke at the full sweep of his arm. Captain Marryat, the novelist (1792–1848) described one huge, raw-boned bosun's mate who flogged left-handed, and had a peculiar jerk in his manner 'that always brought away with it little knobs of flesh wherever the knots fell, so neatly that blood would spout at every blow from the wounds as from the puncture of a lancet'.

Whereas soldiers were flogged at the triangle, sailors were tied to the gratings. In action these gratings were placed over hatchways, but at other times these were kept in gangways and passages. Sailors were also tied over the capstan and over a gun. This operation was known as 'kissing the gunner's daughter'. More extreme than any of these punishments was flogging round the fleet. The delinquent was stripped to the waist, and put into a launch. He was then tied up with his arms extended upon a wooden frame. He was accompanied in the launch by the master-at-arms, who stood beside him with a drawn sword and counted the number of blows, a doctor, a drummer and a fifer plus the crew. The launch was preceded by the despatch boat, and this would visit each of the ships in the fleet, preparing the way for the launch. The two musicians would play a march, and the launch would be rowed to each ship in turn; the number of lashes was divided by the number of ships to be visited, and abreast of each ship the sentence of the court martial would be called out to the assembled crews. After each session, the man's shoulders would be covered with a blanket. Bloody, and half-crazed with pain, with the salt spray dashing against his back, the victim was often more dead than alive by the time he got through the total punishment, a punishment that could take several hours.

Music was used to drown the groans of the victim. To outsiders, this seemed an added sadistic perversion. The bosuns' mates came from each ship in turn, and were thus fresh. So too were many of the cats, and the size that had been worked into the cord had not been removed by washing.

This ceremony was no eighteenth-century relic of the so-called age of reason. Although a Royal Commission had given the thumbs down on flogging round the fleet in the 1830s, no new laws or recommendations had been issued. In 1844 in Chinese waters the yellow flag, the signal of punishment, was hoisted from the *Agincourt*, and two attempted deserters were flogged round the fleet.

Many officers were saddened and sickened by the spectacle, and Lord Fisher, First Sea Lord 1914–15, related in his memoirs how, in his early days at sea, he had seen eight men flogged and had never forgotten it.

The general public had only a vague idea of what went on in the Royal Navy, and provided that it remained invincible that was all they cared. Government probes into discipline and disciplinary methods went for little; short of sending an observer out on every ship in the Royal Navy there was little even the most assiduous minister could do. He knew that at sea a captain was supreme, and whether or not he was a tyrant no one would know. There were Captain Blighs in plenty, but precious few Mr. Christians. Aggrieved sensibilities were laid against the probability of being strung up for mutiny, and most men preferred to keep quiet, and wait for promotion. It is therefore pleasant to resurrect an unsung hero of 1848, J. Warren of the ship *Andromeda*, a bosun who was dismissed the service for refusing to inflict corporal punishment 'lawfully ordered' on a seaman.

Those naval captains accused of being especially cruel could smugly point to the chaotic conditions on board merchant ships, where the captains had no power to inflict corporal punishment, and the crew played on this.

Of course, a naval captain had a number of options. There was 'starting', the use of ropes' ends or knittles and canes on men who were slow or slack, ducking at the main yard-arm, gagging (similar to a scold's bridle), spread-eagling, the wooden collar (a portable pillory), carrying a capstan bar (akin to the army and prison shot-drill), and the barrel-pillory. Spread-eagling was usually practised on drunks; they were placed upon the standing rigging of the mizzenmast, feet and arms stretched wide. The barrel-pillory was a mild punishment brought in about 1840. A delinquent was placed in a barrel on the quarter-deck, wearing a fool's cap, and on the barrel was written the nature of his offence. It is doubtful whether the seafaring man, inured to floggings, startings, duckings, foul food and rough weather, and the heavy hand of any officer, midshipman or captain, was ever susceptible to ridicule.

V CRUELTY TO ANIMALS

17

Animals for Pleasure

THERE WAS NO shortage of sympathy amongst the Victorians for animals, but it largely depended on what the animals were. In the row over vivisection, even the most staunch anti-vivisectionists found it hard to conjure up much concern about experiments on living frogs, and dog-lovers were sanguine about experiments on cats. Many of the organisations formed to protect animals went off at half-cock, such as the Fellowship of Animals' Friends (1879) with the Earl of Shaftesbury as president, John Ruskin's St. George's Guild, or the Dicky Birds Society which numbered 8,000 members in 1883.

Amongst sportsmen there was a contempt for what they considered wishy-washy sentimentality, and bull-baiting, cock-fighting and dog-fighting persisted despite legislation. A bill to abolish bull-baiting was thrown out of the Commons, chiefly through the influence of William Windham who made a speech in favour of the custom in May 1802, and although it was made illegal in 1835 it still went on. It was usual in Britain for the horns of the bull to be sawn off, gunpowder exploded at its feet, and a cat or a firework tied to its tail. Because of the nature of the sport it was difficult for bull-baiting to be carried out in secrecy. The last bull-baiting in Britain occurred at the Agricultural Hall in 1870, when Spanish bull-fighters were used. Despite protestations that they operated 'without the infliction of cruelty' the secretary of the R.S.P.C.A. accompanied by police entered the ring and stopped the event. The Spaniard was fined.

Cock-fighting was still carried on, though ostensibly it was prohibited in Great Britain in 1849. Brought in by the Romans, cock-fighting was heavily patronised by royalty. Henry VIII added the Royal Cockpit to his palace in Whitehall, and to the Stuarts the sport was known as the 'royal diversion'. Cromwell tried to cry halt to the royal diversion, but the Restoration brought it back in all its glory.

Cocking-mains usually consist of fights between an agreed number of birds, the majority of victories deciding the main, but two varieties were particularly opposed by the abolitionists, the 'battle royal' in which a number of birds were 'set' in a pit and permitted to fight until one was left, and the 'Welsh main' in which eight pairs were matched, the eight victors paired amongst themselves, then four, and finally the last two.

Few towns in the United Kingdom were without their cockpits, and provided the opportunities for sporting gentry to lay bets before the rise of horse-racing. Large amounts of money changed hands, and at Lincoln in 1830 a main took place at which the stakes were 5,000 guineas the main and 1,000 guineas each match. Tempers ran high at the meetings, and in 1838 there was a riot at Hanworth, causing the death of an inspector of the R.S.P.C.A.

In Wales and some parts of England cocking-mains took place regularly in churchyards, and sometimes inside the churches themselves. The public schools were strong on cock-fighting, especially on Shrove Tuesday, and parents were expected to contribute towards the upkeep of this tradition, the money they donated being known as 'cockpence'. Public-school participation in the sport continued long after it was illegal.

In most places cock-fighting went on without let or hindrance, for the local gentry and the magistrates were frequently amongst the audience, and the police turned a blind eye to the occurrences. Apprehension was caused amongst the devotees when, on 22 April 1865, thirty-four people were fined at Marlborough Street court for being present at a main, and this gave encouragement to the abolitionists. In 1875 there were eighteen successful prosecutions, though this was only the most minute fraction of the mains that took place during that year. In country houses with their own cockpits there was complete freedom from interference. Cocking-mains took place in Mayfair at which the Prince of Wales, later Edward VII, was present.

Cocks were fought from the age of one year, their wings were cut, and their tails reduced by a third. The hackle and rump feathers were shortened, and the comb was cut down close so as to present a lesser target. There were two kinds of spurs, the short heel up to an inch and a half, and the long heel, between two and two and a half inches in length. A main could be a fearsome and bloody occasion, but this did not prevent society women from enjoying the spectacle. Cock-fighting appealed right across the social board.

This was not true of dog-fighting, which was a favourite diversion of costermongers. The best variety was the bull-terrier and its relatives, raised for bull-baiting. These had 'sporting trims'—their ears were cropped short so that opponents had little to get a grip on. This habit was offensive to many people, even though cropped ears was often an attribute of the fashionable dog. However, none of these expressions of distaste was of the slightest consequence to the costermonger class.

The dog-fighting supporters were insensitive rather than deliberately brutal, and the owners had a rough affection for their animals. The dogs were matched by weight, and young animals were first of all set against 'old gummers', fighting dogs past their best who knew the tricks but did not have the equipment, particularly teeth, to really injure the newcomer. The newly-fledged dog would then be matched against a 'taste dog', a nondescript animal with strength and spirit. Vulnerable parts of its body were shaved to show the fighting dog where he could most effectively attack. These bouts often ended with the death of the taste dog. At matches, however, dogs were seldom fought to the death. Ratting was more to the taste of the genteel than dog-fighting, and appealed both to the aristocracy and the dog fanciers. The sport was to see how many rats a dog could kill in a given time.

Dogs for ratting came in all shapes and sizes, from the five and a half pound Tiny who wore a lady's bracelet as a collar and got through two hundred rats at a go, to scarred and battered terriers. The proprietors of the ratting houses could have as many as two thousand rats on the premises ready to be sent into the pit. Good quality rats could fetch a shilling each, and the providing of rats was a subsidiary trade of the lower orders.

Ratting was certainly not for the squeamish. Henry Mayhew gives an interesting vignette:

The moment the terrier was loose he became quiet in a most business-like manner and rushed at the rats, burying his nose in the mound till he brought one in his mouth. In a short time a dozen rats with wetted necks were lying bleeding on the floor, and the white paint of the pit became grained with blood. In a little time the terrier had a rat hanging to his nose which, despite his tossing, still held on. He dashed up against the sides, leaving a patch of blood as if a strawberry had been smashed there.

In dog-fighting, ratting, and cock-fighting, the betting was as important as the spectacle, and the callousness involved in the preparing of the animals for battle went unnoticed. The preparations were seen

Whether or not the 'Piano of Cats' can be taken seriously, the fact that such a concept could be illustrated in a popular journal is food for thought. (*Picture Magazine*)

as a honing process, making the animal more efficient at doing what it did anyway—protecting itself from an attacker. But bull-baiting, dog-fighting, and cock-fighting were minority sports, relics of a previous age. One looks elsewhere for the mass exploitation of animals, parading under the guise of sport.

Bernard Shaw put one point of view with superb brevity:

To begin with, sport soon bores me when it does not involve killing; and when it does, it affects me much as the murder of a human being would affect me, rather more than less; for just as the murder of a child is more shocking than the murder of an adult (because, I suppose, the child is so helpless and the breach of social faith therefore so unconscionable), the murder of an animal is an abuse of man's advantage over animals.

The Victorians would have shrunk at this description, for the sportsmen were usually decent humanitarian men who loved their wives, their families, their dogs and their horses. By tradition there were certain animals they could murder, certain they could not. The Prince of Wales was applauded when he shot a stag; there would have been a stunned silence had he shot a cow.

The murder of an approved animal was often the unimportant end-product of a social situation. If a fox got away, no one sulked or became depressed, for there was more pleasurable ritual to come— hunt ball, hunt supper. Otter-hunting was a more studied essay in murder, for the otter was not so fly as the fox. Rabbit-coursing was not even murder, but certain execution; the rabbits, bemused and dazed, were shaken out of sacks, and would as frequently run into the jaws of the hounds as away from them. Similarly with the hunting of tame deer, much of it, for no clear reason, taking place around Reading. These trusting creatures were impaled on iron railings, entangled in barbed wire, were driven into ponds and canals where they drowned.

There are three grades of animal assassination: execution, murder and wholesale slaughter. To argue against any of them in the Victorian age was ill-bred, for there was a convention that they were all manly. An official of the Humanitarian League asked, 'Yet what could be more flagrantly and miserably *unmanly* than for a crowd of men to sally forth, in perfect security themselves, armed or mounted, with every advantage of power and skill on their side, to do to death with dogs or guns some skulking terrified little habitant of woodside or hedgerow?'

Such objectors were dismissed as namby-pamby. The *Irish Field* asked:

Do these hyper-humane faddists ever consider how, by doing away with many of what they are pleased to call spurious sports, they would be taking the actual bread-and-butter out of the mouths of thousands of men and their families? Hunting, shooting, and other sports give employment to such a vast number of people, directly and indirectly, that it would be nothing short of a national calamity if they were discontinued for any cause.

A point of view, if such a contemptible apologia can be termed a point of view. Certainly the humble protectors of grouse and pheasant, the gamekeepers, who at the turn of the century numbered about 100,000 would have shared the opinion of the *Irish Field*.

Today gamekeepers are as concerned about conservation as anyone, perhaps more so, for they realise the importance of preserving the balance of nature and the interdependence of the various species, but in the nineteenth century their views were narrow, and a high proportion of them had been recruited from the poacher fraternity. Gamekeepers were, in essence, private police, eager to tackle accidental trespassers with the same violence as they dealt with poachers.

To some degree, gamekeepers were justified in arming themselves to the teeth and taking with them savage bull mastiffs. When caught by a gamekeeper, a poacher would often fight back, and pitched battles of immense ferocity took place in isolated copses and woods. The poachers sometimes used a 'poacher's gun', a murderous weapon disguised as a walking stick, and just as the gamekeepers set traps for them using spring-guns activated by a thread so did the poachers retaliate, lying in ambush or setting their own guns.

The radical newspapers, such as *Reynolds News*, identified with the poachers, whom they saw as the unfortunate poor trying to eke out a living by catching rabbits for the pot, and around London estate-owners ordered their gamekeepers to play it cool. But away from the Metropolis, the great land-owners gave their gamekeepers a free hand with intruders, and captured poachers often appeared at court drenched in blood and severely wounded. It was a rare magistrate indeed who tood the side of the poacher.

The country folk were always on the side of the poacher, and the gamekeepers acerbated class differences and suspicion. A select parliamentary committee in 1846 investigated the poacher, and found that he was generally far superior to the average agricultural worker in intelligence, that he rarely broke any law but the Game Laws, and that he was not regarded as a criminal by his neighbours.

It was the system that one should blame. A gamekeeper was good at his job if there were partridges in the fields, pheasants in the covers, and grouse on the moor. All other wild creatures were forfeit. It seems incredible to us that less than a century ago one gamekeeper hazarded his life to descend a Scottish cliff for the purpose of killing a golden eagle with a seven-foot wing-span. There was no reason to kill it;

it was just there, of no value, as it was neither grouse, partridge, or pheasant.

The gamekeeper was paid for exercising his primitive hunting instinct. The gentleman paid. But, wrote W. H. Hudson, 'the gentleman, like the gamekeeper, cannot escape the reflex action of the gun in his hand. He too, has grown incapable of pleasure in any rare or noble or beautiful form of life until he has it in his hand—until he has exercised his awful power and blotted out its existence.'

One conservationist, E. B. Lloyd, made a short list of the creatures he had seen strung up by gamekeepers: stoats, weasels, moles, hedgehogs, crows, jackdaws, magpies, jays, owls, sparrow-hawks, kestrels, merlins, woodpeckers, nightingales, and nightjars. One keeper was asked why he shot nightjars. He replied, 'I don't believe a word about their swallowing pheasants' eggs, though many keepers think they do. I shoot them, it's true, but only for pleasure.' Nightingales were killed because their singing kept the pheasants awake at night, and a whole heronry was blotted out because their cries disturbed the sacred pheasant. By the end of the century this cavalier attitude had almost exterminated the kite, the peregrine falcon, the harrier and the raven.

The gamekeeper was able to rationalise his killing, but others were not. These were the people stigmatised by the naturalist Sir Harry Johnston as 'often not nearly so interesting, physically and mentally, as the creatures they destroy'. These were the people who set off in yachts to destroy the seals that bred on the shores of isolated Scottish islands, contemporaries of the gun-happy Americans who were then engaged in slaughtering the buffalo.

Several of this happy band claimed that wild animals *preferred* to be hunted. Sir Herbert Maxwell, one of the members of the Prince of Wales's set, declared that a pigeon would rather accept life 'under the condition of his life being a short and happy one, violently terminated'. As well ask a battery hen whether it liked being a battery hen.

The upper classes, of course, had an answer for everything. To turn to H. Seton-Karr, M.P. for St. Helens.

If a person experiences pleasure in the chase, such as in fox-hunting or deer-stalking, or even in lion-hunting, the rights and wrongs of that natural instinct are a personal matter between that man and his God. That, in common with all carnivorous creatures, we do possess God-planted instincts of the chase is a fact.

The lower orders also had 'God-planted instincts of the chase', but they put them to financial use. They slaughtered pretty birds by the thousand to provide trimmings for hats. In an eight days' shoot, 10,500 miscellaneous coloured birds were shot on behalf of the millinery trade.

The lower orders also liked to bet on their sports and shooting matches were organised. Between Stratford and Tottenham railway stations an observer counted thirteen shooting parties. They were after linnets and sparrows, and were backed by innkeepers who were betting men. In Epping Forest the shooting parties were in competition with the bird-trappers, who limed trees, caught singing-birds, put them in cages, and sold them in Club Row, the animal section of Petticoat Lane which, despite all efforts of animal-lovers, still exists.

Thanks to these various categories of sportsmen, many varieties of animal and bird life disappeared. Given the chance, they would have made every creature extinct (with the exception of grouse, partridge, and pheasant, fox, stag and otter).

There were conservationists battling against the massed forces of indifference, Cassandras crying woe, but they were a target for the humour of *The Times*. What about a Butterfly and Caterpillar Protection Society? A Battersea Dogs Home? How about a 'home for £5 notes dropped in the streets?' To rationalists, killing for sport was not only morally wrong, it was ludicrous. George Bernard Shaw made this point lucidly:

> To kill as the poacher does, to sell or eat the victim, is at least to act reasonably. To kill from hatred or revenge is at least to behave passionately. To kill in gratification of a lust for death is at least to behave villainously. Reason, passion, and villainy are all human. But to kill, being all the time quite a good sort of fellow, merely to pass away the time when there are a dozen harmless ways of doing it equally available, is to behave like an idiot or a silly imitative sheep.

There was a degree of brutality in the annihilation of harmless creatures, but it was not of the same order as that inflicted on performing animals, forced to carry out tasks that were not natural to them.

Performing animals were an essential part of the mass entertainment known as the circus.

The popularity of the circus in London dates back to 1770 when Philip Astley (1742–1814) started one in Lambeth. Astley's Amphitheatre existed until 1841. The modern circus derives from the American showman P. T. Barnum (1810–1891). In 1871 he established 'The Greatest Show on Earth' a travelling show of circus, menagerie, and freaks, and this became a target for emulation by cut-

Bear-baiting had been stopped by law, but bears were still used in circuses, and cruelly treated. *(Picture Magazine)*

price circus managements and theatre proprietors. The demand for trained animals led to the establishment of places on the continent where they were broken in and trained, and in due course they were brought to England.

Writers on the trade in performing animals hastened to add that London theatre owners were not party to the cruelty involved in rehearsals, which took place in cellars or in the very early morning on stage when it was thought that no one was about. However, the theatre managers of Victorian London were no fools, and if the profits were coming in they were not over-scrupulous how the animals were trained or treated. Most outsiders were reluctant to interfere; one dog trainer was interrupted during a rehearsal when he was engaged in putting a new dog that he had obtained from Battersea Dogs Home through its paces:

> He was in a rare rage; he lashed and dragged and jerked, the dog got more and more terrified, until at last his temper got the complete mastery over him, and he—strangled the poor beast.'

The Mr. X who had witnessed this 'was not in a position to interfere in the matter' though willing to give details to the Fellowship of Animals' Friends.

Acrobatic dogs were trained to walk on their fore feet by sticking needles in a piece of wood and tapping the hind legs repeatedly to induce the dog to keep its balance. Whips used in elephant and bear turns had short spikes in the butt, and occasionally a hook as well. English law afforded no protection to wild animals, and often trainers took advantage of this.

It was rare for an animal trainer to be brought to book. They usually covered their traces very well. An R.S.P.C.A. inspector who suspected that performing elephants at a music-hall show in the Midlands were being ill-treated persuaded a veterinary surgeon to go to a rehearsal pretending to be an artist taking part in the programme.

> It is a serious business, at each end of the stage there is stationed a groom armed with a spiked pole, ready, I suppose, in case the elephants turn upon the woman-trainer. She was wielding a heavy whip, and under the thong there must have been a sharp spike and a crook or hook as well. I saw her stab the elephants under their trunks, and in any tender part she could reach, in order to make them sit on iron stools about a foot in diameter without letting their hind feet touch the stage boards.

The inspector saw the elephants and the injuries, but the trainer maintained that they had been caused by a rough passage across the Channel. The groom maintained that the only whips used were small cane sticks, but by interviewing other members of the cast the full story came out, and although the trainer, his wife, and the elephants went to another town the R.S.P.C.A. official tracked them down, and a sympathetic J.P. signed a warrant for the trainers' arrest. They were fined a few pounds, and left for the Continent to carry on their vocation.

The passing of the Wild Animals in Captivity Protection Act in 1900 did something to alleviate the distress of performing animals, and signifies that a loophole in the law needed to be filled, but it was an act almost totally without teeth, and the derisory fines were equably paid.

It is much to the credit of Queen Victoria and Edward VII that they abhorred cruelty to animals, and gave a lead to humanitarianism. In 1874 Queen Victoria sent £100 for cats and small birds, and when Edward VII came to the throne he abolished the Royal Buckhounds that had been in existence for 700 years and were used for hunting tame deer. The king was no opponent of blood sports, and was as fond of shooting anything that moved as the next man, but at least he preserved a sense of perspective. Things could not be too one-sided.

18

The Work of the R.S.P.C.A.

IN 1924 THOMAS HARDY wrote a poem to com-
memorate a hundred years of the Royal Society for the Prevention of
Cruelty to Animals. It began:

> Backward among the dusky years
> A lonesome lamp is seen arise,
> Lit by a few fain pioneers
> Before incredulous eyes.

The fact that the last line does not scan is perhaps a subtle reminder by
Hardy that a certain sloppiness and lack of attention to detail were
characteristics of the pioneers of the movement. Certainly Richard
Martin, M.P., who got the R.S.P.C.A. off the ground, had his heart in
the right place, but he might have managed to pass a few hard-hitting
laws through parliament had his mind been in less of a muddle through
the necessity to compromise. Certainly any idea of restricting the
pleasures of the upper classes, whether or not they involved cruelty to
animals, was curbed.

In parliament and outside, Martin was the butt of gibes and mockery,
and the oft-quoted love of the British for animals had yet to make an
appearance. The early days of the R.S.P.C.A. were handicapped by
lack of funds, by the refusal of magistrates to take much interest in the
ill-treatment of animals, and by animal-lovers being split into various
species. Martin had succeeded in getting an act passed in 1822,
directed mainly at the lower orders who used animals as beasts of
burden or were engaged with animals as a job. The new society paid

particular attention to the men who took cattle to Smithfield Market, and in six months a man employed to keep an eye on them secured the conviction of sixty-three men for cruelty to animals.

There was some argument as to what constituted cruelty and what was worthy of prosecution. The Reverend G. Hatch suggested that a man might be prosecuted for breaking the leg of a horse but not for beating it; the beaters but not the maimers could be rehabilitated by tracts and pamphlets (an illusion that was shared by religious propagandists).

The formation of the R.S.P.C.A. did achieve one definite result; it made people think about their obligations to animals, and made the more thoughtful feel ashamed by their transgressions. It had been no disgrace for a gentleman to sell off his old racer or hunter for £4 or so to the coal mines to draw coal, but with a new deal for animals in the air, and the radical newspapers alert for any opportunity to attack the high-born, he thought twice about it.

Martin's act of 1822 protected cattle, including horses, but did not protect domestic animals. Surprisingly it had been ruled that bulls did not qualify as cattle, and bull-baiting went on. Publicity, rather than the law, worked for the Society, and decent newspaper-reading men and women were horrified by the stories that they read, of sheep torn to pieces by dogs, of eyes knocked out and legs broken by drovers, of calves with their legs tied together packed in carts for market, and muzzled to stop their moans being heard by the public, of pet cats being skinned alive for their fur (it was easier to skin a live animal than a dead one). An act to protect all domestic animals went through in 1835; Martin did not live to see it. He had died in 1834. The first major success of the Society in promoting a prosecution under the new bill was at Lincoln Assizes in 1837, when the organisers of a bull-baiting contest were tried and found guilty.

A fillip was given to the Society by Princess Victoria in 1835; when she was crowned in 1837 she renewed her patronage, and in 1840 she allowed the Society to use the prefix 'Royal'. She was especially distressed by the cat-skinning, and she carried the general public with her, though the trade still went on.

There was some uncertainty about cruelty to horses. They were regarded as indispensable, for the whole Victorian economy depended on horse-power and the railway-engine. It was accepted that men would get all the work they could out of their horses, and at Holborn

Hill and Ludgate Hill the R.S.P.C.A. employed three powerful horses to assist in drawing goods waggons up these hills. The carters, knowing that these trace-horses would be provided free of charge for their benefit, over-loaded their waggons.

The canal operators were enlightened men who instantly dismissed any bargee ill-treating one of his horses, but such men were in the minority. A man who lit a fire beneath his horse's belly to encourage it to pull an over-laden cart out of mud was fined a modest amount, and there was little supervision of the most ill-used category of old and decrepit horses—those drawing cabs at night.

One cabbie who was asked if he let his horses ever have any rest riposted, 'Rest? My 'osses rest when they're dead.'

The Society's inspectors were few and far between, and could not hope to be at hand for the thousand-and-one incidents that called for their attention. It was all very well covering the holiday beaches to see if there was any cruelty to seaside donkeys (there was) but the procession of sheep and cattle to Smithfield Market (closed in 1855) was too much for officials of a private society to watch over, though the City Police did prosecute occasionally. In 1846, when the Society had been established more than twenty years and was making headway, 160 salesmen at Smithfield sold 226,132 head of cattle, 1,593,270 sheep and lambs, 26,356 calves, and 33,531 pigs, most of them driven in from outside London. A good deal of cruelty was carried out under cover of darkness, and the animals were maddened and goaded by the drovers' torches. Some diminution in cruelty in the approaches to Smithfield occurred when gas lamps were provided.

In 1837 the R.S.P.C.A. underwrote 270 successful prosecutions, twice the number as in 1836, and declared the Earl of Carnarvon, the chairman of the Society, 'every year shows us that our sincere efforts are at length beginning to be triumphant'. But the figures for prosecutions were infinitesimal compared with the amount of cruelty that went on; the public were sending in complaints of cruelty to animals at the rate of 250 a week.

The Society was handicapped by the assumption that animals had been put on the earth to help mankind, literally. Horses pulled the nation's road transport, omnibuses, carriages and cabs, ponies worked down the mines, and dogs were used to haul loads that were often too much for their strength. Birds supplied feathers for hats, and cats supplied fur for cheap muffs. The position of animals was not unlike that of working-class children; what would one do without their cheap labour?

Dogs were used as beasts of burden because they were cheaper than donkeys, horses and ponies, cost less to feed, and a dog-cart paid no tolls on the road. The owners of dog-carts got off lightly; a single dog had been made to pull a load of five hundred pounds at twelve miles an hour, and had been goaded on until it dropped from exhaustion. The driver was fined ten shillings. In some parts of the country dogs were let out to children (often beggars) for a penny a day, and the hirers of the dogs were nominally obliged to feed them. Attempts to make dog-carts illegal were met by the routine argument that to do so would deprive honest working men of their living (and make them a burden on the rates).

A tribute should be paid to Bishop Wilberforce ('Soapy Sam') of Oxford, a subject of a good deal of malicious gossip. It was he who managed to sway the House of Lords and get a bill passed. He told his lordships that in those parts of the country where dog-carts were used the animals had been traced for as much as twenty miles by blood-stained pad marks on the road, and it was not uncommon for dogs to be driven hard for up to fifty miles until they could go no further. They were then destroyed, and a fresh dog put in the harness. Although the dog-cart should have been rendered obsolete in 1855, the year of the act, it is evident that it was still being used late in the century.

Roaming dogs were treated with great suspicion, and throughout the nineteenth century there were a number of rabies scares. As rabies was invariably fatal there was reason for the apprehension, though not for the shoots that took place in the London streets when anything that moved was considered fair game. The obsession with rabies even led to the invention of a combination ladder and walking stick—the ladder was run up when the owner was attacked by a dog.

To cope with half-starved homeless dogs, many of them coldly discarded by tradesmen and costermongers when they were too old to work, many of them pets that had inconsiderately grown up (a phenomenon still with us and dealt with in the same way), the Home for Lost and Starving Dogs was opened in 1861, founded by Mrs. Tealby of Islington, her brother the Reverend Edward Bates, and a Mrs. Major. Compared with the adulation heaped around Richard Martin these genuinely philanthropic people have had less than their share of glory. The Dogs' Home started in Hollingsworth Street, north London, but was moved to its present site, Battersea, in 1871. Between 1885 and 1895 206,000 dogs were received into the home.

The R.S.P.C.A. did good work in pressing charges where dogs had been chained up year after year. In one case a dog had been chained up for nine years; another dog had been kept in the same room, without ever leaving it, for seven years. In such cases magistrates awarded a small fine, many of them thinking that a dog was lucky to be fed for such a length of time. Nor were magistrates especially severe on dog-stealers. Fortunately for dogs, they could not be made into something else, and the stealing of dogs was only undertaken on a blackmail basis. The owners paid the thief to get their dogs back. In two years an organised band of thieves cleared £970 by restoring stolen dogs.

The Society was also successful in prosecuting butchers and farmers for cruelty to cattle, and the bleeding to death of calves to obtain white meat was brought to the attention of the Home Secretary, who claimed that he had directed inquiries to be made but no case had been brought to him. There was less success in putting an end to packing animals in railway trucks and in waggons far too small for them, and magistrates threw most of such cases out of court. The drovers were too ignorant and were aghast at the suggestion that they should be considerate to creatures that were soon to die anyway. It was as though, one man remarked, the animals were Christians.

Many such as Angela Burdett-Coutts the philanthropist, thought that sheer unadulterated ignorance and contempt for common humanity could be combated at school, and children's branches of the R.S.P.C.A. were formed. But many of them blenched when details of children's cruelty to animals were revealed in the columns of newspapers. Among these cruelties were killing a thrush by sticking pins in it, roasting live hedgehogs, and a ghastly roll call of mutilations. R.S.P.C.A. officials were placed in an unenviable position when it came to the prosecution of youngsters who had no conception that they were doing anything wrong.

There was some ambiguity, too, when it came to the slaughter of animals. The operators of slaughter-houses considered themselves as innocents unjustly accused of heinous sins, scapegoats for the eaters of meat. Even the most committed of animal-lovers thought twice before venturing into a slaughter-house; there was no institution more private. It was common knowledge that animals were skinned while they were still alive.

The difficulty of adequate inspection of slaughter-houses and the methods used for killing the animals were immense, for in the 1870s there were 1,500 slaughter-houses in London alone. The R.S.P.C.A. made a great effort to abolish private slaughter-houses, and issued 20,000 copies of a pamphlet setting out the various methods of humane killing. In 1882 the London Model Abattoir Society was formed for providing sanitary and less inhuman ways of killing

Hundreds of thousands of beasts were brought to Smithfield every year, and the driving of them often involved intense cruelty despite the efforts of the R.S.P.C.A. (*Old and New London*)

animals for food. The 1890s saw development of the captive bolt pistol, but the R.S.P.C.A. humane cattle killer, very similar to the one used today, did not come in until 1907.

Had the R.S.P.C.A. the requisite funds, many of the reforms in the law could have been pushed through earlier, though cruelty to animals always caused a greater stir than cruelty to children, and Dickens complained that the attention awarded to animals would be better directed towards cruelly-treated children. There was increasing compassion towards animals as the nineteenth century wore on, especially among people who took a lead from the queen.

Household pets—and there was no clear distinction amongst the poor between dogs, cats, fowl and pigs—suffered from what might be termed the kicking order. A husband beat his wife, she beat the children, and the children took it out on the animals. Pets were outlets for despair and disgruntlement and served as surrogates for 'Them'. Unquestionably deliberate efforts by means of tracts and pamphlets and newspaper coverage to make people kinder to animals had a backlash, and those who had been indifferent to animals, neither cruel nor kind, found an impish satisfaction in causing suffering to those animals that were handy just because they were told not to.

19

Vivisection

VIVISECTION ALWAYS HAS been, is, and always will be an emotive issue. Its meaning cannot be glossed over; it is literally the cutting (*sectio*) of living (*vivus*) animals, and it was extensively practised by the Victorian medical profession. Even those who shrank from doing experiments themselves conceded that they were necessary. One of these was Charles Darwin, a timid and kindly man:

> I am fully convinced that physiology can progress only by the aid of experiments on living animals. I cannot think of any one step which has been made in physiology without that aid. No doubt many surmises with regard to the circulation of the blood could be formed from the position of the valves in the veins and so forth, but certainly such as is required for the progress of any science can be arrived at in the case of physiology only by means of experiments on living animals.

This statement, made before the Royal Commission on Vivisection in November 1875, is worth quoting at length. It is the statement of a responsible man making a responsible judgment. But when asked whether pain should be inflicted that was not absolutely necessary, Darwin was at one with the abolitionists of vivisection. The practice 'deserves detestation and abhorrence'.

This was the crux of the matter. Anaesthetics had been introduced early in the Victorian reign; ether was used as an anaesthetic in 1846, Dr. Simpson used chloroform in 1847. Many experiments on living animals were carried out using anaesthetics, but a powerful core of medical men considered anaesthetics unnecessary and limited the usefulness of the experiments. They were contemptuous of what they termed sentimentality, and could not understand the mentality of those who objected to the infliction of pain on animals; it was, they said, a special form of imbecility. Some of them went a step further. Pain was a necessary ingredient of life, and the giving of anaesthetics not only to animals but to women in childbirth was a retrograde step (Queen Victoria would not have agreed; she found anaesthetics very acceptable during labour, and scattered honours about like confetti).

The abolitionists had the established church on their side. The Bishop of Durham, Dr. Brooke Westcott (1825–1901) declared: 'I find it absolutely inconceivable that God should have so arranged the avenues of knowledge that we can attain to truths, which it is His will that we should master only through the unutterable agonies of beings which trust in us.' Archdeacon Wilberforce (1841–1916) believed 'that this practice panders to the very lowest part of human nature, which is our selfishness engendered by fear'. Westcott and Wilberforce were joined by important figures in art and literature. Ruskin resigned the Slade professorship of art at Oxford because it was proposed to endow a college for vivisection. Many of the people involved in the crusade against vivisection spoiled their chances of making a real impact because they dispersed their energies. The anti-vivisection movement sheltered temperance advocates, women's rights, devotees of spiritualism and animal magnetism, and theosophists. One of the latter group was Anna Kingsland, who put a curse on two of the leading French vivisectionists; much to her pleasure, they died shortly afterwards. Harriet Martineau, a key figure of Victorian economics, famous for her hypochondria and ear-trumpet, Frances Power Cobbe, an ardent propagandist of women's suffrage, both raised their voices against the barbarity of the experimental laboratory.

It was a matter of history that the great physiologists of a past age such as William Harvey and John Hunter had made many of their discoveries by using living animals. Hunter, born 1738, made many observations on the nature and circulation of the blood. Claude Bernard, one of the vivisectors ostensibly struck down by the curse of Anna Kingsland, had discovered the vaso-motor nerves by experimenting on rabbits. One of the pioneers of brain surgery, Sir Victor Horsley, made the first ever operations on the spinal column, and stated that 'the technique of that operation I owe entirely to experiments on animals'.

It is debatable whether these discoveries would have been made except by experiments on living animals, and certainly vivisection led to advances in bacteriology. In 1881 Koch discovered the bacillus of the tubercle, and in 1890 the immunising of animals against diphtheria proved to be a much-sought breakthrough into methods of controlling killer diseases. The erroneous doctrine that tetanus was due to acute inflammation of a nerve was disproved by Nicolaier by inoculating rabbits with garden mould rich in microbes. The first attempt at coping with rabies took place in 1885, and owed much of its success to Pasteur's experiments with rabbits.

The end of the nineteenth century saw vivisection taking new paths, with the inoculation needle taking over from the knife. By the start of the first world war, 95 per cent of experiments on living animals were inoculations, and this succeeded in robbing the anti-vivisection movement of much of its fire. The chief use of experiments by the Victorian medical profession was for the advancement of physiology. This was what they claimed, and this was what the abolitionists refuted.

The abolitionists could not disguise the fact that discoveries of great moment had been made by physiologists of the eighteenth century, but they could speculate whether the experiments made in nineteenth century laboratories were done for any purpose except curiosity and in demonstrating Hunter's and Harvey's theories and findings to students. The experimenters were their own worst enemies; they were arrogant, self-satisfied, and clearly took pleasure in their calling. When they moved outside their field and plied scorn on the use of anaesthetics for childbirth or even ordinary surgery, then the general public were justified in stamping many of the experimenters as inhuman sadists who were using vivisection as a cover for their own diabolical pursuits.

Until 1876 there was no control over laboratories. Continental experimenters had a free hand. Typical of the kind of man the anti-vivisectionists would have liked to strap to his own table and poke around inside was Dr. Emanuel Klein, a lecturer at the Medical School of St. Bartholomew's Hospital, author of a handbook for the physiological laboratory widely read by other experimenters and students. He never used anaesthetics except when the cries or screams of the animals he was working on 'inconvenienced' him. He entirely disregarded the sufferings of an animal. He claimed that the administration of chloroform to dogs distressed them as much, if not more, than the operation itself. Klein came from Vienna, where, he said, the public were too well-behaved and intelligent to offer their opinions about what was going on in experimental laboratories. He admitted that he did under-cover experiments in rooms owned by London University unbeknown to the university administrators.

There were humane doctors, such as Dr. A. de Noé Walker, who, while appreciating the value of experiments on animals, deplored those operations carried out to demonstrate a point to students; by depriving animals of food experimenters rediscovered that the result was starvation. Walker was contemptuous of such men, and of those who instilled disease into animals and let them die in agony. He maintained that indifference to pain made the experimenters callous in their day-to-day life, and this was transmitted to students.

This was affirmed by James Mills, a veterinary surgeon in the Woolwich Arsenal, who was taught at Edinburgh. Medical and veterinary students would gather together in their lodgings and carry out experiments on dogs and cats which they had hunted down in the street or caught by poisoned bait. The principal of the veterinary college, William Williams, was well aware of what was going on; he could hardly fail to be so when the students carried experiments out on a horse in the college quadrangle, but the nearest the students got to a rebuke was when they opened up their landlady's cat. Mills, who had taken part in these activities, admitted that the students did it out of curiosity and boredom, and that nothing was learned from their experimentation.

Indignation amongst the public varied, depending on what animals were used. The experiment in which a dog's stomach was opened up and a live frog popped in to demonstrate the digestive process created a furore, though not on account of the fate of the frog. Boiling frogs alive, an aimless exercise to vivisection moderates, was not greeted with the horror that relatively painless operations were received when they were carried out on dogs and cats, especially dogs. Had the experimenters confined their attentions to frogs, known as the physiological animal, the Society for the Abolition of Vivisection, founded in 1875, would have lost much of its support.

Public opinion was more powerful in the nineteenth century than in any previous age, and the climate of thought forced the government to appoint a Royal Commission, resulting in a bill being passed in 1876 to regulate vivisection. Vivisectors were to have a licence. The medical profession was furious about this legislation, considering that the government had no right to meddle in its personal affairs and asserted that the number of experiments carried out was not so large as the public thought. In 1881 Professor Ferrier experimented on the brains of living monkeys under anaesthetic, and was prosecuted, but this failed. R. T. Reid's bill for the prohibition of vivisection was talked out in 1883.

One thing that the Royal Commission did do was to obtain statistics. This had never been done before. No one knew who was experimenting, or on what. The London teaching hospitals and medical schools were obliged to open their records. King's College, London, performed the most experiments, between two and three hundred a year, most of them for demonstration purposes. The animals included 150 frogs, 25 rabbits, 10 dogs and 5 cats. Of 120 experiments carried out at University College, 100 were on frogs. The total of dogs used in experimentation each year in the London hospitals and medical schools was less than forty; it was clear that the annihilation of the dog population, as feared by the abolitionists, was a long way off, and this figure of forty was only a fraction of the number of domestic dogs killed through cruelty or neglect in the home. But no one speculated how many animals were experimented on by students or amateurs.

It was certain that the act cut down on the number of experiments, for in 1883 only 44 licences were issued in Great Britain, resulting in 535 experiments. This number went down the following year to 441. Lecturers without licences were more concerned with keeping their jobs than amusing the students with experiments.

Abolitionists believed that the official figures were false, and that thousands of experiments went on behind closed doors. They were convinced that they were the victims of a confidence trick, and redoubled their efforts to get vivisection banned. Propaganda abounded, for they now had something concrete to go on—the Blue Paper issued by the government after the Royal Commission, which became required reading. It was clear that there were cruel callous men carrying out experiments; they had suspected it before, and now they knew. Dr. Klein in particular was perfectly set up, for not only had he brazenly admitted his attitude towards vivisection, unlike many of his colleagues who covered up as best they could, but he made the cardinal error of trying to amend his statement. His fumbling attempts to establish what he really thought were published for all eyes to see in an appendix to the report of the commission. He fell into the same trap as Dr.

Pembrey, head of the Physiological Laboratory of Guy's Hospital, at a later inquiry.

Pembrey did not believe in anaesthetics. 'I admit that I have done painful experiments and I am not ashamed of admitting it. They are absolutely necessary. I want to show that pain is part of the scheme of nature, and that we must recognise its existence.' He explained that if an animal is bound down on its back it often passes into a condition of hypnosis, and that anaesthetics could therefore be dispensed with.

Yet even he, though his attitude was damned by the commission as untenable and absolutely reprehensible, did not vie with Dr. de Cyon:

> The true vivisector must approach a difficult vivisection with the same joyful excitement, with the same delight, with which a surgeon undertakes a difficult operation. . . . He who shrinks from cutting into a living animal, he who approaches a vivisection as a disagreeable necessity, will never become an artist in vivisection. . . . He who cannot follow some fine nerve-thread, scarcely visible to the naked eye, into the depths, if possible sometimes tracing it to a new branching, with joyful alertness for hours at a time. . . .

Happily for the medical profession, the de Cyons of the age were rare, and paranoiac dissertations of this type are far more common in Victorian pornography and in the casebooks of Stekel and Krafft-Ebing than in medical literature. Klein, Pembrey, and de Cyon, however, provided the nourishment on which the anti-vivisection movement fed. They were, inadequately hiding their propensities under jargon, classic sadists.

The anti-vivisectionists had the support of Queen Victoria. In 1879 it was proposed that the new medical school at Edinburgh be called Victoria College. Only on the condition, warned the Queen, that there should be no rooms for vivisection. In 1882 a book on vivisection was presented to her. She made no bones about her attitude—'the subject causes her *whole nature* to boil over against these "Butchers" (Doctors and *Surgeons*)'.

Few could look coolly at the whole topic, and disputes were never conducted at less than shouting pitch. There was rarely any common ground between the antagonists. The vivisectionists openly admitted that they were cruel; but they claimed that their cruelty was justified. In a passably civilised age, their opponents could only rage and fume.

The vivisection issue is still with us. Though it rarely boils over today. Buchenwald and Belsen have conditioned us to other things.

VI   SEXUAL CRUELTY

20

Persecution of the Outsider

RESPECTABLE VICTORIANS WOULD have huffed and puffed if it had been suggested that their frenzied victimisation of those who strayed from the path of sexual normality was assuaging their own guilt, that they themselves did things in the dark hours of the morning which they refused entrance to their waking consciousness. The most unlikely characters were 'bondage' people, and oral sex—fellatio and cunnilinctus—was probably only marginally less common in the nineteenth century than it is today, rendered respectable by articles in the glossy women's magazines.

If respectable men were honest, they would have defended themselves by claiming that although they did these things they only did them to women, not to other men. To women, but not necessarily to wives. W. T. Stead seized upon the dishonesty of this viewpoint when commenting on the trial of Oscar Wilde in his magazine *The Review of Reviews*:

> If Oscar Wilde, instead of indulging in dirty tricks of indecent familiarity with boys and men, had ruined the lives of half a dozen innocent simpletons of girls, or had broken up the home of his friend by corrupting his friend's wife, no one could have laid a finger upon him. The male is sacrosanct: the female is fair game.

Stead made the point that the criminal law takes no account of burdening society with a dozen bastards, that young men of the type courted by Wilde were very able to take care of themselves, and under no circumstances could they bring a child into the world as a result of their corruption.

Those who left the path of normality were not necessarily sophistic-
ates of the Oscar Wilde set with their talk of 'feasting with panthers'.
Nottinghamshire miners habitually practised buggery on their wives
as a form of birth control. Homosexual behaviour in the public schools
was well-known to everyone who had attended Eton, Harrow, Rugby
or Winchester. Dr. Vaughan, headmaster of Harrow, was forced to
resign his post when his homosexual proclivities were brought to the
notice of Dr. Symonds, father of the writer J. A. Symonds. But there
was no talk of sending Dr. Vaughan to gaol; he found a comfortable
sinecure elsewhere.

Until 1885, when Labouchere, editor of *Truth*, a Member of Parliament, and a formidable lecher, introduced an amendment to the
Criminal Law Amendment Act, the law regarding unnatural offences
was blurred and ambiguous. Unless behaviour was outrageous, as it was
in the Boulton and Park transvestite case of 1870 with gaily dressed men
flaunting their wares in theatres, the music hall, and the Strand, the
police preferred not to interfere. The amendment to the 1885 act
altered all that. Indecent practices between males, or 'outrages on
decency' whether committed in public or in private, were considered
worth two years' hard labour. It became open season on perverts, and
the amendment became a blackmailer's charter.

Henry Labouchere (1831–1912) had been educated at Eton and had
knocked around the world until he became M.P. in 1866. His weekly
journal *Truth*, started in 1877, was a powerful force in exposing
corruption and cruelty, and one is at a loss to know why he decided to
undertake a crusade against homosexuality, or why the supporters of a
bill entitled 'An Act to make further provision for the Protection of
Women and Girls, the suppression of brothels and other purposes'
should have fed in the new material.

The clear-cut provisions of the amendment rendered the task of
jurymen easier, for under previous legislation even the most reactionary
of jurymen thought twice about condemning a homosexual to a term of
penal servitude, the length of which was determined by the judge and
could be a very long spell indeed. Only in 1828 was the death sentence
for unnatural offences abolished.

Homosexuals were not the only minority group who were languish-
ing in prison under the old regime. In the analysis of crimes for which
the 8,983 male prisoners in the English convict prisons on 6th May
1878 were sentenced to penal servitude, there were 112 entries for

bestiality (sexual intercourse with animals), five attempts at bestiality, and only eleven for sodomy. 388 were in prison for rape. To judge by the infrequency with which the charge came up, sodomy was no threat to the stability of England. The police was aware of the reluctance of juries to inflict crushing sentences, and as a case thrown out could send a detective-constable back on the beat a good deal of latitude was given to the 'margeries' and 'pouffs' who plied their trade around Charing Cross.

The Oscar Wilde case is significant in that it demonstrates the British middle-class public at its most savage. It was clear that no one had come to any harm—Wilde's associates were the flotsam and jetsam of the fringe underworld who happily turned to blackmail when it suited them, and there is no question that Wilde's tormentor, the Marquis of Queensberry, was responsible for more human unhappiness and tragedy than Wilde himself.

Wilde was dangled as a spectacle. He was as good as a live show at the Alhambra, a dog-fight in Whitechapel, a cock-fight in a discreet Mayfair house, or a bout of bare-fist boxing in some scruffy arena. He was arty, he was soft, and he was vulnerable, and the tattered traditions of fair play were thrown in the corner. The dock was his pillory, and his aesthetic word-play was the equivalent of the condemned man's lamentations. The oh-so-clever quips that had had theatre audiences rolling in the aisles fizzled in the court of law like fireworks left out on a damp night.

The trials of Oscar Wilde are a matter of history. Here was a celebrated dramatist prosecuting an eccentric peer for criminally libelling him, the libel having been uttered to save the peer's son from homosexual involvement with Wilde. When Wilde lost his case the Crown instigated proceedings against him under the 1885 Act, and he was found guilty and sentenced to two years' imprisonment at Reading Gaol.

Moderate opinion found it difficult to get itself published; the voice of reason can be overheard in the comment of one gentleman who said that he did not mind what people did as long as they did not do it in the street and frighten the horses, but even such an enlightened approach was treated as overt approval of perverse behaviour. The vendetta against Wilde discomforted reformers attempting to make homosexuality respectable.

The story starts with the introduction of Lord Alfred Douglas to

Reading Gaol, where Oscar Wilde was imprisoned. (*Illustrated Times*)

Wilde by Lionel Johnson, the baby-faced aesthetic poet who was told in good faith by fashionable hostesses at dinner parties to go out and play with the children in the garden. Wilde was nearly forty, Douglas twenty-two. Wilde became infatuated with Douglas, bombarding him with letters, telegrams, inscribed copies of his books, and other presents. Douglas was flattered and fell under the Wilde spell. Unknown to him, Wilde had been having homosexual adventures since 1886, the probable outcome of his unwillingness to have sex with his wife; he had caught syphilis at Oxford when an undergraduate, and this had recurred.

A copy of a letter from Wilde to Douglas referring to Douglas's 'rose-red lips' and 'madness of kisses' fell into the hands of Douglas's father, John Sholto Douglas, the eighth Marquis of Queensberry. Copies of this particular letter had been circulating fairly freely, and Wilde had already been tapped by a blackmailer on its account. At no time could this 'prose-poem' (as Wilde called it) have fallen into less sympathetic hands than those of the Marquis of Queensberry. Born in 1844, he had been divorced by his wife in 1877. He was a tyrant in the home, and openly preferred the society of whores and the pugilistic fraternity. His second marriage in 1893 ended in annulment in 1894. As a young man he had been a lightweight boxing champion, but the Marquis of Queensberry's rules, advantageous as they were to fisticuffs, had no part in his private life.

In addition he was an atheist, for no very clear reason. He scandalised his family when he refused to take the oath in the House of Lords, dismissing it as 'Christian tomfoolery'. He hated his wife and his children (four sons and a daughter); when his eldest son was created a peer in his own right the marquis blamed Lord Rosebery, then prime minister, and went at him with a dog-whip.

When first introduced to Wilde, the marquis was charmed, but the agreeable conversation about atheism, a good subject for Wilde's *bon-mots*, was soon forgotten. He wrote to Lord Alfred Douglas, damning the 'most loathsome and disgusting relationship' and his son replied with a telegraphic quip, 'What a funny little man you are.' The marquis then went round to the restaurants frequented by Wilde and his boy friends, warning the managers that he would be violent if he found the playwright there with his son. The general public had not yet caught on, but there was talk about family scandal, and the politician George Wyndham, Lord Alfred's cousin, intervened. A lawyer's letter was sent to Queensberry demanding an apology for the abusive letters he was posting.

Queensberry refused, and visited Wilde at his home, making a scene. Wilde told him to leave, and ordered his servant never to allow the marquis, referred to as 'the most infamous brute in London', to enter his house again. Not surprisingly Queensberry stopped his son's allowance, but also, the mark of a bully, began to involve his ex-wife through her father, claiming that she was encouraging their son to carry on with the association. Wilde was a 'damned cur and coward' and to his son the marquis wrote, 'You reptile. You are no son of mine and I never thought you were.'

This, then, was the man the public applauded for his righteous stand on sexual morality, a whoremonger with the tastes and appetites of an East End tough. At the first night of *The Importance of Being Earnest* on 14th February 1895, the marquis was there with his prize-fighter companions, but police ringed the theatre and he could not get in and he left 'chattering like a monstrous ape' but not before depositing a bouquet of vegetables at the stage-door.

The persecution continued until Wilde decided to counter-attack on grounds of libel. He lost, and was bankrupted. When Queensberry was freed, there was an outburst of cheering in the court which was taken up by those waiting in the street. As Wilde left, prostitutes were dancing in the streets. Queensberry's private detectives had been visiting brothels and the consensus of opinion amongst the madams was that Wilde and his lot were not doing their trade any good at all.

The transcript of the libel action were sent to the public prosecutor and although Wilde was allowed time to fly the country he did not take advantage of this. He was arrested carrying a yellow book under his arm. This was reported by the newspapers, and the public immediately associated this book with the magazine *The Yellow Book*, published by John Lane of the Bodley Head. Irrespective of Wilde never having written for this magazine, an angry mob gathered outside the Bodley Head offices in Vigo Street and smashed the windows. The book that Wilde took with him to the magistrate's court was, as a matter of interest, a novel called *Aphrodite* by Pierre Louÿs.

This was one of the first of the near riots sponsored by the contemporary puritans, and the newspapers realised that they had a coup on their hands and that there was a lot of mileage in moral indignation. *The Echo* declared that Lord Queensberry was triumphant and that they would

not sully their pages with 'probably revolting revelations', a commendable stand that was reversed within twenty-four hours. Minor members
of the aristocracy, such as Lord Claude Hamilton, M.P., congratulated
Queensberry on his sterling behaviour, so did the actor Charles Danby,
and so did the fashionable clubmen who would formerly have seen the
marquis damned.

The snowball was gathering momentum. The magistrate who refused
bail to Wilde considered that there was no worse crime than that with
which he was charged. The papers applauded the magistrate, all except
for one weekly, the sensationalist Sunday *Reynolds News*, and *The Daily
Chronicle*. Even the *Law Journal* was infected by the hysteria, criticising
Wilde's advocate, Sir Edward Clarke, for defending Wilde without a
fee, though it later modified its view. With the exception of Lord
Alfred Douglas, Wilde's friends fled to the continent (these included
the Royal Academician Lord Leighton) leaving Wilde almost alone to
face the music. Literary acquaintances were glad that they did not
share Wilde's Arcadian tastes.

Frank Harris declared, though not at the time, for this celebrated
bon viveur realised what side of his bread was buttered, that Wilde's
arrest

> was the signal for an orgy of Philistine rancour such as even London
> has never known before. The puritan middle class, which had always
> regarded Wilde with dislike as an artist and an intellectual scoffer,
> a mere parasite of the aristocracy, now gave free scope to their
> disgust and contempt, and everyone tried to outdo his neighbour in
> expressions of loathing and abhorrence.

The poet W. B. Yeats had recently moved to London, and suspended
his black magic interests to survey the phenomenon: 'The rage against
Wilde was also complicated by the Britisher's jealousy of art and the
artist, which was generally dormant but is called into activity when the
artist has got outside his field into publicity of an undesirable kind.'

It was only to be expected that Wilde's income abruptly stopped.
An Ideal Husband was taken off immediately at the Haymarket Theatre,
and his name was obliterated from the bills advertising *The Importance
of Being Earnest*. Sarah Bernhardt, one-time mistress of the Prince of
Wales, took the opportunity to refuse to pay agreed advances on the
royalties of Wilde's *Salomé*, in which she would play the lead.

Wilde's creditors considered that they were behaving in a thoroughly moral and patriotic way by pressing, and his house in Tite Street was sold up. The auction was conducted under scandalous conditions, and valuable paintings and furniture and rare first editions were knocked down for trifles. Many of the spectators thought it would be acceptable in the circumstances to steal what they could, and a good deal of small stuff, plus Wilde manuscripts, were whisked away.

Although at the first trial the jury were unable to agree, this was small comfort to Wilde. Released on bail, he had nowhere to go; the Marquis of Queensberry had instructed a gang of thugs to follow Wilde everywhere he went and see that he did not gain admission to any hotel. Thrown out of that monument to Victorian fantasy, the Midland Hotel, St. Pancras, Wilde was pursued over London and ended up on a camp-bed in the home of his half-mad mother and his dim-witted brother Willie.

The marquis gloated over all this, and sent crazed messages to all his family, including the wife of his eldest son Percy who had put up part of the bail money between Wilde's first and second trial. Percy, he informed his daughter-in-law, looked like 'a dug up corpse. Fear too much madness of kissing'. Later Percy met his father at the corner of Bond Street and told his father to stop sending obscene messages to his wife. The result was a fist fight, resulting in them both being bound over at Great Marlborough Street court for six months.

The Marquis of Queensberry succeeded in having an example made of Wilde, but the success was muted. Wilde died in Paris in 1900, three years after his release from prison, but Queensberry had died before, under the impression that he was being harried by the Wilde set. A final touch of irony is provided by the fact that part of the profits of the libel action (the costs awarded to Queensberry) went to Lord Alfred Douglas when he inherited his share of his father's fortune.

The apologists for the marquis who granted that he was not, admittedly, *compos mentis*, claimed that he had the perfect right to try to stop a dangerous and embarrassing relationship between his son and a much older man. In the context of the marquis's known peculiar behaviour on religion and his attitude towards the sanctity of the family, his persecution of Wilde is not remarkable. What is is the eager attempt of the middle classes and certain newspapers to help him. If this persecution, social cruelty at its most flagrant, had been directed against anyone but a homosexual, and a willing victim at that, there would have been more opposition from those elements in society for rather than against toleration.

Lust for revenge against outsiders has never been particularly uncommon in Britain. It was exposed in naked form when the Profumo scandal broke in recent years, but never were so many people willing to jump on the bandwaggon once it had started rolling as in 1895. To some extent, it was the last attempt of the forces of reaction to turn the tide of the permissive 'nineties. The voice of the London *Evening News* was the voice of paterfamilias deploring the overturning of the Victorian way of life: '. . . these abominable vices, which were the natural outcome of his deceased intellectual condition, will be a salutary warning to the unhealthy boys who posed as sharers of his culture'. Far better that Wilde should have infected his wife with the syphilis he had contracted at Oxford, and lived a normal life.

The case revealed that there was in Britain a powerful core of crabbed repressed men and women which, normally dormant, could be sparked off by an appeal to their hunting instincts. These were the people who at one time would have haunted the precincts of Newgate Prison on the eve of an execution, who would have bombarded men in pillories and stocks with potatoes, turnips, stale eggs and stones, who would have been in the wash of any gathering to lynch highwaymen, burn witches' cottages or duck scolds.

They would never have been in the vanguard; they would always have been hangers on. They would never have thrown the first stone, but would have first conned the moral barometer, which in the 1890s was the popular press. In the aftermath of righteous indignation they would not have considered their own inconvenience; at its most banal this could be represented by not turning up to redeem their ticket money when *An Ideal Husband* was taken off, a gesture of self-sacrifice for the good of the country.

The late nineteenth century did not offer the possibilities of venting their spleen that earlier ages had. There were no public hangings, no heads stuck on Temple Bar to jeer at. The mob had to take the chances as they came along.

Although the component members did not realise it, the mob was being swept along by the spirit of the age. It rarely got into top gear when there was some ambiguity. For example, its attitude towards prostitutes was uncertain, for it was well known that prostitutes were supported by public figures, the aristocracy, the younger sprigs of the monarchy such as the Prince of Wales and the Duke of Edinburgh, and, most important, members of its own ranks.

Homosexuals as a group knew that they were vulnerable, that distrust and hatred of them could overflow into violence, and that their only chance of survival was to keep out of the public eye. Both groups had their special castigators who had lost all sense of proportion, and both groups numbered many famous men; in sensible societies their propensities were overlooked. In others they were hounded (many Victorians would have liked to have seen the homosexuals of their age meet the end of the homosexual Henry II—'sleyne with a hoote broche putte thro the secret place posteriale').

In the eighteenth century homosexuality 'gains ground apace . . . will become in a short time a more fashionable device than simple fornication' (*Roderick Random* by Smollett), and there were a number of spectacular trials. In the early years of the nineteenth century the Duke of Cumberland and Byron were suspect. Lord Castlereagh committed suicide probably because he was being blackmailed by a gang who had threatened to denounce him as a homosexual. In 1833 and 1841 the M.P. William Bankes was arraigned on committing acts of indecency. On the first occasion he was acquitted, on the second he fled the country.

Yet most cases were not publicised. As with prosecutions for bestiality, reportage was not permitted. It was a subject few wanted to meddle with, for fear of the consequences. Christopher Millard wrote to *Reynolds News* asking 'Why does not the Crown prosecute every boy at a public school or half the men in the Universities? In the latter place "poaderism" is as common as fornication, and everyone knows it.' At Oxford and Cambridge and in both Houses of Parliaments there were men who could give the answer why. Many of them remembered Canning's reputation for propositioning any pretty new members, if not Canning himself (he died in 1827). And Disraeli's sexual behaviour had often been the topic of speculation. That the public prosecutor did not exert himself on behalf of the submerged middle classes out for a witch-hunt was only to be expected. The class differential must be preserved whatever the consequence to private morality.

Homosexuals were the most vulnerable group, but the possessors of aberrations and anomalies were also hounded and victimised, even when anomalies turn out to be aspects of normality. The Victorians ran a campaign against masturbation remarkable for its hypocrisy and ignorance of the facts, and the medical profession offered dire warnings. Dr. Acton wrote in 1857 that 'self-indulgence, long pursued, tends ultimately, if carried far enough, to early death or self-destruction'. The venerable Dr. Henry Maudsley in *The Physiology and Pathology of Mind* (1868) declared that 'the habit of self-abuse notably gives rise to a particular and disagreeable form of insanity, characterised by intense self-feeling and conceit, extreme perversion of feeling, and corresponding derangement of thought'. These views were echoed by the writers of popular medical handbooks for the home, such as Dr. Spencer Thomson's *A Dictionary of Domestic Medicine* (1856).

Not surprisingly these proscriptions engendered anxiety (which is a distortion of the fear instinct), and it is difficult not to believe that a good deal of pleasure was felt by medical men and their myrmidons when spreading the word. As long ago as 1923 M. Marcuse put the percentage of men and women who have masturbated at some time or other at 98 per cent, and one is therefore surely not wrong in supposing that a large proportion of the population felt that over their heads lurked a special kind of doom. Many of these people would be of the reading and introspective breed, and sexual anxiety became confused with religious doubt. Especially at public schools and universities there were a large number of cases of boys castrating themselves to prevent 'pollution', a term that was used by Dr. von Krafft-Ebing (1840–1902) in *Psychopathia Sexualis*. There were also a number of suicides, though it is difficult to say how many as it was considered more decent to blame suicide on worry over examinations.

Parents were advised to watch out for the symptoms—a lustreless expression, pallor, and unsociability—and the more assiduous bought infibulation devices for their sons, but daughters were more difficult to deal with. No doubt many parents and doctors thought their threats and exhortations were for the best, but there remains an element of psychological cruelty, the deliberate deprivation of a pleasure which, for human nature alters little over a few generations, the parents themselves had indulged in.

In the present age, society has come to terms with perversions of the sexual instinct, provided that they do not affect others not involved. What goes on in the privacy of a bedroom is of no concern to anyone other than the participants, though there are still sexual perversions that are on the statute book—bestiality, for one.

What went on in nineteenth-century bedrooms was felt to be of concern to everyone. It was thought desirable to establish a sexual norm. By the very necessity to keep matters secret, curious sexual behaviour acquired extra charge, and the chasm between public and private acts was not to be bridged. The refusal to acknowledge, even to oneself, what one was doing could lead to a form of schizophrenia; it was an age when visitors to specialised brothels had pseudonyms and the madams of brothels and bawdy-houses acquired a quasi-religious character as a kind of confessor, exemplified by the practice of calling a brothel madam an abbess.

Fetichists and transvestites were incomprehensible to the Victorian purists, and sex-changes, of which a number were recorded, were considered ludicrous and obscene. Brothels were often completely kitted out with all kinds of costume, with decor to match; favourites were a nun's outfit and the long black dress.

Kleptomaniac-fetichists were the most vulnerable. The forty-five-year-old shoemaker who in 1876 was found in possession of three hundred female articles including chemises, drawers, night-caps, garters, and a doll had little to say for himself, especially as he was wearing one of the chemises.

These were the solitaries, without position, without defence, often inarticulate and feeble-minded, scapegoats for an age that did not pretend to understand. They were wholly outside the ring of compassion that the Victorians had, despite themselves, evolved.

21

White Slave Traffic

THE VICTORIANS ACCEPTED prostitution with a good deal more commonsense than the present age credits them with. Many prostitutes chose their trade dispassionately; it was easier, more profitable, and even healthier than being a needlewoman, a mill hand, or a factory worker. There were risks from venereal disease, but these were no greater than from consumption or from cholera and scarlet fever that periodically came to ravage the slums. Prostitution was one of the few ways, except marriage, that a poor girl could escape from her class and her background. Such girls could scarcely go down in the social scale, and an intelligent pretty girl could, if she decided to be a prostitute, graduate to become a *poule-de-luxe*, a well-treated mistress, or even retire at an early age and live a respectable life in Maida Vale or Notting Hill.

But there is a great difference between selecting a trade and being bundled into one, between a mature woman deciding that the trappings of high life were preferable to drudgery and a child who was bullied, decoyed, and violated, ravished before she knew what was happening. These were the authentic victims of white slavery, a trade that was pursued on a large scale, where there was cruelty right along the line, from government indifference, through brothel-keepers, ponces, and decoys, down to the men who used child prostitutes.

Child prostitutes were highly rated. It was widely believed that raping a child virgin would cure syphilis, and child prostitutes who were not virgins were treated so that they seemed to be to rich clients— broken glass or leeches were inserted into the vagina to simulate loss of virginity.

All reform was wrecked on the archaic grounds that at twelve years old, a child became, magically and over-night, of a marriageable age. Defloration was made respectable by a marriage contract and compliance on the part of the bride. Child prostitution was in law no worse than ordinary prostitution, and the police, anxious as they were to interfere, were hamstrung. In 1835 the London Society for the Protection of Young Females reported that 'it has been proved that 400 individuals procure a livelihood by trepanning [ensnaring] females from eleven to fifteen years of age for the purposes of prostitution'. There were institutions south of the River Thames where young children were broken in.

The whole crux of the matter was consent. A Royal Commission stated that 'a child of twelve can hardly be deemed capable of giving consent, and should not have the power of yielding up her person'. Many thought that the age should be put up to thirteen or fourteen.

The men who were most keen on copulation with young children were not anxious to have a compliant partner, for part of the nature of man lies in the urge to deflower against resistance. The slum girls of London and Liverpool lost their virginities to street boys or relations before paying customers could get at them, and there was a great demand for innocents. It was very important to get them young.

In the 1860s it was reckoned that there were 9,000 prostitutes in Liverpool, including 1,500 who were under sixteen, and 500 who were under thirteen. Few of these children lived in brothels, but carried on their trade from their homes. It was common knowledge that parents would not inquire too deeply into any extra cash that was coming into the house. The lay-out of Liverpool was convenient for outdoor fornication, for, as in many industrial cities such as Birmingham, the houses were 'tunnel-backs', built with a back entry, a long very narrow passage, and the men would copulate with the children against the wall. Sixpence was the top rate. Sometimes the children would do it for a penny or twopence. Most of these tiny whores were far gone in crime, and would also let the men commit sodomy upon them or engage in fellatio; they often operated in pairs, with one girl acting as look-out at the end of the entry. There was very little interference from the police. The chaplain of Liverpool Gaol declared that trying to stop child prostitution was like 'taking a spoon to empty the Mersey' and considered that the incredible numbers of Irish immigrants were partly responsible for the trade, though there is every evidence that the same kind of thing was happening in all the industrial towns, with the children plying their wares under the pretence of selling matches or newspapers.

These young children were not the type demanded by the brothel-keepers of London. Josephine Butler, who worked hard and long to suppress child prostitution, maintained that these girls were 'craving for some little affair of the heart to enlighten the insipidity of their lives' but most observers viewed the Liverpool child prostitutes as incorrigible, cunning and dirty-minded. The London brothel keepers wanted a different class of child, and they spent a lot of money looking for them. One brothel keeper in the Mile End Road said 'the getting of fresh girls takes time, but it is simple and easy enough. I have gone and courted girls in the country in all kinds of disguises, occasionally in the dress of a parson.' They were decoyed, with no inkling of their fate.

One procuress had a responsible position in the sewing-room of an Oxford Street shop, and she recruited children and apprentices from among her charges, saying to them, 'You only need to have a little game with a gentleman, and you will have lots of money.'

Many of the men with a taste for, as it was put, 'unripe fruit', were not in their day-to-day life cruel, but activated by their passions they could inflict serious injury on terrified children. Sometimes these children were brought from the country, enticed from simple-minded parents with the promise that they would be nursery maids in a good home, or sometimes they would be bought from a parent. The cost of a virgin averaged out about twenty pounds, and before the bargain was sealed the child would be examined medically to ascertain that she was, indeed, a virgin. A virgin, naturally, could only be used once, and the cost to the client would depend on his purse. A thorough reprobate, with an obsession over raping virgins, would pay almost any amount of money. A girl was sold to a clergyman for twenty pounds ostensibly to distribute tracts.

A few of the parents did not realise the incredible demand for their virgin daughters. A man in Hackney offered his own daughter for five pounds, another in Dalston eight pounds. They did not put any value on virginity. Why should the fine gentlemen in the West End buy a pig in a poke? They were not to know of the padded rooms, where the girls would scream out without anyone hearing, or of the tying-down ceremonies of unwilling girls in Half Moon Street.

Many men, not necessarily perverse, went to child prostitutes because there was a better chance of them being free from disease. Whereas broken-in child prostitutes tried to appear older, wearing fashionable dresses and adopting the low jargon of their seniors, mature prostitutes attempted to appear younger, often with ludicrous effect—short dresses, long frilly drawers, and girlish curls.

Mr. Dunlap, superintendent of C Division of the Metropolitan Police, told of a case of the former:

> We had two lads charged at my station with attempting to steal from a carriage in Bond Street, and I saw the 'Dialonians', as they are called amongst us [i.e. from the Seven Dials district] waiting round the station for the police van to come. Amongst them was a little child that had high boots buttoned halfway up her legs; she had very short petticoats, her hair was down her back, and she wore a tight-fitting polonaise. I went outside and endeavoured to get into conversation with her. She thought I had something to do with the police; she said she was waiting to see her man go down.

The girl's fingers were covered with rings, and Dunlap reckoned that she would have been younger than thirteen.

C Division of the Metropolitan Police covered the highly respectable area of St. James's, but even there the police found it difficult for shopkeepers to lodge objections against brothels. A shopkeeper in Regent Street had done this several years previously to 1881, when Dunlap was giving evidence to a select committee of the House of Lords, and had regretted it ever since, for the local prostitutes and their fancy men had made life difficult for him. When brothels were raided— and in one swoop the police got sixteen brothel keepers—and children were found, their parents were informed. The parents were indifferent, saying 'I cannot help it; I have to go out to work; what am I to do?' One child was arrested for molesting passers-by, a rare event as possible customers did not usually take action and draw attention to themselves, and when the mother was told she did not bother to attend the court.

One man who knew all about child prostitutes in 1881 was C. E. Howard Vincent, Director of Criminal Investigations. He also knew how the scene differed from that in Europe, and how the Metropolitan Police were hampered by having no clear-cut red light districts, no registration of brothels, and thousands, tens of thousands, of streetwalkers, a phenomenon uncommon on the continent. Vincent also pointed out that the prosecution of brothel keepers did not lie within the jurisdiction of the police but was the responsibility of the parish.

Child prostitution was peculiarly English, and although there were parallels in Europe, European whoremongers preferred adolescents and those who had just achieved maturity. Child prostitution was the base side of the coin; on the other was the sentimental adoration of childhood as a sacred state, the worship of innocence. Because it was wide-spread, child exploitation was not remarked overmuch, whether it was working in the mines or mills, in sweat shops or factories, in the match-making industry or begging in the streets. It was in the interest of child prostitutes to pretend to be older than they were, for if they were under sixteen they could, if prosecuted for molesting, be sent to an industrial school, or reformatory, but if they could persuade the magistrate that they were of mature age they would get off with a nominal fine.

The centres of child prostitution in Europe were Brussels, Antwerp and Paris, and in Brussels in particular there was a demand for English girls for the brothels. Perambulatory prostitution was uncommon in Belgium, and the brothels were run on business-like lines, with government control and inspection. It was a heavily punishable offence to keep anyone under twenty-one years old in a brothel. Those keepers with a police connection always had wind when there was to be an inspection.

To get round the law, the brothel keepers who had imported English girls obtained false birth certificates from Somerset House, a simple operation costing a few shillings. The officials of Somerset House were too busy to inquire into the reasons for requiring birth certificates. The books were spread all over the counter, and the applicant selected a likely name and birth-date, obtained the certificate, and wished it on an under-age girl who had been decoyed to Europe under the belief that she would be an actress or have a position with a family. Many of these girls were themselves from a good family, and the procuresses and *placeurs* went to a good deal of trouble to put on a front. One girl who had been told that she had obtained a 'liberal engagement as governess in the family of the lady under whose charge she then was' was seen on a railway station by a friend, who happened to recognise the 'lady' as a London procuress. These ladies went deep into the country, attending churches and Sunday schools to pick up likely candidates.

Other agents were small shopkeepers, laundresses, and charwomen, and at 'Servants' Bazaars' (a kind of informal labour exchange) the recruiting agents were hard at work. Dressmakers, milliners and seam-stresses were always fair game, especially after the introduction of the sewing machine had made many of them redundant. Male agents were 'spooneys' and ponces, who would seduce a servant girl, promise mar-riage, and then decoy her to Europe. The girls were very vulnerable at fairs, and it was said that 'more young women were debauched at Greenwich fair (three days) than at any other place in England'. The barmaid was a favourite target of the *placeur*; in 1901 there were 27,707 barmaids in England and Wales, of whom 18,251 were under twenty-five. Barmaids were usually comely and pretty, accustomed to being chatted up and not averse to an adventure with a winning young man with plenty of money to splash about. Their abduction cannot really be said to be cruel; most of them were aware of what was going on, even though they did not expect to land up in brothels. But the luring of country girls, the indigent daughters of poor clergymen, shopkeepers' daughters desperate to become governesses on account of their knowledge of French or drawing, this was inexcusable.

Once they had got into a brothel, and perhaps were seduced when drugged or bemused with unaccustomed drink, the once respectable girls despaired. They were told that they had committed a crime, and that unless they complied with the brothel keepers and assumed the names wished on them by the agents who had procured birth certificates from Somerset House they would end up in prison. Some of these girls did, indeed, end up in prison. The Brussels police had to protect themselves, and their corrupt superiors, by seeming to en-force the law.

One of these girls was Helen Cordon alias Adeline Tanner, im-prisoned for giving a false name. She had also been in hospital and gave a lurid account of it:

> Although I had not, when I was sent to the hospital, and never have had, any venereal disease, I was detained there for six months, and during the first half of that time, I was treated there for the illness caused by the cruel examination and yet more cruel lust of which I had been the victim. When I began to recover from that illness, fresh horrors were in store for me, and they commenced to operate upon me for the purpose of making me capable of prostitution.

Young prostitutes were often deprived of their liberty especially when they were victims of the white slave traffic. (*Leisure Hour*)

They did not even give me chloroform, but the students held my hands and feet, whilst the operator seemed to tear and cut away my living flesh, inflicting upon me agonies I can never describe, besides the intolerable shame. This was repeated at intervals, about seven times; and during the operations, my screams and appeals to my tormentors for mercy were heard, as the other patients told me, over the whole building, and the other girls who were there used to cry at the sight of my sufferings. The principal, Dr. ——, seemed to hate me, and take a pleasure in prolonging my torments.

As in many matters involving British subjects at the hands of foreign nationals, the issue was not as cut and dried as might appear from this tale of torture. Thomas Jeffes, the Consul in Brussels, thought that Miss Cordon Tanner had made the hospital scene up to gain sympathy, though it is worth noting that Jeffes averted his eyes from everything that would cause him or his office any embarrassment. He took no action when another English girl, Lucy Nash, made a statement to him that she had been decoyed to the brothel and then raped.

It was not so easy in Paris, for although the demand for fresh English girls was there, the police were less corruptible. A French lawyer, Alexander Treitt, thought it not possible for girls to be kept in brothels against their will because there were regular daily inspections by the police. Brothel keepers also had to contend with the secret police and government medical men. There was also a trade in girls to Lille. One of those who was induced to go there was Eliza Bond, a servant girl, who after visiting Soho Bazaar Registry Office in search of a job was approached by Madame Raffael, a procuress living at 70 Berwick Street, near Oxford Street. She was asked, over a glass of stout, whether she would like to go to France. Madame Raffael said, 'I'll get you a beautiful place there, where you will get more money than you do here; you'll get hundreds of pounds in a few months, and come back to England rich, or perhaps you might get married.'

Miss Bond and her companions left London in March 1879, and were met at Lille station by the brothel keeper Madame Cleavier. A magistrate interviewed her, asked her in English if she would like to stay, and she answered yes. She was then examined by two doctors with a speculum, and the same evening she was taken by a man. 'The man was a foreigner who took me, and I could not understand what he said. I could only laugh at him. I made no resistance to him. It was not the first time I had been with a man, but I had not been walking the streets in London.' Miss Bond was kept locked in the brothel, but through the intervention of the English chaplain at Lille, and despite the threats of the brothel keeper, she managed to get back to England. Although Miss Bond was no country innocent, she seemed genuinely horrified by her imprisonment in the brothel.

Actual physical brutality by the brothel keepers of Brussels and Paris on their English inmates was not common, for it was in the interests of the proprietors to reconcile the girls to a life of bondage, accompanied by dissipation and drink. Those who initially refused to yield were threatened on two grounds—that legal action would be taken against them for stating that they were registered with the authorities with false birth certificates, and that they were liable to debts incurred (food, board, even the *placeur*'s fee). One girl who knew what the score was complained:

> Before I entered the house, I knew it was a Maison de Tolerance, but not that my clothes would be taken from me, or that I should not be allowed to go in and out when I pleased, or that the door would be locked, or that the 200 francs, the fee of the *placeur*, would be charged against me. I was led to believe I should lead a jolly life, but I was much disappointed, I was deceived. I thought I should have had more liberty.

Few people would lose any sleep over the fate of this girl, and the most broad-minded would say that she deserved all she got, but even in this case there was a strong element of psychological cruelty, the exploitation of ignorance. Similar circumstances occurred in the following case, but there is a note of pathos present that demonstrates the cruelty of decoying young girls into brothels.

In October 1874 a letter was received by the Commissioners of the Metropolitan Police at Scotland Yard:

> Dear Sir,
> Pardon me for the liberty I take in addressing you but as I am English subject who was Brought here under the Impression that I was to take a situation as Barmaid & finding that I am in a gay House I want to know if you would be so good as to claime me

come & see me as I will go away and the English people say that
you are good & I am shure that you will come & speake to me that
is all I want & then you will see that I am kept against my will I
cantott speake one word of the Language & you must come as a
stranger & see us all or they will reffuse the entrence. If you are
English you will come to my aid and I will never forget you.

Your Humble Serte
Alice F——r

The letter had originally been sent to the British Consul in Antwerp,
but it had not been possible to deliver it to him. The Foreign Office
made strenuous enquiries, the brothel in Antwerp where Alice had
been interred was investigated, but there was no trace of her. She had
disappeared, the Belgian police said, 'clandestinely'.

Jane M——n was approached in a beer-shop in Kings Road,
Chelsea, and asked if she would like to be an actress by a Mrs. Dunner.
Mrs. Dunner wanted two 'actresses', and Jane's friend Fanny G——r
was contacted. They would 'be dressed in silk, become actresses, and
be able to learn languages.' The next step in the train was a meeting
with one of the leading London *placeurs*, a man named Kleber or
Klyberg, a shoemaker. Other *placeurs* had genuine jobs: 'Albert' was a
Leicester Square hairdresser, Carroty Jack kept a fishmonger's in
Westminster Road. The two girls went to Somerset House, where, on
payment of 3s 7d they obtained copies of their elder sisters' birth
certificates.

When they landed in Rotterdam they were told that they were
going to be prostitutes. Jane protested, but was warned that if the
girls refused they would be 'turned out in the streets, without boots,
and an old ragged skirt on your back.' Klyberg had something of a job
with these two girls, for they refused to enter the brothels he took them
to and created scenes in Rotterdam. He tried to get them drunk,
unsuccessfully, and also made a fruitless attempt to seduce Fanny.
She realised that Klyberg's threats had no basis, so she threatened him
with proceedings in London; he paid her fare back to Liverpool Street
station.

The case of Hephzibah S——t was more pathetic. She was a Welsh
servant girl, in service in Brixton, and was taken to Brussels by Madame
Laurent as a maid. Madame Laurent was a *placeur*, and Hephzibah
found herself in a brothel, unable to contact anyone or get out. Thanks

to persistent enquiries, especially by the local vicar, she was got out and brought back to Britain, but died from consumption contracted in the brothel.

The white slave traffic had elements both of tragedy and comedy. There are grounds for belief that the two girls Klyberg hawked around the brothels of Rotterdam were amateur prostitutes ('dollymops') before they left London. There was certainly no ambiguity about the case of Louisa H——y, an orphan who had recently left the workhouse to go into service. She had been to the theatre, and had been approached by a man and a woman in Oxford Street who invited her home for a meal. She went, and was asked if she would like a hotel job in France.

On arrival in Brussels, she was examined by three women and it was discovered that she was a virgin, and this was confirmed in writing by a doctor later, who sanctioned her admission to a brothel, despite her protestations that she wanted to go back to England, and pronounced her a *fille publique*. She was raped, and taken ill, but even then she was obliged to do her duties. She was made pregnant. She said 'Men wanted me when I was in this condition.' She was always crying, and the brothel keeper sold her to another brothel in the Hague for 1200 francs, but as Louisa was always ill and nearing her time she was turned out with 30 francs, managed to get back to London, and was confined in Lambeth Workhouse.

On account of the testimonies of these girls several Belgian brothel keepers and their accomplices were prosecuted and sent to prison, not for their cruelty and lack of compassion but for using under-age girls. Several *placeurs*, were sent to prison. But it was only the tip of an iceberg. In Brussels alone there were nineteen brothels, and with the close liaison between police and brothel keepers diligent inquiries were rare. Really young children in foreign brothels were kept away from the prying eyes of police or medical officers. Josephine Butler wrote:

> In some houses in Belgium there are immured little children, English girls of some twelve to fifteen years, lovely creatures (for they do not care to take any who are not beautiful), innocent creatures who, stolen, kidnapped, betrayed, got from English country villages by every artifice and sold to these human shambles. . . . The secret is known to none except wealthy *debauchés* who can pay large sums of money for the sacrifice of these innocents.

Government action was conspicuous by its absence, the diplomats in Europe were only anxious to have a quiet life, and the prying was carried out by private individuals such as S. W. Snagge, a barrister, who went to Brussels in November 1880 to see things for himself. The white slave scene in London was exposed by the journalist W. T. Stead in his journal the *Pall Mall Gazette*. To demonstrate how easy it was he bought a child virgin aged thirteen. An early apostle of

BEFORE.

AFTER.

Young girls of twelve or so were often taken from their parents, cleaned up, and placed in brothels. (*Cassell's Magazine*)

tabloid journalism, Stead tantalised his readers with promises of shuddering horror and a maelstrom of vice, and although there was no doubt that Stead received a sexual kick from his inquiries in the under-world he did much to guarantee the passing of the Criminal Law Amendment Act of 1885, which raised the age of consent to sixteen, made procuration a criminal offence, and the penalty for assault on a child under thirteen whipping or penal servitude.

'The daughters of the people . . . served up as dainty morsels to minister to the passions of the rich'—it was a circulation-boosting story, and although Stead received a term of imprisonment in Hollo-way he enjoyed this, saying that he never had a happier two months than those he spent in 'Happy Holloway'. He had been imprisoned because he had taken away the girl without her parents' consent. The proprietors of his magazine, having made their money, took Stead back on the understanding that there would be 'no more virgins', and the English public, their indignation and horror sated, settled back into indifference. The white slave traffic cautiously moved back into gear; it took more than a newspaper stunt to deter the rich who had a thing about young girls.

The publicity did have another effect. Servant girls, barmaids, and simple innocents, were not so easily tricked into going into Europe, and could no longer plead ignorance when they found themselves at the mercy of strange foreign gentlemen in far-off towns.

22

Cruelty for Pleasure—the English Vice

ALL THINGS CONSPIRED to honour flagellation with the title of 'the English vice'. It was the chosen mode of discipline at the great public schools, in the army and navy, in many nurseries, in prisons and reformatories, it was indulged in in the home ('Makes young blood tingle, and keeps old blood warm'), and it was a speciality of many brothels. Like the homosexuality popular towards the end of the nineteenth century, flagellation had its poets and its literature, a pedigree and its hero-figures, such as Richard Busby (1606–1695), headmaster of Westminster, and John Keate (1773–1852), headmaster of Eton. The devotees of the perversion also drew for their philosophy on the English masters and mistresses of the macabre such as Mrs. Radcliffe, and on French writers of a previous age such as de Sade and contemporaries such as Gautier and Baudelaire.

The flagellated reacted to flogging strictly according to class. The poor were angry and resentful, the rich took it philosophically or enjoyed it. The middle classes had mixed feelings about it, but as their wealth grew, more and more of their children were sent to Eton and Harrow for an apprenticeship. The middle classes took their lead from the upper classes, and accepted the maxim 'spare the rod and spoil the child' literally, and liberal chastisement in the nursery was often the fate of a boy or a girl born to the wife of a rising industrialist or tradesman.

The flogging inflicted on the upper classes was a good deal more

decorous than that inflicted on the lower classes. Nobody struck a
working man expecting him to get some pleasure out of it, and floggings were exclusively carried out as punishments. It says much for the
peculiar make up of human physiology that so many people did get
sexual pleasure out of the experience. This was analysed by the psycho-
logist Wulffen in 1913. The initial pain of the first blows gave way
to a warm sensation over the buttocks and gradually over the genital
area. This feeling continued after the flogging, and when this happened
to boys and girls who had had no previous erotic experience there was
frequently a desire to repeat the experiment.

A further distinction between the flagellation of the rich and that
of the poor lies in the region flogged. Prisoners, soldiers, sailors and
all those beaten for official reasons, were flogged across the back and
shoulders. Although there were some enthusiasts who liked being
flogged in this manner, they were a microscopic section compared
with those who wished to be flogged across the buttocks; the former
are the true masochists who wish to be hurt, at one with the church
flagellants.

Of course, many boys at Eton and Harrow found being flogged a
painful and humiliating experience, and looked back on it with horror
and disgust. There were others, though they cannot have been many
(so wide and diverse were the excuses for a swishing) who escaped.
And there were others who forsook the pleasures of the block when they
discovered the delights of heterosexuality. But even after these three
categories have been cleared there were considerable numbers of young
men anxious and often desperate to recapture the lost sensations,
and for them the flagellation brothels thrived.

In 1838 the publisher George Cannon (*fl.* 1815–54) commented that
flagellation 'is a letch which has existed from time immemorial, and
is so extensively indulged in London at this day that no less than twenty
splendid establishments are supported entirely by its practice'. The
leading brothel devoted to the English vice had been that run by
Mrs. Theresa Berkley of 28 Charlotte Street, who in 1828 had created
a flogging machine called the Berkley Horse, a frame on which the
'victim' was strapped down. In the eight years between this invention
and her death she made £10,000 from the curious habits of her clients,
and when she died there was great competition amongst the other
flagellation brothel keepers to take over her exclusive trade. These
included Mrs. James of 7 Carlisle Street, Soho, Mrs. Emma Lee of

50 Margaret Street, Mrs. Phillips of 11 Upper Belgrave Place, Mrs. Shepherd of 25 Gilbert Street, and Mrs. Sarah Potter whose 'Academy' was at 3 Albion Terrace, King's Road.

The connoisseurs were provided with an extensive literature, such as *The Utility of Flagellation* 'as regards the Pleasures of the Marriage Bed, and as a Medicinal Remedy, with its effects on the Functions of the Loin' advertised in *The Town* in 1841. Despite the high price of 5s 6d, this was a come-on, for it was merely a translation from old Latin. *Betsy Thoughtless* was advertised by its publisher William Dugdale as 'a most spicey and piquant Narrative of a Young Girl obliged to excoriate her sweetheart's bum before he could ravish her Maidenhead'. The hardest cored flagellation book was unquestionably *Colonel Spanker's Experimental Lecture* on the 'exciting and voluptuous pleasures to be derived from crushing and humiliating the spirit of a beautiful and modest young lady', dismissed by the bibliographer of erotica H. S. Ashbee as the 'wild dream, or rather nightmare, of some vicious, used-up, old rake'.

The pornography of the time is directed at two distinct groups of readers, the floggers and the flogged. Those with fond memories of their schooldays were more often found amongst the victims; the successors to the Regency bucks, the rakes, the sharps, were the floggers. Like those who flocked to public hangings and anything special in the way of open-air public entertainment, they were connoisseurs of suffering. Many of them divided their time between the flagellation brothels, the scaffold, the cocking main, the rat-pits, the prize ring, and the race-course. They were known as the fancy, and the more sophisticated of them traced their pedigree back to George Selwyn (1719–91) with his 'morbid interest in the details of human suffering, and, more especially, a taste for witnessing criminal executions'. Selwyn would travel to Paris to witness executions, often disguised as a woman to escape notice. In the nineteenth century he became a cult figure to the French amateurs.

It is certain that the floggees outnumbered the floggers, if only for the fact that the prostitutes of London, while having no objection to doing the birching, whipping, fustigating, scourging, needle-pricking, holly-brushing, stinging-nettling, or curry-combing, were understandably reluctant to allow half-crazed enthusiasts to get at them. The sadists amongst the devotees were perforce reduced to fantasying; it is interesting that the fantasies written for this market distinctly resemble each other, both in the writing and the scene-setting (the favourite was a girls' school).

That there *were* prostitutes willing to let gentlemen flog them was brought definitively to light in 1863 when Sarah Potter, one of the brothel keepers in the top flight, was accused of assaulting one of her stable, Agnes Thompson. Police officers brought into the court a number of birch rods and two bunches of dried furze. Miss Thompson's story was that she had been picked up in George Street, seduced, had met Mrs. Potter who had taken her into her brothel, and had then been subjected to floggings by men nicknamed 'Sealskin' and 'The Count'.

Another of Potter's girls, Catherine Stewart, aged seventeen, related that she had been stripped naked and strapped to a ladder in the 'schoolroom', then flogged, receiving a sovereign. On a second occasion she was flogged for ten minutes, and only got half a sovereign.

The ramifications of this odd situation did not escape the prosecution, which urged that the matter should be dealt with summarily by the magistrate, 'for the ends of public morality, to prevent a repetition of the disgusting disclosures'.

Occasionally cases did get through the net drawn by disgusted magistrates, and a 'massage' scandal broke surface in October 1899, when a 'nurse' summoned to Marylebone Police Court was cross-examined:

'What do you know about massage?'
'Nothing.'
'What is the "discipline" you give?'
'Well, it is a treatment.'
'Yes, but what is it? Is it the birch?'
'Yes, it is flagellation, of course.'

The *Daily Telegraph* also broke the unwritten law not to excite readers' sensibilities in an account of a police raid on a brothel:

Sub-divisional Inspector Roberts said that the place was furnished in the usual way of a disorderly house. . . . In the centre of the studio was a large arm-chair with brass rings fixed to the top of the frame. In a wardrobe he found two birches and several wrist and ankle straps, which could be fixed to the chair; in a room on the second floor another birch, and in a box in a lumber-room two other birches or flagellettes.

Those most perturbed by sensationalist accounts in newspapers were as worried by the effect on potential floggers as anything else. A flogging had been witnessed by Llewellyn Williams, M.P., in prison:

> I saw a warder administering twelve lashes with the 'cat'. At first he shrank from administering it, but after four or five lashes had been laid on the naked back, and blood was squirting from it, that warder, instead of shrinking from his task, seemed to be taken with a blood-lust, and could hardly stop himself from inflicting the punishment. A more brutalising thing never happened in my experience.

The floggers nicknamed 'Sealskin' and 'The Count' preserved their anonymity, and so did most of the men on this end of the rod. A few of the floggees, on the other hand, glorified in their obsession, especially Algernon Swinburne, who in the *Whippingham Papers* expounded his philosophy: 'One of the great charms of birching lies in the sentiment that the floggee is the powerless victim of the furious rage of a beautiful woman.' Swinburne is a perfect example of a man whose sexual behaviour was entirely governed by his experiences at Eton, and throughout his life he harked back to those years and the pleasure/pain inflicted by his tutor, Joynes, a man of sufficient notoriety to get himself caricatured in *Vanity Fair*.

Swinburne's case is tragic, for his great talents, even genius, were blocked by his obsession. One of the most perceptive critics of his era, he was one of the first to rediscover Jacobean drama. At times he could look at himself with detachment, and when de Sade's *Justine* was viewed with horror as a harbinger of insanity he brought a refreshing objectivity to the scene. In August 1862 he wrote to Richard Monckton Milnes: 'You see that whether it drives curates or curates' pupils to madness and death or not . . . it has done decidedly little damage to my brain or nerves.'

To us, de Sade seems one of the great bores of all time, but in France in the age preceding that of Swinburne (1837–1909) people were so convinced of the supernatural power of his novel *Justine* that one writer, Frédéric Soulié, made the villain of his novel *Mémoires du Diable* (1837) put a copy of the book into the hands of the heroine with the idea that reading it would drive her mad. The heroine was locked up alone in a dungeon.

The mystique of de Sade was spread wide, particularly amongst those who had not read his books. What appealed to enthusiasts was that he was not merely a writer but a doer; he had picked up a girl and whipped her with a cat-o'-nine-tails, and a broom, taking the trouble to count the strokes (215, 179, 225 and 240 blows).

De Sade gave if not respectability to sexual cruelty at least a philosophy, and his successors in France and England made the most of this. Hacks jumped on the bandwagon, such as George Reynolds (1814–1879) who not only started *Reynolds News* but was a blood-and-thunder novelist. His *Mysteries of London* included a hangman who when not amusing himself with his model scaffold and full-sized dummy was mercilessly thrashing his beautiful niece and humpbacked son. Reynolds was also responsible for a scene where tax collectors in India strip a young woman to the waist and place 'carpenter beetles' on one breast; the other breast they crush in a vice made from supple sticks. Reynolds was catering for masturbatory fantasies, and was rightly scorned by the true cognoscenti; he was not in the same league as de Sade so far as prestige went, nor, for the matter of that, another cult figure of the first half of the nineteenth century, Edgar Allan Poe, whose macabre stories had sinister sexual overtones and that requisite element of the obsessional (in *Berenice* the dead loved one is dug up and her teeth taken out).

Although Swinburne could see the funny side of de Sade—who could fail to when coming across passages such as 'his form of pleasure is to dress in a tiger's skin and bugger mad people of either sex, especially those who think they are Christ or the Virgin'?—he was drawn to the myth as if by a magnet, and his novel *Lesbia Brandon* partakes of obsession. The book has the three basic ingredients of Swinburne's life—desire to be humiliated by a beautiful woman, the remembrance of being flogged at school, and the combination of the two. Both the first and second categories provided the impulse for a good deal of his poetry. The latter occasionally intrudes in a bizarre and embarrassing fashion in his private correspondence, as when he wrote to Monckton Milnes who was about to review his *Atlanta in Calydon* (1865): 'Please, Sir, don't hit very hard this time. . . . I do think it's no end of a chown for a fellow to be swished for his verses when he showed them up in time for school.' It must be remembered that Swinburne was nearly thirty at the time.

Characteristic of his flagellation verse was the *Ballad of Frank Fane*, published in the pornographic magazine *The Pearl* ('a journal of Facetiae and Voluptuous Reading') in 1879, and discovered there by the author in 1967:

> Any boy that enjoys
> A fine flogging to see,
> I give leave to stay here
> With Frank Fane and me.
> They will see his white bottom,
> When they see it again,
> I don't think they'd fancy
> It belongs to Frank Fane.
>
> Now loosen your braces
> And lower your breeks,
> And show your companions
> Your bare nether cheeks.
> Make haste to the closet,
> And bring a good Rod,
> Or I'll cut you to ribands
> You, shuffler, by God!
>
> O! firm was his muscle,
> And supple his wrist;
> And he handled the Rod
> With a terrible twist,
> But muscles grow weary,
> And arms lose their powers,
> There's an end for all nice things
> For floggings—like flowers.

That this doggerel could be written by a poet who was acknowledged to be one of the first in the kingdom (and nearly obtained the Poet Laureateship when Tennyson died) is incredible. It demonstrates the power of a perversion to transform a charming and likeable person into a personality vestige. Swinburne passed from harsh judgment on the 'most abominable bawdry' of de Sade to attendance at an 'establishment' at 7 Circus Road, St. John's Wood, where two rouged and golden-haired ladies 'consented to chastise' gentlemen visitors. Swinburne would have gone along with St. George H. Stock: 'When an elegant high bred woman wields the birch with dignity of mien and grace of attitude, then both the practice and suffering becomes a real pleasure.'

Swinburne reformed in 1879 when he was whisked away by Theodore Watts-Dunton, solicitor and man of letters, and isolated from his one-time friends, the ladies in St. John's Wood, and the demon drink. Simeon Solomon, a friend of Swinburne, was not so fortunate. Born in 1841, Solomon was a member of a celebrated painter family, and his weird fey paintings are highly sought after. Solomon attacked normal sex and those who find 'an amusement, nay, a satisfaction, in copulating with vulgar and often diseased persons of the opposite sex, and vaunted his own tendencies, declaring that his affections were 'divided between the boy and the birch'. Solomon died in a London workhouse in 1905, abandoned by all.

Swinburne and Solomon notwithstanding, most people with this 'letch' preferred to keep it to themselves. Surprisingly some did not know that they had it. One of these innocents was the Reverend Francis Kilvert, who was activated by sensationalist High Art paintings and young girls, standing by swings to see if they wore any drawers. One comment on one girl so deprived was that her bottom seemed to be in 'excellent whipping condition'. Wonderingly he asked in his diary, 'Were bottoms so formed that they might be whipped?'

Kilvert did not attempt to interfere in a part of the border country between England and Wales that was evidently flagellation mad. He even co-operated, and one girl, Fanny Strange, was brought to him in her 'shimmy' while he was still in bed: 'I held her hands while Joseph and Charlie [Fanny's brothers] whipped her on her naked bottom as hard as ever they were able to flog her.' Not surprisingly after this robust treatment Fanny was taken ill, but everyone, including Kilvert, thought that it was advisable to continue the medicine as before. The most incredible passage dealing with Kilvert's quirk and his curious relationship with Fanny Strange is surely:

I asked her mother if it would shame the girl and have a good effect if I were to whip her myself or if she were to flog her in my presence. 'No', she said, 'she is so hardened that she wouldn't care if I made her strip herself bare and then flogged her on her naked bottom before you. You can whip her as much as you please.'

The motivations of Kilvert were transparent, but many of those who were excited by flagellation, for and against, concealed the interest they felt under a cloak of duty and indignation, hanging on grimly to the deposed theory that the wholesome birch was a purifying influence, echoing Dr. Keate's words 'Be pure of heart, boys, or I'll flog you.' A London magistrate, Mr. Fordham, regretted that he could not flog an Italian who insulted an English girl. Perhaps he realised the truth of de Quincey's comment that corporal punishment is to the male what rape is to the female, and 'its peculiar and sexual degradation'.

The Reverend Benjamin Waugh, closely connected with Stead in his white slavery investigations, wished to get a whipping clause in the Youthful Offenders Bill of 1900, on the ground that the birch would be a 'reasonable penalty' in the case of a boy charged with incest with his own sister. Lord Aberdeen was all for flogging procurers, and the President of a Society for the Abolition of Capital Punishment was reported as saying that in dealing with murderers, persons who were 'mentally diseased' he 'would not exclude personal chastisement from the treatment.'

The operators of the white slave traffic were the favourite candidates for flagellation, but the mixed motives of those advocating this, and the muddled thought surrounding the topic, were cleverly pinpointed by Bernard Shaw:

As to the flogging from which all our fools expect so much, it will certainly give a lively stimulus to the White Slave Traffic. That traffic makes a good deal of money out of flogging, which is a well-established form of vice.

If any man doubts that this is the real secret and nature of flogging legislation, let him ask himself this question: Why, out of all the many methods by which pain can be inflicted on a criminal, is this particular method chosen? . . . Flogging is not more deterrent; on the contrary, the same men get flogged for the same offence again and again. Why, then, is flogging chosen? Why do people frantically keep protesting that it is the only punishment that these people fear—that it put down garrotting—that its opponents are sentimentalists—any absurd and ten-times disproved falsehood, put forward recklessly in the agonies of a ridiculous longing for this relic of the Cities of the Plains? The answer is obvious. The Act is a final triumph of the vice it pretends to repress.

The afficionados of flagellation were not amenable to reason. Whether they were floggers or floggees, whether they wanted to whip procurers or the users of their services, fifteen-year-old boys who committed incest on sisters or the sisters themselves for permitting it, criminals, soldiers, sailors, schoolgirls for playing with themselves or schoolboys for not getting their Latin verbs right, they produced their own justifications, ranging from the Bible to popular medical books. Some were more selective than others: the British Anti-Mormon League only wanted to see the birch used on Mormon Elders.

Bernard Shaw was right. Books on flagellation were (and are) good sellers; accounts of flagellation cases in the newspapers were widely read. Behind the lace curtains of their villas in Holloway, the contemporaries of Mr. Pooter were busy at it, but at what no one could say with much certainty. Flagellomania was, said Shaw, 'a special disorder of the imagination'. For every practitioner, for every obese middle-aged man who was perfunctorily chastised by a bored half-naked whore in a brothel, there were a hundred timid explorers of fantasies. They read about it, and left it at that, for even the most obedient wife might take umbrage at being handed a birch rod and told to get on with it; not everyone had been inculcated into the mystique.

A Select Bibliography

Anon, *Habits of Good Society* (*c.* 1855).
Anon, *Hanging and Scenes Witnessed before the Gallows* (1868).
Anon, *Undercurrents Overlooked* (1860).
Adamson, J. W., *English Education* (1930).
Adderley, James, *In Slums and Society* (1916).
Andrews, William, *Old-time Punishments* (1890).
Arnold, R. A., *History of the Cloth Famine* (1865).
Babington, A., *The English Bastille* (1971).
Barry, J. V., *Life and Death of John Price* (1964).
Bartlett, D. V. G., *London by Day and Night* (1852).
Beames, T., *The Rookeries of London* (1850).
Berry, James, *My Experiences as an Executioner* (1972).
Booth, Charles, *Life and Labours of the People in London* (1889–1903).
Booth, Michael, *English Melodrama* (1965).
Branch-Johnson, W., *The English Prison Hulks* (1957).
Bremner, C. S., *Education of Girls and Women in Great Britain* (1897).
British Weekly, Tempted London (1889).
Brown, J. B., *The Home: in its Relation to Man and to Society* (1883).
Bryce, James, *Studies in History and Jurisprudence* (1901).
Bullocke, J. G., *Sailor's Rebellion* (1938).
Burn, W. L., *The Age of Equipoise* (1964).
Butler, Josephine, *Personal Reminiscences of a Great Crusade* (1896).
Calcraft, William, *Life and Recollections* (1871).
Cane, Edmund du, *Punishment and Prevention of Crime* (1885).
Carlyle, Thomas, *Past and Present* (1843).
Carlyle, Thomas, *Latter-day Pamphlets* (1850).

Chadwick, Owen, *The Victorian Church* (1966).

Chambers, J. B., *The Workshop of the World* (1961).

Chesney, Kellow, *The Victorian Underworld* (1970).

Claver, Scott, *Under the Lash* (1954).

Clay, W. L., *The Prison Chaplain* (1861).

Cleveland, A., *Woman under English Law* (1896).

Cobbe, Frances, *Essays on the Pursuits of Women* (1863).

Cobden, John C., *The White Slaves of England* (1860).

Collinson, J., *Facts about Flogging* (1905).

Cooper, W. M., *A History of the Rod* (1870).

Decker, C. R., *The Victorian Conscience* (1952).

Dicey, A. V., *Law and Public Opinion in England* (1914).

Dodd, G., *Days at the Factories* (1843).

Dunbar, J., *Early Victorian Woman* (1953).

Dymond, A. H., *The Law on its Trial* (1865).

Earle, A. M., *Curious Punishments of Bygone Days* (1896).

Ellis, Havelock, *The Task of Social Hygiene* (1912).

Engels, F., *Condition of the Working Classes in England in 1844* (1892).

Escott, T. H. S., *Society in London* (1885).

Escott, T. H. S., *Social Transformation of the Victorian Age* (1897).

Evans, E. P., *Criminal Prosecution and Capital Punishment of Animals* (1906).

Ewing, A. C., *The Morality of Punishment* (1926).

Fairholme, E. G., *A Century of Work for Animals* (1924).

Fay, C. R., *Life and Labour in the Nineteenth Century* (1920).

Féré, C., *The Sexual Instinct* (1900).

Ferri, E., *Criminal Sociology* (1895).

Fielden, J., *Curse of the Factory System* (1836).

Fison, Mrs. W., *Hints for the Earnest Student* (1850).

Gavin, Hector, *Sanitary Ramblings* (1848).

Glaister, J., *Textbook of Medical Jurisprudence* (1931).

Godwin, G., *London Shadows* (1854).

Godwin, G., *Town Swamps* (1859).

Greg, W. R., *Why are Women Redundant?* (1869).

Gregory, B., *Sidelights* (1903).

Greenwood, James, *Curiosities of Savage Life* (1863).

Greenwood, James, *Unsentimental Journeys* (1867).

Greenwood, James, *The Seven Curses of London* (1869).

Greenwood, James, *The Wilds of London* (1874).

Greenwood, James, *Low-life Deeps* (1876).

Griffiths, A., *Chronicler of Newgate* (1884).

Griffiths, A., *Secrets of the Prison House* (1894).

Grisewood, H., (ed), *Ideals and Beliefs of the Victorians* (1949).

Hadden, R. H., *An East End Chronicle* (1880).

Hammond, J. L., *The Age of the Chartists* (1930).

Harper, C. G., *Revolted Woman* (1896).

Harris, E., *Treatment of Juvenile Delinquents* (1877).

Hart, A. T., and Carpenter, E., *A Nineteenth Century Country Parson* (1954).

Hartshorne, A., *Hanging in Chains* (n.d.).

Hewitt, M., *Wives and Mothers in Victorian Industry* (1958).

Hibbert, C., *The Roots of Evil* (1963).

Hird, F., *The Cry of the Children* (1898).

Hollingshead, J., *Ragged London* (1861).

Home, C. S., *Nonconformity in the Nineteenth Century* (1907).

Houghton, Walter (ed), *The Victorian Frame of Mind* (1957).

Housden, L. G., *The Prevention of Cruelty to Children* (1955).

Howard, D. L., *The English Prisons* (1960).

Hutchins, B. L., and Hamson, A., *A History of Factory Legislation* (1903).

Inglis, K., *Churches and the Working Classes in Victorian England* (1963).

Ingestre, Viscount, *Social Evils* (1853).

Ingestre, Viscount (ed), *Meliora: or Better Times to Come* (1852).

Ives, G., *History of Penal Methods* (1914).

'Dr. Jacobus X', *Discipline in School and Cloister* (1901).

Jardine, D., *On the Use of Torture in the Criminal Law of England* (1837).

Jay, A. O., *Life in Darkest London* (1891).

Jay, A. O., *The Social Problem* (1893).

Jay, A. O., *A Story of Shoreditch* (1896).

Jefferies, R., *The Gamekeeper at Home* (1877).

Jefferies, R., *The Amateur Poacher* (1879).

Jephson, H., *The Sanitary Evolution of London* (1827).

Jerrold, B., *A London Pilgrimage* (1872).

Johnston, G., *England As It Is* (1851).

Johnston, H. M., *Children and Public Houses* (1897).

Keating, P. J., *The Working Classes in Victorian Fiction* (1971).

Kingsmill, J., *Chapters on Prisons and Prisoners* (1852).

Knight, C., *Passages of a Working Life* (1864).

Krafft-Ebing, R. von, *Psychopathia Sexualis* (1925).

Laver, J., *The Age of Optimism* (1966).

Lawrence, J., *History of Capital Punishment* (n.d.).

Letchworth, W. P., *Report on Deprived and Delinquent Children* (1877).

Linton, Mrs. L., *The Girl of the Period* (1883).

Logan, W., *The Great Social Evil* (1871).

London, J., *People of the Abyss* (1903).

Mach, E. C., *Public Schools and British Opinion* (1930–41).

MacMaster, John, *Divine Purpose of Capital Punishment* (1892).

Mallett, Mrs. C., *Dangerous Trades for Women* (1893).

'Manchester Operative', *Stubborn Facts from the Factories* (1844).

Marshall, H., *A Historical Sketch of Military Punishments* (n.d.).

Mayhew, H., *London Labour and the London Poor* (1851–52).

Mayhew, H., and Binny, J., *The Criminal Prisons of London* (1862).

McGregor, O. R., *Divorce in England* (1957).

Mearns, A., and Preston, W. C., *Bitter Cry of Outcast London* (1883).

Merryweather, M., *Experiences of Factory Life* (1862).

Midwinter, E. C., *Victorian Social Reform* (1969).

Miles, W. A., *Poverty, Mendicity, and Crime* (1839).

Milne, J. D., *Industrial and Social Position of Women in the Middle and Lower Ranks* (1857).

Mitchell, W., *Rescue the Children* (1886).

Monger, A. W., *Children's Rights* (1886).

Morrison, W. D., *Juvenile Offenders* (1896).

Murray, E. C. G., *Side Lights on English Society* (1881).

Nadal, E. S., *Impressions of English Social Life* (1875).

Neate, C., *Considerations on the Punishment of Death* (1864).

Neff, W. F., *Victorian Working Women* (1929).

Norton, C., *English Laws for Women* (1854).

Oldfield, J., *The Penalty of Death* (1901).

Pare, W., *Plan for the Suppression of the Predatory Classes* (1862).

Parry, L. A., *History of Torture in England* (1933).

Pearsall, R., *Worm in the Bud* (1969).

Petty, J., *History of the Primitive Methodist Connection* (1864).

Pike, L. O., *History of Crime in England* (1873).

Pinchbeck, I., *Women Workers and the Industrial Revolution* (1930).

Plint, T., *Crime in England* (1851).

Pratt, E. A., *Pioneer Women of Victoria's Reign* (1897).

Praz, Mario, *The Romantic Agony* (1933).

Prescott, E. L., *Flogging Not Abolished* (1897).

'Prison Matron', *Female Life in Prison* (1862).

Reiss, E., *The Rights and Duties of Englishwomen* (1934).

Ritchie, J. E., *The Night Side of London* (1857).

Rogers, J., *Reminiscences of a Workhouse Medical Officer* (1889).

Romilly, H., *Punishment of Death* (1893).

Rose, M., *The East End of London* (1951).

Salt, H. S. (ed), *Killing for Sport* (1915).

Salt, H. S., *The Flogging Craze* (1916)

Scott, G. R., *History of Corporal Punishment* (1938).

Scott, G. R., *History of Torture Throughout the Ages* (1940).

Sherard, R. H., *The White Slaves of England* (1897).

Shoberl, F., *Persecutions of Popery* (1844).

Simon, Sir John, *English Sanitary Institutions* (1890).

Sims, G. R., *How the Poor Live* (1883).

Smith, B. L., *Brief Summary of the Most Important Laws Concerning Women* (1854).

Stekel, W., *Sadism and Masochism* (1935).

Stoughton, J., *Religion in England, 1800–50* (1884).

Strachey, R., *The Cause* (1928).

Swain, J., *Pleasures of the Torture Chamber* (1931).

Tallack, W., *Penological and Preventive Principles* (1896).

Taylor, W. C., *Notes of a Tour in Lancashire* (1842).

Temple, N. (ed), *Seen and Not Heard* (1970).

Thompson, E. P., and Yeo, E., *The Unknown Mayhew* (1971).

Thompson, F. M. L., *English Landed Gentry in the Nineteenth Century* (1963).

Tonna, C., *The Wrongs of Women* (1844).

Trist, S. (ed), *The Under Dog* (1913).

Unwin, Mrs. J. C., *The Hungry Forties* (1904).

Wightman, Mrs. J. B., *Haste to the Rescue* (1862).

Wing, C., *Evils of the Factory System* (1837).

Woodham-Smith, C., *The Great Hunger* (1962).

Wright, A., *The Unexpurgated Case Against Woman Suffrage* (1913).

Wright, T., *The Great Unwashed* (1868).

Yeames, J., *Life in London Alleys* (1877).

Yelyr, R. G. van, *The Whip and the Rod* (1941).

Young, G. M., *Early Victorian England* (1934).

There are also a considerable number of novels, autobiographies and biographies that contain interesting material, though their inclusion would stretch the bibliography to an inordinate extent, and such inclusion is not really warranted when the relevant material is compressed into no more than twenty pages. Of especial interest is Hodder's life of Lord Shaftesbury, Cecil Woodham-Smith's *Florence Nightingale*, Phyllis Grosskurth's *J. A. Symonds,* and Una Pope-Hennessy's *Charles Dickens.* Even more fascinating, because less self-conscious, are the volumes of gossip by chatterboxes such as Lady Dorothy Nevill and Lady St. Helier.

Notwithstanding the information found in the books mentioned in the bibliography, the most fruitful sources are, first, the newspapers and the periodical press and, secondly, the Parliamentary Papers ('the Blue Books') covering inquiries, often stringent and penetrating, into abuses and anomalies, public and private. Because of the formidable task of wading through thousands of thick folios, each one running to six or seven hundred pages, it is perhaps not surprising that much of the information presented in these Parliamentary Papers has, until now, remained there.

It is often forgotten how complete the reportage was in Victorian England; only in sexual matters was there any restraint, and even then semi-underground papers such as *Night and Day* and *The Town* broke the taboo. Acts of cruelty and savagery were reported not only in the Sunday newspapers, such as *Reynolds News* and the *People*, but in *The Times* and the *Daily Telegraph*, and the crusading weeklies such as *Truth* and the *Pall Mall Gazette*. The middle classes, so assiduous in preserving their innocence and the innocence of their servants, could not find a way to muzzle the press. It is from the press that one gets the fullest picture of Victorian cruelty and callousness.

Index